Morning Glory Ever-After
(The Story Continues)

Gloria Ann Hawker

SunRise Publishing
Albuquerque, New Mexico 87120

Library of Congress Control Number: 2015914674

Morning Glory Ever After   The Story Continues / Hawker

ISBN 978-0-692-52650-7

EDITOR: Sylvia Adamsko
COVER ART: Hannah TM and Mary Munoz

Address All Inquires about this book to:
Gloria Hawker

Damom15165@aol.com

ALSO BY GLORIA ANN HAWKER

"Morning Glory" Diary of an Alien Abductee

6/1/15

Dear Gloria,

Thank you for letting me read your manuscript. I hope my editorial comments and proofer's marks are accurate and helpful. For any errors on my part, I apologize. Feel free to disregard any of my suggestions that doesn't meet with your approval (after all, this is you, telling the story of your life!)

Gloria, your story is amazing in every way. Most important to me is what it says about you. OMG! Gloria, you are such an inspiring model of strength, courage, love, open-mindedness, resourcefulness and the power of the mind to transform negative energy into positive reality. That's breath-taking! Of this, you are a Master... and a credible example of what is possible for any of us in our lives.

Thank you for writing these books, Gloria. They let us see you, and that is a powerful gift to us all.

Love, Susan

INTRODUCTION

In January of 2001, my "secret life" was revealed when "Morning Glory" Diary of an Alien Abductee was published. Amazingly, I succeeded in reaching the "one" abductee I had intended to reach through my story. I have touched many lives of alien/milab abductees who are "experiencers" of this phenomenon, living their "secret life" with alien species. Millions of these humans also experience the darkest side of these abductions, those which occur within their own governments. Contracts are signed by both entities (alien species and humans) within each sector of governments, world-wide, on planet earth. These signed contracts agree to allow humans to be abducted by the alien species in return for the alien's advanced technologies. Governments often use a special military "entity" to carry out their abductions. These government abductees are called Military Abductees, or "MILAB."

My life has changed drastically since "Morning Glory" Diary of an Alien Abductee was published. The years have passed quickly bringing many exciting and new features into my life. They have been exciting to me because I have met other abductees who eventually contacted me seeking their unknown reality in this phenomenon. They were looking for guidance and answers to their own questions. They wanted to be able to understand more about themselves and come to accept where they are in their lives today. Many of them were farther along than I was because they were "open-minded" about their abductions. When my own experience began, I was very "closed minded," a non-believer with regard to other species living in the vastness of the Universe. These new alien abductees are looking for friendships within this phenomenon because of their need for further understanding, and acceptance. Friends tend to share knowledge of their alien or MILAB experiences which allows them to know and feel that they are "not alone." And yes, there are many thousands of humans experiencing the alien/milab abduction phenomenon.

In today's society as well as in past years, no matter where you live in this world, the majority of people do not accept the concept of alien/milab experiences. Often our abductions are called "dream experiences." But these "dream experiences" are just as real to us as you holding this book, feeling the weight of it in your hands, and reading the words on the page. Perhaps, when you first picked up this book you felt the smoothness of the cover. As you opened it and turned the pages your fingers felt the paper that my story is printed on.

Think about your surroundings, become aware of the environment around you. Listen to the loud or the quiet sounds of other humans, or notice the quietness of the room you are sitting in. Perhaps another person is in the same room with you, either speaking or sleeping. Listen to their tone of voice or their breathing. What exactly is in your "awake" environment right now? When another human being touches you with their hands you feel the warmth of their skin against yours. The touch of another human skin is exactly like a touch from the finger of a non-human alien, except aliens don't feel warm. Use all of your senses to listen to your surroundings, to taste sweetness or sour flavor of your food. Notice the texture of the food in your mouth. Is the temperature in your environment warm or cold to you right now? Look around the room you are in. What is in the room? Are there pictures on the walls, a table, and a lamp?

You have just experienced what it feels like to be in a "real time dream experience". The only difference is, you *know* where you are, at present. During a "first" abduction experience, the abductee does not understand how he/she got into this predicament and cannot recognize the unfamiliar space he/she is in. The abductee looks around with wide open eyes trying to investigate the surroundings (if allowed to do so). The activity is so overwhelming to the unsuspecting abductee that some will simply close their eyes tightly, thinking what a horrible dream they are having and just wanting to "wake up." Sometimes the light is so bright above you that it distorts what you are able to see. There are Beings performing what seem to be medical procedures on your body. If you are an abductee, your nose, eyes, ears and genitals may be experiencing pain. If you are female, you may be implanted with an alien embryo. If you are male, your semen may be extracted.

Hey, wait a minute!!! This is supposed to be a dream. I am not supposed to feel pain but this hurts. I'm asleep, remember? So why am I feeling their touch? What are they doing to me and what sort of instruments or tools are they using? Who are they? Where am I? I need to get off of this… What am I lying on? Why can't I move?

"Sorry, this is your reality for the moment, so shut up and quit moving your head!" These words are in an unknown language, but you hear them in your own language, in your own head. How did they communicate with me? I heard no voice, saw no lips moving. What the -----is going on here?! You finally figure it out. You are not asleep. You are awake in real present time. There is strange equipment dangling above you that is used on your body by strange looking, bug-eyed Beings with pear-shaped heads and slits for mouths. Perhaps a disgusting Reptilian being is performing the same procedures, violating your body in some manner, in the strangeness of the sleeping moment.

Yes, you go to sleep like any other human being, but it just takes a touch to your temples with alien or human fingers to sedate you in sleep mode until they are ready to wake you up. You find yourself lying in a strange room with strange beings towering over you. If you are a MILAB abductee, you see humans standing over you. Alien species and humans also have other ways to paralyze and keep abductees in sleep mode until they are finished with them. They may even allow you to be awake and aware of what is happening to you. When you are returned to your own environment you may be awakened in the same manner you were put to sleep. As an abductee you may return to your bed to wake up the next morning with a real life dream experience that you cannot comprehend. This depends upon whether or not the alien species or the human abductors (MILAB) allow you to retain the memory of your abduction. The alien species have taught MILAB human abductors this technique and other ways to keep the abductee asleep and paralyzed while being abducted.

You are laughed at and called crazy and insane, even though society today is warming to the concept of extraterrestrial beings INVADING your world and ABDUCTING humans.

Back to the original subject: why do "humans" need to find and be with other abductees? The reason is that their new friends already accept what has happened to them. For many, these real dream experiences have been taking place since childhood, through their teenage years, and into adulthood. Therefore, they understand, have compassion and share knowledge of what they have already lived through. Most of all, they know that they are NOT ALONE in this phenomenon, even though abduction is difficult to accept. They need to have vital information of their experiences confirmed. Through this process we have all found more understanding, teaching and learning from one another. It appears that each human alien abductee has certain knowledge or intelligence in many fields of this phenomenon. Many of these human alien abductees have revealed their own truth to inform and share knowledge with those who are just beginning to realize their own involvement in the process of alien/military/government abduction.

In Morning Glory I wrote the truth about a warning and eventual attack upon me that I still live with today. In order to distinguish between our elected government officials and those Shadowy Figures who work with the aliens on secret projects, I will hereafter refer to them and their activities, as the "rogue" government. Certain rogue government officials who were involved in this phenomenon told me, "If I talk, I will pay." The message was to "not talk" and not reveal vital information. I have been trained by the alien species that work with rogue military/government. These people train each selected alien abductee to work in specific fields of known alien technologies, including medical, nuclear, laser, chemical and biological laboratories.

I was trained to investigate in the medical, chemical and biological laboratories with some training in nuclear and laser technologies. It is quite strange for me to talk about it because I cannot carry on an intelligent conversation about the knowledge I was given. As I read the daily newspaper, books, magazines or listen to news of new developments in these fields, it seems as if I already know the information. Perhaps you, the reader, understand, but I don't. I am just a "student" sitting in a cinder-block classroom with my "military teachers" and scientists who wear white lab coats over their brown colored uniforms.

Previously, I was falsely accused of "talking" and the consequences I suffered are still ongoing today. What has happened in the lives of my family and who was taken away from us February 16, 2005 is unspeakable and detrimental. I cry every day. My soul is in turmoil, fighting and arguing within myself, searching for the truth.

Two other families who were warned "not to talk" contacted a good friend who is a researcher in this phenomenon. Both families experienced the same outcome of events: One has lost a loved one, and another is living with an aggressive cancerous brain tumor.

The above occurrences happened one week prior to and one week after the sudden passing of my husband, Fred. As of this writing, the identities of the two other families remain confidential. The only information I've been given is that they are also alien/milab abductees. I pray there is an answer for each of our families within the research this person is conducting. One wonders if the loss of our husbands or wives due to quick and painful death came from the ensuing threats of "Don't talk. If you do, you'll pay."

The humans who make these threats will face their own demise one day when they meet their maker! In that, I find some comfort.

FORWARD

The following review of <u>"Morning Glory" Diary of an Alien Abductee</u>, turned up on the internet. After reading it, I felt compelled to send an email to Debby.

<u>"Morning Glory" Diary of an Alien Abductee</u>, August 27, 2004 By <u>J. Frawley "Debby Frawley"</u> (North Carolina) -

This review is from:
"Morning Glory" Diary of an Alien Abductee (Paperback)

First I'd like to say I bought Gloria's book at a book signing. On meeting this lady I was at once struck by something special in her. She was the soft spoken person and answered all questions, some painful all spellbinding. I bought the book; you cannot put this down. It delivers, its real, it's scary, it's sad, its amazing. Be surprised, be very surprised there are VIPs described in her story that you will never look at the same again! I know I haven't!! It is also one of the best written books in general that I have ever read. I have re read it just to enter her world again. From the first page you are in Gloria's world going through this along side of her. She has also mentioned maybe writing another book (meaning there is still a-lot she is not telling us yet). On one hand I respect the pain on the other she is a genius at letting that pain go on paper. At our meeting she alluded to and dare I say these more formidable beings not of this earth, not to say many beings were who you would bring home to mom. But these few Gloria promised in a future book. I can't believe there are more beings scarier than I already here. Gloria has just touched upon this subject. But this is one meaty book.... I want more. This book will educate you it is full of information about many beings all different. I also want to say I hope Gloria is well as she became ill while being with these beings. It will amaze you at why she has been chosen and what she was chosen for!!! If you are looking for a book on this subject, without a doubt get this one, you will read things you can't imagine!!!! I only wish to see Gloria at another book signing and give her a big hug for her courage and the sheer enjoyment she gave me with her written words. I've yet to read another book that I admired more!!!

Dear Debbie,

The inspiration in your written words did inspire me to begin writing again on my memoirs of having lived with this unusual phenomenon of alien/milab abductions in my life. After reading your blurb on Amazon.com I stared at your words and as if it were a mind boggling reaction I said to myself, "It is time, now to fulfill a promise I made to many people."

I previously started writing after my husband's death but my heart was just not into writing. Realizing once again many experiences within this phenomenon had happened in my life since "Morning Glory" Diary of an Alien Abductee was published.

To wake up one day feeling alone in this world without my soul mate, along with my father and mother all who died within a three year period, leaving me with the feeling as if they left me to be the "Family Matriarch" of my two younger siblings and my own children. I found out this is not the case at all as we have bonded to one another. Why I had felt so alone is because I have lived with familiar loved ones who always surrounded me in my life. I have four loving children and five grandchildren. Two beautiful granddaughters one who was born just a couple of months after my husband, father, grandfather, left us.

Knowing and respecting that each one of my children has their own lives and families; life is so different for me. In reality my new life began "alone." With lessons learned I've come a long way in learning and knowing myself in this new life with new friendships being made. I feel I have survived with the help and love of my children. I do have another special person now in my life but he cannot accept this part of my life and sadly I cannot share my deepest secrets, secrets such as the explorations and experiences in this given phenomenon. After ten years since my husband's passing I miss *his* sharing of *his* secrets of what he thought might have occurred to him during any one of his experiences within this phenomenon. I miss terribly waking up in the morning feeling our arms around each other and the first day's kiss which welcomes in a new glorious day with whatever is dealt to the both of us in life for that day. The first year of mourning is a catastrophic affair. I could continue on writing on this subject of losing loved ones but that is another book.

Since the loss of my husband my life has been quiet in regards to having abductions with any of the different alien extraterrestrials or military/government. At least this is what I am led to think. If there are any memories these memories have been "covered up" by someone else other than myself. In reality the invading parties had split up my life into normal and abnormal. Having the sense of "normalcy" in my life is great now. I often wonder why these alien extraterrestrials and military/government have stayed away and not bothered me since the death of my husband.

In recent months, I have found myself thinking more about these universal beings and finding that I do actually miss them, that is what I consider, the good universal beings, meaning those who I finally accepted into my life and yes, the hybrid children I have. The various different Greys', Nordics, and other universal cultures, which had become part of my life, and I have never forgotten my daughter Winsha. I often wonder about her welfare and how much she has matured. What has she accomplished in her life since the last time I was with her? Does she remember me? I pray that one day I can visit her again. I found only very cruel and malevolent Reptilians although I have heard that some are benevolent. I still have much disrespect and hatred for the high-priority military/government people who are involved in this phenomenon and who continue to disrupt human life within this phenomenon working for their gain to be the first with technology and information given through signed contracts from the Universal Federation dating back to the Hoover and Roosevelt era.

DEDICATIONS

I dedicate this book to my soul mate, my husband,
Fred Walter Hawker.
Who left us on February 16, 2005
Together we made and lived through many discoveries
that we made as one.
I miss you deeply

I dedicate this book to a very special lady
who was a researcher/hypnotherapist and dear friend
to many abductees.
Barbara Bartholic *was an outstanding, loving and caring human.*
I know she is looking down from Heaven
and still guiding me with her love.

I honor a special and dear friend who passed over
on August 21, 2011 who is greatly missed.
Budd Hopkins *was a true pioneer who was respected*
within and beyond the UFO community.
I am grateful for his care, concern and guidance
that developed into a most rewarding friendship.
I deeply benefitted from his direction and compassion over the years.

On September 27, 2004 we lost another soul.
Dr. John Mack
I never dreamed it possible I would personally meet and be able
to work alongside with Dr. John Mack.
Dr. Mack formed PEER (Program for Extraordinary Experience
Research).
I was invited to join PEER as a hypnotherapist.
I was able to draw upon a reliable source of
knowledge to be able to guide my clients through their traumatic
abduction experiences.
Dr. Mack's teachings and his compassion will never be forgotten.

13

I have also lost another dear friend.

Gabe Valdez *passed away on August 7, 2011.*
Gabe and I met through some mutual friends sometime in 1999.

Gabe investigated the phenomenon of cattle mutilations in and around Dulce, New Mexico. He also researched the phenomenon at Mt. Archuleta and the apparent underground bases located there. He was interested in the UFO phenomena including extraterrestrials.

Gabe told me that if ever I needed his input to help people who are experiencers (abductees) or with my own abductions to contact him.
I have missed this courteous, caring human being who also gave of himself to many other people.
A dear friend is now gone.

*June 7, 2015 **Julie Shuster** left us.*
She is in peace and no longer in pain.
She was someone very dear to me.
I found her to be a very warm, loving, and understanding woman.
She accepted where I was in my life when I met her.
With her guidance and direction I was able to better accept who I am in this unusual phenomenon.
Thank you Julie for being on my "Road of Life."

THE DIARY CONTINUES

When we help others
and strive for the best possible outcome,
We discover Blessings in our Lives
that we never could have imagined.

S.F. Adamsko

"Morning Glory" Ever-After

SO...ONCE AGAIN IT BEGINS ...

OCTOBER, 2000

For a period of three weeks I received strange phone calls that began the first week of October, 2000. The phone calls occurred every other day and at the same time each day. I heard the same man's voice speaking through constant static that was on the phone line. The static made it seem as if the person was using some source other than a telephone line to make this call. The sound I was picking up reminded me of what you hear from a ship that is out to sea calling in to land. I often wondered if someone was trying to communicate with me using satellite or if they were actually calling from a ship. The same message was always repeated: "At 5:07 ..STATESIDE.......NOVEMBER 7TH." The man would speak slowly and at times the same message would be repeated so that I would understand his message. I don't know what this message meant or who it was for. Why I was given this message is unknown. Was it just a coincidence? Is it possible the caller had the wrong phone number? The question is: why was I getting these calls at the same time every other day with the same message? I found this to be strange and it made me feel uncomfortable. What was this particular warning about and who was behind it? Was this occurrence really going to happen? And to whom I wondered?

I have a friend who worked with the Secret Service here in Albuquerque. I did contact her with regard to these phone calls and she began to look into the matter for me. The investigation eventually ended up in the hands of the FBI. The FBI, after questioning me, told me this would be documented and if the calls continued our phone line would be tapped to find the reason for and the source of these calls. The calls eventually quit. The FBI never followed up as they'd said they would, by staying in contact with me. Over time, my friend would occasionally ask about the calls. I had hoped for some kind of information to ease my mind.

I explained in "Morning Glory" Diary of an Alien Abductee that I am a (MILAB) military/government abductee as well as an alien abductee. I began to believe this message was somehow related to

17

our Government. Was this message a warning about some kind of devastation to happen here in the United States or somewhere else in the world? I never found out who this person was or where the calls originated.

AUGUST 25, 2001
"ANGELINA"

In the government section of <u>"Morning Glory" Diary of an Alien Abductee</u>, many times I mentioned seeing and becoming acquainted with an older lady and a younger lady. During these encounters we would see each other either onboard an alien space ship or here on our planet earth at one of many unidentified military installations. In either situation we were not allowed to speak to one another. However, we did find ways to communicate with each other through facial expressions, whispering to each other very quietly when no one was watching, or by using our fingers or hands. We normally found each other on board an alien ship working in the medical/chemical laboratories. On earth we would be in secluded secured "class rooms" where we were taught medical, chemical and biological warfare. Even to this day, I could not explain to the reader "what I learned" during these God awful classes. I feel as if my brain does not maintain the studies or learning of what I was taught. I did discuss how the gray block building was guarded and how we were being guarded by men in camouflage uniforms, armed with machine guns and directions to shoot to kill if need be. I believe we three became quite close when an unknown substance was injected into my tongue after I was accused of "talking." I wrote about this matter in the government section of "Morning Glory."

I don't know when or where Louise gave me her name as "Angelina," but during the many times we were together I knew her as "Angelina." When Louise and I finally met in person in California, we agreed that the older lady's first name was Grace. About a year or so before Saddam Hussein was killed, Angelina (Louise) and I had an experience together. I don't really know how the government or our military was able to do this without the knowledge of the dignitaries who were in attendance at a meeting in a very classy beautiful room that we suspected was in Saddam's palace. The dignitaries were not aware of our presence as we stood and walked behind them. They sat at a large, sturdy, beautiful gold table with gold-like chairs that appeared to have red velvet backing on them. Sitting in the chairs were approximately six to eight dignitaries from Iran, Iraq, and Egypt. I failed to document the other countries that Iraq was "friends" with at the time who were in attendance at this meeting.

Angelina and I found each other in a darkened room and we were led out of the room into the larger brightly lit room were the meeting was taking place. I do know that Angelina and I could see each other but somehow the dignitaries were not aware of our presence. When we woke up in the darkened room, someone placed an item - camera/microphone or some other new technology-onto our clothing so that the meeting could be viewed by someone not in the room. I did not care to know who that "someone" was. My notes (if they were correct) stated that the discussion concerned the stolen green substance (K-LITE) that I had written about in "Morning Glory." This green substance (K-LITE) ended up in Saddam's hands and he had the small stolen vial hidden in water somewhere. This substance can be mixed with other chemicals and made into a medical derivative (by-product) to cure cancer and other health problems, or be made into bio-warfare products. Bio-warfare products were being discussed that evening by the dignitaries. Speaking of new technology how was it possible for Angelina and myself to be present at this meeting without anyone seeing or hearing us while we were all in the same room together?

On Saturday, August 25, 2001, Angelina and I again found each other. A dear friend of ours, Eve Lorgen who had listened to each of our stories, finally made the connection between Angelina (Louise) and myself. If it had not been for Eve, we would not have had any confirmation of our real-life shared experiences. This confirmation – meeting Angelina (Louise), validated my experiences with the universal alien/government/military – and was an important event in my life. There are no words to express the emotions resulting from actually finding another human who has shared the same abduction experiences with me. I am so grateful Eve. Thank you.

On the afternoon of August 25th Fred and I sat in a booth at Denny's restaurant in Apple Valley, California waiting with anticipation for the moment to arrive. Was Louise going to show? Would I recognize her? Would we know each other? I had so many questions swirling in my head....

The meeting time came and went. Fred and I walked out of the restaurant. I had wanted to wait a few minutes more to see if she would come. There was a bench near the front door so we sat down. A car drove up. In the car was a lady I thought I recognized. The lady got out of the car and stood there by the open door, then slowly walked toward me. I recognized her immediately and she recognized me. Tears flowed and hugs held tightly. We went inside the restaurant and spent the afternoon talking away, renewing our memories, ourselves and our lives. Between us, Louise and I have had many major health problems. Yes, we both believed our government/military and possible universal aliens were to blame for our health problems because we had been exposed many times to an unknown substance. Louise told me that day, as I understand it the Greys also healed Louise's uterine cancer. Supposedly, her cancer was thought to be spreading to her liver and kidneys. The Greys abducted Louise and healed her like they also healed the complications I was having in my diseased lungs. Evidently the Greys informed her that she was going to become very ill and die. I was told that she did die twice but because she is allergic to iodine. She was revived again by the Greys. Her doctors were shocked and amazed at her recovery.

SEPTEMBER 20, 2001

Weekly phone calls began again. I was unsure if this was the same man who had called several times in October, 2000. These phone calls would occur at the same time on any given day during the week. I would answer the phone with "hello," then there would be silence on the other end of the line for a couple of seconds. The man would not say "hello" but apparently would just listen to see if it was me who answered the phone. Then he would proceed to say some numbers. Each of the phone calls followed the same scenario.

I recognized the same voice repeating the same numbers. I believed these numbers to be the date of some occurrence. The numbers were: 5171978. I did research on the numbers 05/17/1978 but found nothing significant that might have occurred on that date. It was always the same man's voice – a voice that I could not identify. The calls continued for a month and a half. Then the man just stopped calling.

OCTOBER, 2001

The date was not documented.

I hadn't felt any symptoms of an oncoming abduction. I felt as if I had slept well - until I woke up on the Grey's ship. I found myself lying on a familiar table with a warm soft blanket around my body. There were three Greys standing around the table. I experienced pain in the area around my lungs and my breathing was somewhat labored. My vision cleared and I noticed a Grey on my right holding a large, deep, silver-colored bowl. He came closer to me and showed me what was in the bowl. The substance appeared to be dark pink in color with black running through it. The Grey told me the substance in the bowl was tissue from my diseased lungs. He said the scrapings were tissue from the lower part of my lungs. He said they were trying to repair the damage in my lungs. The Grey told me telepathically that I needed rest, so another Grey touched my temple and I apparently fell asleep.

Waking the next morning in my own bed, I experienced some discomfort in both lungs which continued for about three days. My breathing was not as labored as it had been in the past. But my body continued to feel lethargic and tired, as was the norm for me since coming down with this disease. In a documentation in "Morning Glory" Diary of an Alien Abductee, I wrote about what the government/military did to cause my diseased lungs. I have what is known as interstitial lung disease. My death was to have occurred within two-years of receiving the diagnosis.

I did not notice any immediate difference in the condition of my lungs or health since the night the Greys worked on me, other than my breathing seemed to be somewhat better. Seemingly out of nowhere I gained back a sudden burst of energy the following spring. The tiredness and lethargy dissipated. Experiencing newfound life and good health, I realized that I was once again able to do things I had not been able to do for several years. The feeling of being active and having extra strong energy produced great excitement within me.

I was once again able to walk in the evening with my husband and daughter. My newfound endurance continued to build until we were walking almost two miles a day. I soon found myself riding a bicycle with my family down our favorite path. I was able to ride two and one half miles, keeping up with my family as we pedaled our bikes. I thanked the Greys many times over for healing me again.

"MYSTERIES OF THE MIND"

After the publication of <u>"Morning Glory" Diary of an Alien Abductee</u> I was invited to be a special guest on several different radio programs. My story would be heard throughout the United States and Europe. I want to tell you about one weird experience that happened at this particular time.

I was invited by Mr. and Mrs. Alex Merklinger to be on Alex's "Mysteries of the Mind" radio program that aired nightly on Millennium Radio Network. I met with Ardeth Merklinger, Alex's wife, before the airing of "Mysteries of the Mind." We met at a quaint tea house in Old Town (located in Albuquerque).

Arriving at their home, I was greeted with love and warmth. I found Alex to be an excellent radio host. He always made me feel comfortable speaking about my abduction life experiences. On the radio, my story would reach a large listening audience.

The interstitial lung disease that I describe in <u>"Morning Glory"</u> made its presence known during this time. Was I once again falling under the control of someone not wanting me to "talk"? In past months, I had been free of the constant uncontrollable coughing I had become accustomed to. My lung situation appeared to be improving. That Friday after dinner, as we relaxed and enjoyed conversation, I realized I'd done hardly any coughing. Alex

22

excused himself and went outside to the radio studio. Ardeth and I joined him soon afterward.

During the news section of the program I excused myself to use the restroom. Ardeth followed me back to the house to do something in a different room. After using the facility, I began walking back outside to where the radio studio was located. As I got near the kitchen door, I felt as if there was no air getting into my lungs. As I began to gasp for air, the uncontrollable coughing began. I could not catch my breath. I had never experienced an attack like this before. Ardeth came into the kitchen and saw what was happening to me. I could not respond to her questions. I began to feel quite dizzy. I thought I was going to fall to the floor. After trying to get water and mints into me, Ardeth went into the guest bedroom and came back with my Albuterol Inhalation Aerosol.

During the brief period of her absence, I had the distinct feeling that someone else was in the room with me - someone who had caused this to happen. I felt a presence but did not see anyone other than Ardeth when she walked back into her kitchen. I regained my composure as the incident faded and I was able to breathe normally once more.

During the second segment of the radio program, I began to cough once again, making it difficult to speak and respond to Alex. With Alex's and Ardeth's help, the radio program turned out to be a good one in spite of the coughing episode.

Alex invited me to return to "Mysteries of the Mind" the following week.

A week later, I again found myself at the home of my lovely host and hostess. When airtime rolled around, I was excited about reaching the audience and furthering my true story.

The first half of the program went quite well, and at the newsbreak, I excused myself to use the restroom. As Ardeth and I walked from the studio to the house, we stopped to admire some beautiful stars in the night sky. We searched for different types of lights or even space ships they thought they might have seen while sitting on their patio.

Their home was located in an area far from city lights that distort the dark sky.

I waited for Ardeth in her kitchen by the outside door. Unexpectedly, I felt very congested. A burning sensation in my lungs traveled up my esophagus, once again triggering a coughing attack like the one I had experienced the week before! Realizing the cough was uncontrollable at this point; I drank bottled water, quickly used the inhaler, and sucked on mints. Nothing controlled this horrible cough. I was quite dizzy, and felt as if I was going to fall to the floor. Ardeth and I do not know how long I stood there trying to get the coughing to stop.

It was close to airtime, and I was not ready. Finally, having the situation somewhat under control, we walked back to the studio.

I had not thought much about this unusual situation until some time after being on "Mysteries of the Mind" radio program. I remembered an investigator I had worked with for several years, who had cautioned me when I was writing "Morning Glory" Diary of an Alien Abductee. His warning was this: If the alien species or military/government did not want me to write and publish my story, they would find ways to thwart my attempts.

The investigator also stated that the same would be true if I decided to speak out using mass media (radio, T.V) or presentations (lectures, workshops). His information came from other knowledgeable people within the UFO/Alien abduction phenomenon who *had* spoken out through the media and had written books on this phenomenon.

Reflecting back on the coughing occurrences that transpired while being a guest on "Mysteries of the Mind," I felt that someone had *not* wanted me to speak out on those particular evenings and had somehow caused the unusual coughing attacks. Having been on many other radio programs, I had never before experienced anything like what happened during "Mysteries of the Mind."

In the end though, I felt as if I'd prevailed over the situation and won a battle with *whomever!*

JUNE 2002 HOOPER, COLORADO
UFO WATCH TOWER

I had been asked by Judy Messoline to be a speaker at the UFO WATCH TOWER in Hooper, Colorado. I spoke about my alien and MILAB experiences to an audience of other alien abductees and people interested in the phenomenon. The Watch Tower is located near the west side of the San Luis Mountains and the Sand Dunes. It has been reported that there is an underground base located in the San Luis Mountains with much alien activity.

Combating the strong summer winds that carried heavy smoke from a southwest Colorado forest fire, I thought, *"Well, if this is the only problem we will encounter then let that be it."* Little did any of us know what we would encounter that Saturday evening; and, as the night worn on, what I would eventually encounter.

The gathering of people was very intimate and we were getting to know each other. We listened to other people's stories of abductions or sightings which were quite interesting.

I was excited to meet other well-known authors at this workshop. A film crew from Denver, Colorado had come to enjoy the weekend but had a venture in mind: to film and interview speakers and other interested people who attended the weekend. At various times during the long weekend the three men actually filmed and interviewed me. My speech was chosen to be filmed on Saturday afternoon. I became quite nervous, as this was only the second time I had spoken out about my "secret life" story.

Our accommodations, while we attended the workshop, were an RV trailer that belonged to Judy Messoline, owner of the property and UFO WatchTower. Camping next to us were some close friends who are also abductees. Other campers would walk by our campsite in the evening and stop and talk while we prepared a late night supper, or made S'mores and hot coffee.

We enjoyed the evenings and chatted with everyone, having fun with the crew who filmed our group at night. The dark night sky was filled with many stars that cannot be seen in a well-lit city such as Albuquerque. The long weekend went very well until Saturday night when a spectacular UFO event was witnessed by all of us.

We were sitting around the campfire about 10:30 p.m. with a few of our new friends. Suddenly, four people came running from the Watch Tower into our campsite, hollering for us to turn off our camp lights. They had been witnessing some unusual lights in the night sky. We quickly turn off the camp lights and before we knew it, there were many other campers at our site looking skyward at several small, round, lighted objects. At first, they were hard to see, as they would zig-zag very fast and high in the sky.

"Are they airplanes?" someone would holler out.
"Are they coming out of the San Luis Mountains?" another one asked.
With much excitement, one person said, "Look! They are going into the San Luis Mountains."
"Watch their pattern of flight." someone added.

The lights on the objects would just blink out. Then the objects returned, with lights lit, in close proximity to their original location. The film crew got out larger cameras and filmed the objects. We were all standing in the cool evening air, watching several of the objects do their "amusing dance" for us as we looked through binoculars. Another camper obtained some type of red light that he pointed towards the objects to guide us when we lost sight of them. The objects continually disappeared and reappeared.

The time was 11:30 p.m. I was standing outside looking upward when some type of powerful energy hit me. Fumbling around in the dark, I took several steps to where I knew there was a chair. I had to sit down quickly because my body began to shake and I had a "knowing" of something that was going to happen that evening.

"Yes. They are here. They are looking at us, as we look at them. They are looking at you and they know you are here." I was told telepathically.

Mary and Sylvia quickly joined me while I sat near the safety of Mary's truck. Other campers soon joined us where we were standing and sitting. Mary knew something was wrong and I did not want to tell her yet what I was experiencing. My head spun wildly and a strong headache began to take hold. Sylvia asked if I was "OK," and I snapped at her, feeling very dizzy.

Mary asked again, "Are you all right?" and I told her "*NO!*" She grabbed my body and held me tightly. I told her what I was feeling and that "they" were going to come that night. "Yes," I told her, "*they were the ones up in the sky.*"

I regained my composure but had that gnawing feeling for the rest of the evening. The excitement grew as we watched the "dancing objects" that were streaking across the night sky. Everyone gave in to tiredness around 12:30 that evening. We all called it a night and people disbursed to their own campsites.

I lay sleepless for awhile, tossing and turning quietly so not to wake Sylvia. I tried to reason out why I went through that nonsense earlier. If "*They*," meaning the aliens, were there watching over us, well, they did not hurt us. So get over it, Gloria and get some rest! I could not rest, knowing that "reported" Reptilians were that close to me in those mountains. Were "*they*" Reptilians who had contacted me earlier that night?

I asked for God's protection now, knowing that Abe, Mary, and Hannah, were sleeping in their tent not far from our trailer. I think I fell asleep only to awake at some point during the night. I felt the trailer walls vibrate very hard and I put my hand against the wall. I was trying to figure out what was causing the vibration when the entire trailer began to shake, as well as my bed.

I called out to Sylvia but got no response. I thought someone was just having fun by shaking the trailer to scare us. I could hear Sylvia's heavy breathing while she slept through this on the bed in the back of the trailer. She never did answer when I called out to her.

Suddenly, I saw through the window across from my bed, a very large bright white light shown through the closed curtains, illuminating the trailer and the outdoors. I cautiously sat up and pulled open the curtains to see who was trying to "scare" us. No one was there.

Abe, Mary and Hannah did not stir during what I thought was a loud commotion. I saw no one. Everything was quiet except for the noise coming from the shaken trailer. I pulled back my sleeping bag and stepped in the direction of the light that was coming through the windows. As I pulled back the curtains, the light was in the process of going up into the sky, illuminating the other campsites. The tremors stopped! It was so quiet outside and inside the trailer that you could have heard a pin drop. I stood in the same spot, listening to Sylvia's breathing. I called out to her once more, but again, no response. Before I got back into bed, I looked outside one more time, but nothing stirred. All was quiet and once again very dark. I asked myself if I should chance going outside to wake Mary and Abe. Instead, I lay on my comfortable bed, awake for some time, waiting for the sun to come up.

Somehow, I did finally fall asleep.

The questions I had when I woke up were, ***"What caused this occurrence during the night?"*** And... ***"Who had done it?"***

In the morning I asked THE question. The response was, "No one heard any noise or saw anything during the night." Sylvia did not feel or hear anything strange. Mary, Abe and Hannah did not hear or see anything either.

This particular campground has a reputation for campers experiencing "unknown phenomena" at times. It is not known if these phenomena are alien related or not.

JULY 18, 2002:

I awoke this morning to an electronic sounding man's voice constantly repeating to me these words: "WITHIN MY BIRTHING CUP I WILL FIND." I don't know the meaning of what he was trying to tell me. Did these words come from an alien source? I don't know. These words were repeated several times until I was fully awake.

I tried to understand the meaning of what I was being told. Does it have to do with something when I was born? What is a birthing cup? Is the birthing cup my own uterus? But I no longer have a uterus. So was I being told something of the past before I had a hysterectomy? Had I held many hybrid babies in my birthing cup? Does anyone know or can anyone tell me what this birthing cup is, and what these words mean? Please let me know what you may think this phrase means.

JULY 23, 2002:

On this day I was again awakened by the same electronic man's voice, repeating over and over until I was fully awake. His words were:

"INFORMATION WILL SOON EXPLODE"

I quickly responded as if I knew to whom I was speaking. I asked, "When will this information explode?" The response from the man was, "Soon."

Shockingly, right in front of *my* face was a Grey's face. "You're a liar!" I said. I repeated this to him twice. "You have told me this before!"

With a stern look, his face faded away from me, and I found myself lying in my own bedroom, in my own bed.

Okay. I waited all week for information to "explode." Did this mean I would be told something else? Would information soon be revealed through the media with regard to aliens and UFOs? I waited every day for further messages from the Greys or the news media. I heard nothing. Understand that the aliens "timing" of moments, minutes, hours, days, months and years is a lot quicker than our own realization of time. So in alien time, was this information to come about in *our* time, meaning a month …several months….a year…. or many years from now?

Why do they have to speak to me in riddles? Why can't they just come and tell me the full story and the truth? Perhaps they *have* told me the truth and it lies dormant in my unconscious mind?

29

JULY 30, 2002
4:14 A.M.

I was awakened again with the same message: "SOON INFORMATION WILL EXPLODE." But this time I heard some kind of music in the background. I did not recognize it as being American music. Along with the music, I immediately saw a black box that had some type of lines drawn through it. The meaning of this scenario is unknown.

AUGUST 24, 2002

Fred and I felt agitated with some disturbing phone calls. These calls came nightly or every other night and interrupted our sleep. The phone calls happened over a period of three to four weeks. Since the phone is on my side of the bed, I am the one that answers the phone. I listened to a slow beeping sound on the phone, thinking someone miss-dialed and was sending a fax. But this was not the same sound you hear when someone is faxing a message. To verify this, I handed the phone to Fred on several occasions and he confirmed it was not a fax machine. The calls were made at the same time between 2:00 a.m. and 4:00 a.m. These calls happened at least twice a night during the noted time frame. As the calls progressed I quit answering the phone and just let it ring. Then I would dial our message service to pick up the message. There were no messages left. But when I "accidentally" answered the phone again, the slow beeping sound would occur. On that night, I *did* answer the phone and listened to the beep. Then I just hung up. Before the phone was back in its cradle some type of trance came over me and I fell asleep quickly. This was unusual after one of these phone calls. I would normally remain awake wondering what was happening and who was doing this. Was it some kind of joke? Whether I fell asleep quickly or was put into a deep trance, it did not take long to get into what I thought was a dream state.

I found myself in an unknown room that had a square wooden table with chairs and a wooden bookcase full of books. To my amazement there was a man who resembled my primary-care doctor. This man was attended by two other black haired women. One woman was sitting at an easel painting some of my alien abduction experiences. As she painted, the experiences came out of her unusual easel in a 3-D format (a live action picture of the abductions). The easel had no paper on it. I was actually looking at my past abduction experiences with the aliens in a 3-D format! This was so unbelievable to witness and actually see this happen! The two women and this doctor began to argue about each painted 3-D experience that I saw. The argument between them was that these abductions never happened and were untrue. "There are no such alien species in our universe or any universe." I was told. I argued back, stating how wrong they were. Would I be so dumb as to not believe in my truth? What were they trying to "play me for?" I angrily asked them, "Who are you? And what do you want with me?"

They never answered my questions but struggled to convince me otherwise - to change my beliefs in this phenomenon. I felt this encounter with these three people was not a dream but a vivid realization. I tried to wake up from the trance or real life dream and get away from these people. I felt myself fighting to wake up, but before the "quickening" of waking up happened, I heard a man's voice talking to me and repeating over and over that "they are not finished with me yet".

In a snap, I was fully awake and the man repeated those same words to me. I looked around the dark bedroom. I saw no one. But his voice was right there by the side of my head and it felt as if he was standing there by my bed! I felt as if someone, perhaps government, was trying to deprogram me.

FEBRUARY 20, 2003
2:00 A.M.

I abruptly woke up to a loud electronic tone in my right ear. The tone was excruciating. I thought it was the fire alarm going off. I immediately woke Fred and excitedly told him, "The fire alarm is going off! We need to get up and find the source of the fire!"

He said he did not hear the fire alarm and it was not going off! I asked him, "What is that sound I heard." He repeated himself,

31

saying that he could not hear any sound anywhere. Fred turned over and went back to sleep.

My right ear began to vibrate so hard the skin was moving in and out from my head. As I grabbed and held my ear, I realized that the whole right side of my face was in pain, and my right eye seemed to be pulsating inward. I quickly sat up in bed. Then suddenly I heard a man's voice yelling at me. His voice was coming from inside of my ear: "CODE ORANGE, CODE ORANGE!" I looked around the room, thinking this man was in our bedroom, but did not see anyone.

"CODE ORANGE, CODE ORANGE!" he shouted again even louder. I thought these directives were coming through the radio and my ear was just sensitive. The area immediately below my right ear began to pulsate even more so I pressed my hand harder to my ear and the area below. I was quite fearful and bewildered. I had no idea what this directive meant. I cannot even explain the upset feelings I had because of what was happening to my face while listening to these directives.

The man then spoke and said that this transmission was being sent to me by satellite. This would be the mode they would use to contact me so I would know.

"Know what?" I said. I was then instructed to go outside to the balcony, which I did not do. I told this "male voice" that I would not follow his instructions. Immediately, I was shown a vision and was instructed to drive to the Sandia/Kirtland Air Force Base gate at Truman and Gibson Blvd. (In the vision I was shown which gate I was to drive to). I was given directions to park my car west of the gate located on the south side of Gibson Blvd. After parking I was to get out of the car and walk to the front of the guard facility. A man whom I would recognize would be there to take me onto the base. I was not given a reason why I was to be there. In this vision I saw myself walking through the guard shack at the entrance of the base, and then meeting the military man whom I would recognize.

This is where this story gets weird. I know that I did not get out of bed and drive myself to the place in my vision. I was sitting up in bed in a dark room, listening to a male voice telling me that I was receiving his directives by satellite. At that moment a helicopter flew over our home. The helicopter hovered over our large balcony. I remember saying to myself at that moment, "Oh my God, they are coming for me since I did not obey this man's voice." The man then told me I would have further contact with instructions and they would use this mode (the satellite) to contact me.

I remember being grabbed, having my hands tied and roughly being put aboard a low flying craft. The craft flew from the east to the south side of the city. I was allowed to see the lights and where we were traveling. Just as it had been in the vision, I saw the guard shack, and recognized Gibson Blvd. We flew over the guard shack and the helicopter landed. I was then pulled from the craft by the man who had taken me from my bed.

I do not remember when this actual abduction ended. I woke up in my bed the following morning, *fully clothed*.

My memories soon came flooding back. The small black helicopter landed south of the gate in a darkened area. The military man who took me from my bed was dressed in camouflage. Yes, he had roughly pulled me out of the helicopter. Then we walked north about a half block away to a dark late model car. In the meantime, another man ran from the guard shack. There were no street lights nearby, making the area somewhat dark. I did not recognize the military man I was supposed to know. He had been standing near the south end of the guard gate. He was dressed in military blues. When he saw me, he spoke to me in an angry tone of voice. He said that I would have made life easier if I had listened to the directives. Instead, I had to be picked up!

As we approached the car, a man in the front passenger seat got out and opened the rear passenger door. I was put into the back seat. The car was parked on the west side of a north/south street. I turned to see who was sitting next to me and to my surprise, it was LOUISE! "GLORIA!" she said when she recognized me. Louise lives in Apple Valley, California. She and I have had many MILAB experiences together (which I wrote about in "Morning Glory" Diary of an Alien Abductee).

Louise has not been in good health. I was shocked that we were meeting once again. We were driven some distance with our eyes covered, to another dark area of the base – a place Louise and I had been taken before. When the car stopped we were taken out of the back seat and the blinders were removed. We walked a short distance to a concrete facility. A door was opened and if I remember correctly, the concrete walkway sloped down a bit to a level concrete floor. We had an entourage of three military men, two in back and one in front, guiding us. We were told to keep our heads down and not to turn them. If we disobeyed, the blinders would be put back on our eyes. What I could see were concrete walls and doors opening into other rooms. I don't know how far we walked before entering a large, open laboratory where military women and men worked alongside with some Greys and other entities. My memory ends there.

Since that night it has been quite difficult to contact Louise or even find her. I don't know if she still lives in Apple Valley, California. I would someday like to have the abduction confirmed by her as well.

A question that I have is this: A helicopter landed not far from Gibson Blvd., a large, east/west thoroughfare. There had to be someone who witnessed the landing of that helicopter. Why did they not question that landing at such a weird hour? Also, the Veterans Hospital is not that far from the area where we landed. There is a lot of activity at all hours of the day near the hospital. Another point, if I have the area correct, there is not a whole lot of open space for a helicopter to land.

AUGUST 29, 2003
DURANGO, COLORADO
FRIDAY/SATURDAY LABOR DAY WEEKEND
TRIP WITH MY HUSBAND FRED

DOUBLETREE HOTEL
2:00 or 3:00 A.M.

Something suddenly woke me up and I realized the dark room was spinning fast. Looking around the room, I could not tell if the bed was doing the spinning or if the whole room was spinning. While the room or bed was still spinning, I saw three shadows. Two of these shadows were on my left side of the bed. I looked at them and they quickly walked to the end of the bed to join the third shadow. I felt as if I was no longer in the room but in a dark space with these "alien shadows."

The front of my left leg, below the knee and about three inches above the left ankle, in an area one inch wide felt as if the shin bone of my left leg was being drilled into. I felt a deep pain in my leg; I wanted to cry out but could not. The pain did not spread around the leg as I would have expected but felt as if it remained in that one area where they were drilling into the bone. For some reason I felt as if my leg was raised up and was being supported by something. Then when my leg was again lowered, the dark space in which I was being held, stopped spinning.

When I woke up, I realized I was back in the hotel room. I could not turn my body toward Fred. I immediately stretched out my right arm to touch Fred. To my surprise I could not feel him lying in bed. I quickly sat up in the large king size bed and dragged my body and numb left leg over toward a black, long shape. I thought it was Fred's body, but was unsure because of the contorted position he seemed to be in. Realizing it *was* Fred lying there, I woke him up and told him about my leg and what had just transpired. He paid no attention to me and went back to sleep.

Lying next to him, I grabbed onto his warm body. I wanted to turn on the light but was afraid to look at my leg. Instead, I brought my left leg toward my body and began rubbing the painful area until I fell asleep. When I woke up in the morning, the leg was still quite painful. I examined the area where I felt pain and strangely, did not find any bruising or cuts. What I *did* find were two round ¼ inch needle marks. They were brown in color and just about one inch above the area in question. I rubbed my hand over the affected leg and found a round deep indentation where I had felt the leg being drilled into. Some bone seemed to be missing in this area which indicated that perhaps bone *had* been removed. The pain subsided later that afternoon. Within one month the bone grew back completely.

At this point I would like to jump ten years ahead to February, 2013. The first of February I did not document the day when my lower *right* leg became quite painful. I examined the area about four inches above the ankle at the center of my leg. I found a deep indentation of apparently missing bone. As of March 17, 2013 the pain has subsided, but I have a deep indention in the bone. I have no memory of what might have caused this.

SEPTEMBER 2, 2003
TUESDAY, A.M.

I was taken into this experience readily. I abruptly woke in the darkness with a man who was dressed in camouflage military dress, standing on the left side of my bed. I had not heard any low flying helicopters that would have aroused me. Before I could move my body I was injected with a needle that held some type of chemical to put me back to sleep.

When I awoke for the second time, I found my neck turned downward and resting on my shoulder. My neck was in a lot of pain and I assumed the pain was coming from the way I had turned my neck downward towards my shoulder. I heard the motor of a vehicle and smelled dirt. I raised my neck up to look around and saw I was in the back seat of a vehicle. I soon realized that I had ridden in a vehicle like this before. Looking around the inside of this vehicle I saw a man who was dressed in military camouflage uniform and appeared to be an American. He was the driver of this vehicle that looked like the inside of a jeep. I turned my head to the right and saw another man who sat next to me. He had dark brown or black hair and was also dressed in military camouflage. I was in a daze and not coherent. I just did not care, but I was thinking about where I was being taken. Just realizing that I was in some kind of vehicle with two military men riding on a rough dirt road was enough for me for the moment.

The windows of the vehicle had been covered with a dark sun screen which made it hard to see outside. I could barely see out but with the bright sun outside I knew it was day light. I was quickly reprimanded to not look through the windows as there was nothing to see outside and to keep my vision downward. I quickly followed his orders because I noticed a gun on a rack between the passenger and driver side in the front of the vehicle. The man who sat next to me also wore a gun on his belt. I do not remember if I was still in my night gown or what I was wearing. I wondered how I'd gotten into this situation and where I was being taken. I felt like a prisoner who had committed some crime.

The vehicle eventually stopped and the man who was sitting beside me was the first to get out. He grabbed me and pulled (dragged) me out of the vehicle while holding onto my neck. I was instructed not to look back to see what I had been riding in. Hearing the door slam shut we began walking while he held onto my neck. He did not have such a strong hold on my neck that I could not turn a little bit and see that the vehicle was camouflaged with browns and greens and that it was a Hummer. I also got a quick glance at my military "escort" who stood approximately five feet seven inches tall and was somewhat "stocky." He appeared to be an American/Hispanic. He spoke fluent English. This man told me he had orders to bring me to India and show me the desolate parts of India first. I thought to myself and literally said out loud, "Sure.....Yeah, right, how did we get to India so quickly?"

Fully awake, thoughts began to fill my mind like, "Where am I really?" and "How many minutes or hours have passed since I was brought here?"

In the distance I noticed some dark skinned people surrounding what appeared to be a small fire. As we walked toward them they indeed appeared to be East Indian people from India. Making note of the situation the military man pointed out to me how these people were dressed. They were dressed in East Indian clothing, not American dress. The men were dressed in old white shirts and white or khaki pants. Some of the men had slight tears in the material of their shirts. The women were dressed in colorful shirts with a long skirt that had designs throughout the material. I noticed that most of the men had not shaven their faces so they "sported" a dark shadow, and I saw some men with heavy beards. I thought men from India did not grow hair on their faces but....this is what I saw.

These people began to stare at me and seemed to have a fearful look in their eyes. The women were kneeling on straw mats on the ground cooking some type of food in a large gray pot over an open pit fire. I could smell a familiar spice (which is curry) that the women used in the food that was being cooked. The food the ladies were cooking appeared to be brown in color and soupy. I listened intently to the women's conversations as they spoke quickly in their own language while covering up their mouths with their hands so I could not hear what they were saying. Evidently I must have had a frightened look on my face because the conversation stopped and the women just stared at me with bewilderment. Standing next to the military man I noticed about five Indian men who came and stood close by. They gathered around in a circle speaking excitedly also saying something in what sounded to me like an Indian language dialect.

A small girl and boy around the ages of eight or nine years old approached us as they carried water in a galvanized pail from a water well. The water was for cooking and with what water was left in the bucket, the people began to wash their faces.

I looked around the area and noticed some stone houses that were connected together. They reminded me of Native American built houses on pueblos in New Mexico. My military "escort" proceeded to walk me toward the stone houses accompanied by a few of the Indian men. As we walked closer to these homes I saw that the stones were rocks of different sizes that had been cemented together.

The military escort had not lessened the hold on my neck during this whole time and my neck was hurting from his hold on me. As we approached the stone houses I was led inside of one of the homes. It appeared that my escort was searching for someone as he was asking questions of the Indian men in their dialect. It appeared that my escort kept repeating the question over and over again. The men just shrugged their shoulders, extended their arms outward and made facial expressions that told me the person in question was not there.

Looking quickly at the interior of this home I saw one large room, with folded blankets, a wooden cabinet that held clothing and other miscellaneous items. I then was led out of this home by my escort and we walked toward where the ladies were cooking. The military man spoke with them as well. Their facial expressions became sad.

My escort then turned my body by twisting my arm, using strong fingers that pinched me. We began to walk toward the water well. I didn't understand why I was shown the water well other than that the water he brought up had brown sediment in it. While standing next to the water well I smelled a strong odor of sewage, and I saw we were quite close to a small ditch that was filled with raw sewage. This was confirmed to me because I saw a man who was using the ditch to urinate into. This man thought nothing of a woman standing and watching him urinate. The small ditch ran throughout the property and also held solid human waste.

The military man released his hold on my neck but held my arm tightly. I was instructed to walk backwards. Frightened again, I thought, "What is it he does not want me to see?" Taking small steps looking downward at the brown uneven dirt, my escort demanded I close my eyes and keep my head down as he turned me around. He threatened me by reminding me that I knew what would happen to me if I did not follow his instructions! He did not know I had peeked and saw the Hummer when we arrived at this place. I was forced into the vehicle but had trouble stepping up into it so he helped me inside and I stumbled onto the seat. I don't know why he did not want me to see this vehicle.

After getting into the vehicle I was told I was going to be taken to the U.S. Counselor's home. My escort/guard who sat next to me covered my eyes with a black blindfold. The driver of this vehicle gave the instructions to do so. The man who sat next to me did not check to be sure he had covered my eyes completely. This left me able to see somewhat through the sides and top of the blindfold. Because of that, I kept my head turned away from him. A short conversation took place and my escort said once again that he was to show me the poor and desolate parts of India. I asked him "why" but he did not answer.

I felt that we traveled in the vehicle for about one hour. The dirt road felt bumpy and I could smell dirt again. I peeked through the blindfold and there were no other buildings around until we reached a smooth paved road. Not until then did I see better living conditions and many more East Indian people. I don't know the name of the city I was taken to.

Eventually we arrived at the destination and when the vehicle stopped the door opened and the blindfold was removed by my escort/ guard. I was invited to step outside the vehicle, not dragged as before. I saw a black wrought iron fence surrounding a large two story beige/ blondish stone house. My military escort chose to stand and walk again on my left, holding onto my reddened arm. He always seemed to stay on the left side of my body. I asked myself, "Why?"

I don't remember if I was told the name of the American Counselor I was to meet and speak with. My escort/guard knocked on the heavy dark wood door and a small Indian man answered the door welcoming us. It felt as if we were expected. This small Indian man was dressed quite nicely in a dark suit and white shirt. He spoke in broken English. My escort/guard spoke in an Indian dialect to this man. I was pushed into the entryway of the foyer of a room and I quickly glanced around. I saw a beautiful room that held expensive looking East Indian furniture and accessories. About twenty feet away I noticed a small Indian woman dressed very nicely in East Indian dress but with a white apron on. She had a warm smile on her face as she stared at me. After my escort and the man conversed seemingly about the whereabouts of the "American Counselor" we were guided up a wooden stairway to an office that held a wood desk and leather chairs. Against the opposite wall stood a large table that held what appeared to be a topographical model of land and an ocean.

I waited in anticipation to meet this American Counselor, thinking to myself, "He will help me find safety and let me know why I am here." We waited a few minutes then an American man walked through another door that had been closed. He was about six feet tall with blondish hair, and a strong muscled body. His age might have been around fiftyish. He immediately shook my hand and invited us to sit down. I was offered some hot tea which I accepted because I was very thirsty. The lady whom I'd seen downstairs brought me the tea. It was delicious and I sipped it slowly. The tea made me feel relaxed and at ease. I did not even question whether the tea had been drugged or not. It just tasted good.

The conversation that took place between the two men was in an Indian dialect. I thought this was so that I would not know what they were talking about. We were asked then to step toward the table that held the topographical model of land and an ocean. I saw white buildings coming out of the ocean. Apparently, I failed to see the land these buildings were built on. The two men, now speaking in English, said these buildings held some

type of nuclear and advanced laser technologies given by the alien federation. They also spoke about some type of test that would occur at some future time.

At this point I don't remember what other directives were given me by the American Counselor. He spoke to me in English as he explained the reason I was chosen for this project. This U.S. Counselor told me that a nuclear test was to occur on the ocean floor and could cause disastrous outcomes such as monstrous tidal waves and earthquakes worldwide. These white buildings were to be built with something inside of them. I don't remember what they said was to be inside the buildings. My mind was spinning fast and therefore, not paying attention to what I was being told.

Apparently the tea was drugged as I don't remember anymore until I woke up the next morning in my own bed. Little bits of memory came back to me as I lay in bed. I immediately began to write down my memories. I remembered the phrases "government testing" and "using people." I thought more about the memory and it seemed to fade quickly, I tried hard to reflect on the experience. I remembered the sentence, "A small nuclear bomb with some technologies from an alien species that this government works with….the cause and effect remains unknown." My mind was once again controlled to "forget" until future world events occurred.

I ask myself, "What was the reason behind my being abducted and taken to India to meet this 'Counselor'? What part do I have in this plan? Had I unknowingly worked in the lab that I spoke of in "Morning Glory" on this project with the universal aliens and my own government?"

Until this date I have doubted this experience! When I entered the American Counselor's home and office, for my own confirmation, I did see a small American Flag in the Counselor's office. I also saw certificates on his office wall stating he was an actual American Counselor. I didn't know what to look for in an embassy office.

My question is, did the rogue U.S. government put me into a hologram test like I had been in before? Was mind control used on me so that I would not remember? Up to present date I have not been taken back to India. I have a source though who did visit the desolate poor areas of India. This person confirmed what I had seen there. I have so many questions to ask, but whom do I ask?

JUNE 1, 2013
CONFIRMATION

I recently spent some time in the Tacoma and Seattle area of Washington. I met with a cousin who had been working on indigenous children's programs in India with the very poor. During our conversations, he told me about the living conditions where he had worked in India. He described the water wells, the stone built houses, the open sewage system that is still being used and the way the poor people dress. He told me that the poor people use animal or human waste to plaster the outside of their houses! He also described the way the "rich" people of India build their beautiful homes. Unknowingly, my cousin confirmed what I had experienced in India. To have confirmation was quite shocking because now I had to deal with the whole experience of literally being there. Once again I asked myself "Why?" How was I taken there so quickly and for what reason? I was given the name of Dharaui/Mumba's a shadow city and eyesore in the middle of India's financial capital. The person who gave me this information said I have described such a place.

ONE YEAR LATER
OCTOBER 24, 2004

Regarding my experience in India, I was given this article by an unknown lady named Brenda who works with a doctor who is a paranormal researcher that I know. The doctor does not want to be identified. Here is the article:

"Sources in the Government and UFO researchers opine like America. India is on the verge of gaining military and civilian technologies from extraterrestrial visitors! Another major superpower?

According to some UFO researchers and think-tanks all over the world, India's recent experiences with countless UFO's near the Himalayas are significant. India is one of the nations in the world with largest number of technocrats and education is regarded as one of the major pride in every Indian family. According some inner circles in the Government and the defense establishments, India is on the verge of gaining technologies for civilian and military purposes from the extra-terrestrial cultures. Some strongly feel India and American are the two champions of free speech and democracy. And that is why they may have chosen India to lead the world to the order of the Universe. According to many the order of the Universe is to live peacefully, share knowledge and be spiritually elevated. And India is just ready to lead the world towards that. Which other nation can gain futuristic technologies and not gobble up the world?

Indian's Air Force, Navy and Army will gain immensely from these technologies. The main theme of these technologies is anti-gravity driven vehicles and spatial motion control in 3D. Some say America thirty years back was offered vehicles and spacecraft that ran based on anti-gravity. America's biggest secret research is on that. The Stealth technology that makes a flying vehicle invisible to radar or similar electronic eyes is also from the extra-terrestrial know how, researchers say.

India may gain immensely from these technologies and become a super power. India technocrats and dedicated military personnel will be able to harness these technologies and bring peace to the world. India is probably the only country that spiritually inclined. That makes a big difference. Those who have a close encounter with extra-terrestrial beings say they are spiritually elevated and the energy levels are very high from those beings. It is also said that final frontier of science and technology will come from integration of human spirituality and modern science and technologies.

India is also learning about the order of Universe – the common courtesy and the law of the Universe. Some say year 2012 is when they will land on earth. And for that matter India is one of the chosen countries for pilot projects.

I found this news article helpful in understanding my strange experience in India. However, I found it puzzling that 2012 was the date when extra-terrestrials were expected on earth because everyone involved in this phenomenon knows that universal beings have been on our planet earth for thousands of years.

I discussed this experience with a few researchers and friends who are either alien abductees or who work with and have knowledge of these phenomena. I don't yet know what to make of my experience in India including what I was shown by the U.S. Counselor.

OCTOBER 2003
VISIONS

I heard the familiar electronic sound in my ear and realized it was a communication to me from an unknown source. After the electronic sound stopped I was shown a vision. In the vision I recognized New York City since I had been there before. I found myself standing on a beach. I was looking out toward the ocean, when I saw the waters begin to recede farther and farther out, away from the beach. I saw nothing more than jumping and dying fish, seaweed and different layers of the ocean floor. Someone was hollering "Tsunami." I was then lifted up above the ocean from where I saw and experienced the turmoil of a major earth quake centered far out in the ocean. I saw the rolling waters and a huge wave traveling over the layers of ocean floor. Then I was quickly taken back to the beach in New York City where I found myself standing on the rolling ground. Then I was again lifted up above the ground to see the tsunami hit buildings, flooding the center of New York City.

A couple nights later I had another vision in which I experienced the devastating explosion of Mt. Rainier located near Seattle, Washington. I was standing nearby the volcano and actually felt the heat of the molten rock being spewed everywhere.

As of this writing these visions have yet to come true.

NOVEMBER 1, 2003

I woke up to something touching my back and it felt like a finger. I quickly turned over to see who was touching me. No one there! I heard noises outside the bedroom. They were coming from the connecting office. I got up to go to the bathroom thinking, *"It is just my imagination."* I was wide awake and as I walked through an open doorway from the bedroom into a short hallway that leads to the bathroom, I turned my head. Through the open dining room that connects to the living room I saw the very tall dark shape of a man's shadow facing toward the living room. I ran in fear into the bathroom, closing and locking the door behind me. I was thinking, *"He is coming after me."* After several minutes, I realized the house was very quiet, so I unlocked the door and walked back toward the bedroom, looking rapidly through the area. To my relief and amazement, the dark shadow of a man was not there. I went into our bedroom and then a strange thought came into my mind that the man had probably already entered our bedroom. I found Fred still sleeping soundly. I suddenly felt a strong presence in the room. I lifted my leg to quietly get back into bed thinking, ***"Darn this imagination of mine."*** I no sooner got that thought out in my mind than I felt a strong presence approach me from my left side. The "presence" jumped in front of me into our bed leaving a depression on the bed. I actually saw someone's hands grab my sleeping husband. I don't remember if I blacked out at this point or if something just blocked out the memory that took place.

When Fred woke up in the morning he sat up in bed and exclaimed, "Something happened during the night!" He would never talk about what happened even after I approached him on the subject several times.

NOVEMBER 13, 2003

Again I heard another electronic sound in my ear, accompanied by a vision. I was taken back to New York City to the same beach. I found myself witnessing a repetitive scenario of the earthquake. I felt the ground rolling violently and knew from before, that the earthquake was somewhere far out in the ocean. I was lifted up once again high above buildings, this time hearing screams coming from the people that were below me. There was nothing I could do to save these people. I helplessly watched high ocean waves hit buildings and saw the walls of these buildings come crashing onto people as they drowned. I saw cars, and buses being tossed about.

I saw huge waves of rolling earth. They seemed to cause devastation throughout the connecting states across the United States working their way in a straight line toward the state of Washington. Then I found myself standing on a dark rim in the middle of somewhere. I saw hot molten lava and hot black liquid beginning to spew from a large hole. I could feel the burning heat, as I was bathed and burned. I was then lifted to a safe distance where I observed what seemed to be all hell breaking loose. I was told I was experiencing the worst eruption the earth has ever had. All towns surrounding Tacoma and Seattle were completely devastated.

I was also shown the aftermath of this large earthquake and erupting volcano that devastated much of the United States. I saw what appeared to be a nuclear winter. Many lives were lost. I was not sure what species put me though this hologram. I was told telepathically that this is to happen in our future. Who is to say that one day it could not happen? I would like to know who instilled this vision in me and for what reason! Who controls such visions given to certain abductees? Who is studying our emotions toward such horrific events? What are they learning from us?

The November 1st and 13th visions were experienced by many abductees.

Many of them waited in fear, knowing that the two visions they experienced would happen soon. These visions never became reality. I feel that perhaps a study was conducted by the universal aliens to observe our emotions and reactions to the magnitude of such destruction. Was the study done for the good of human-kind? Perhaps they seek to help if these events actually do occur? If in fact, universal aliens did conduct these "holograms" would they be here to help survivors in the aftermath?

FEBRUARY 25, 2004

I was awake around 3:30 a.m. lying in bed and just staring directly into the connected room that we use as our office. I was looking directly at the glass brick window. I watched as two blue circles of lights passed through the brick glass window to the outside. I do not know from where these blue lights originated within the house. They passed over my head, into the office and exited through the brick glass window. I just laid there in bed watching this.

MARCH 2, 2004

When I woke up I was laying on my back. Directly in front of me, some feet away, I saw two men dressed in the familiar white lab coats. They were doing something at a counter top. I could not move my body and I felt quite drugged. I could not see clearly since I was not wearing my contacts or eye glasses. I thought to myself, *"They did not do whatever they do to my eyes to make me have the 20-20 vision I experience when I am abducted even by the military."* Looking around the brightly lit room to see if it looked familiar to me, I saw medical equipment that reminded me of a hospital operating room. I became more coherent and felt more awake. I felt something inside my mouth on the left side that seemed to travel down my throat. It was uncomfortable. I pressed my tongue along the object that was in my mouth. *"A tube"* I thought. *"It feels like a plastic round tube."* I kept pressing my tongue against the object, following it with my tongue. The plastic tube ran to the outside of my mouth and was pressing against my chin. As I touched the long protruding round tube inside my mouth I felt it running down my throat. My throat hurt (like a mild sore throat) when I swallowed.

I tried to remain calm and not shake with fear. I said to myself, *"I have not experienced this type of abduction and experimentation in such a long time. Am I just dreaming or is this actually happening to me again?"*

I focused on my environment, hoping this was just a dream. *"If I am dreaming why do I feel this tube in my mouth and pain in my throat? The pain.....the pain..... Oh my, I feel something that*

hurts on my bottom. I feel something protruding OUT of my…. bottom (anus). It does not feel right…. WHAT IS GOING ON HERE? WHAT ARE THEY DOING TO ME?"

I moaned. The two men looked at me. One of them walked over and said "She is awake." There was no sympathy from him at all. He turned and walked back to whatever they were working on at the counter.

I thought if I could just move my hips by pushing or rolling over a little I could determine what the object was that seemed to be coming out of my anus. I realized I was still quite drugged and therefore, I could not roll over or even move my arms.

I tried to slightly rub my hips and cheeks over the table but excruciating pain shot upward into my body. The pain traveled far into my body, shocking me into a memory of a medical test I had experienced. The memory was of a colonoscopy to locate colon cancer. This procedure is done by inserting a tube that has a small camera into the anus going to the colon and searching for polyps or tumors within the colon. I had been hospitalized for the colonoscopy.

In the year 2003 I experienced a form of gastro-esophageal reflux, though the doctor was not certain about the diagnosis of GERD. The medications the doctor prescribed were not helping the reflux.

Soon after eating I would vomit up food with a burning acid. This would last until late into the night.

I also underwent another test for reflux. A tube going into my stomach was inserted into my nose and mouth. A small computer was then attached at my waist, to be worn for approximately forty-eight hours.

When I left the hospital, wearing the unit, it was functioning perfectly. When I returned to the hospital, the test results were inconclusive because the computer had malfunctioned at some point during those forty-eight hours. I did not choose to repeat the test. I was sent back to the hospital for another test. For that procedure, I had to fast, and then eat radiated scrambled eggs. After a three hour period, the food I had ingested, rather than moving into the intestines like it should, traveled backward into the stomach near the tube that carries food from the esophagus. Thus, I would bring up the acid and food.

At one point there was some excitement about what was being seen on the monitors. The radiologist ran out of the room and brought back another radiologist to view what they saw on the monitors. They spoke quietly amongst themselves. This information was never documented on the medical forms.

The monitors were large and I was in close proximity to them. What I saw on the monitors was the outline of a fetus lying in the bottom of my stomach.....along with the scrambled eggs I had eaten. The outline was larger than just the scrambled eggs! I did not dare say anything or ask any questions about what this was. I already knew.

I discussed this procedure - using the stomach for implanting hybrids - in Morning Glory. I had asked how I could still be used as an incubator for producing hybrid babies after having had a hysterectomy in 1984. I was told by Mr. Budd Hopkins that the aliens were now using my stomach for this purpose - as an incubator for the production of hybrid babies.

Once again, I found myself lying on a table in an unknown space, not knowing where I was, and not feeling safe. Many thoughts entered into my head. *"Why am I being tested in this manner again? Who*

51

requested these tests? Who are these men? Where am I?"

I was awake and I heard a pulsating noise coming from a machine. The tubes coming out of my body were hooked up to the machine. The machine was pulling something out of my body through the tubes. After a time which felt like forever, two men came to where I was lying and told me to open my mouth and they removed the mouth tube. They rolled me over onto my left side and pulled the long tube from my anus. As they removed the tube, it felt as if my entire intestine had been invaded. The men did not talk much to each other, and even less to me. One of them sat me up while the other one had his back toward me doing something to the machine. He then walked away from us. I could not see what he was carrying. I happened to look downward. On the white sheet was brown liquid. I suspected it was liquid "feces" that had come from me. My body felt limp and I thought I was going to pass out and fall off of the table. As the second man rolled away a small black square machine, I blacked out.

I awoke the next morning in my bed, with this memory and feeling tired. I felt no pain from the previous night's process other than a sharp pain in my left lung as I breathed in and out. The lung pain remained with me all day. I experienced no pain or soreness around my anus or in my throat. I did find the usual needle marks or bruising --- a good indication that something did occur. Even when I have no memory of abductions but experience the "day after" symptoms, I always confirm with the needle marks, and bruising.

The following week I could not get any restful sleep. The nighttime feeling of anxiety about this past scenario would wake me at odd hours of the night. Yet, when I did sleep then wake up around 2:00 or 3:00 a.m., I felt oddness within myself. It was as if something *had* occurred, but I did not have any memory of it.

I would lie awake, and knowing something was not right. I thought I had been abducted during these times, but I did not recognize any abduction symptoms. On several occasions, I would wake up with soreness in my throat, and intestinal pain, to where I had to rush to the bathroom barely making it to the toilet. I would experience a bad case of painful diarrhea that would last for most of the day. Then after a period of time I felt great as if nothing had occurred. I just wanted to say, "Go figure!"

APRIL 27, 2004
STOPPAGE OF TIME? WHAT HAPPENED?

Monday, 4:00 p.m: While I was on the telephone my right nostril began to bleed. For awhile I continued to blow out thick, dark red tissue. I realized this had happened many times before.

Fred and I had a late dinner. After cleaning up from dinner I looked at the kitchen clock. The time was 8:14 p.m. I went into the bedroom and Fred was sound asleep. For some reason I glanced at the bedroom clock. The time was 8:15 p.m. I decided to take a shower. During my shower my nostril began to bleed heavily. The bleeding continued as I dried myself off. When I left the bathroom and went back into the bedroom I glanced at the clock again. The time on the clock said it was 8:15 p.m. I thought the clock had stopped because the real time should have been after 9:00 p.m. So I went into the kitchen to get the correct time to set the bedroom clock. The kitchen clock also read 8:15 p.m. I thought to myself that this couldn't be right. So I went to the living room clock and that clock also read 8:15 p.m. Both the kitchen and living room clocks run on a battery. The bedroom clock runs on electricity. I walked back to each room checking the times on the clocks. All clocks still read 8:15 p.m. I sat on the bed in a dazed state feeling somewhat strange. I don't know when I came out of this dazed state. I looked once again at the bedroom clock and the time was still 8:15 p.m. Fred was waking up from his nap and I commented to him that the time was 8:15 p.m. I went into my office, checked that clock against all the other clocks for the next half hour and yes, the clocks kept moving with the correct time. I don't understand this timing error or what happened earlier in the evening. I *DO* remember being in the shower.

A little later memory came back to me from earlier that same afternoon. Around 2:00 p.m. I heard a familiar male voice calling out my name. He called out my name twice, and I said to myself,

"Oh forget it and go away." This happened again around 3:00 p.m. with the same male voice calling out my name. I said, "Sorry, I'm busy and am not going to pay attention to you".

Perhaps I should have paid more attention to the person or Being that called out to me. I did not sleep comfortably that night because I kept trying to figure out the missing time. My nose bled consistently into the night.

MAY 21 and 22, 2004

On this night I took out of the drawer a clean set of pajamas and laid them on the bed. While putting on the top of my P.J.'s, I looked down at the right hand sleeve as my arm went through. On the cuff of the right sleeve I saw large splatters and circles of what looked to be fresh blood. I followed this blood up the arm and saw 1/8 to ¼ inch round circles of splattered blood on the sleeve. These spots also appeared to be fresh blood. I moved my head downward while slipping on the top of the pajamas attempting to button it up. To my surprise, I saw more splattered blood on the right front side of the top. The spots were the same size as those on the sleeve.

Fred, who was already in bed, looked toward me and exclaimed, "What is that on the back of your P.J. top?" I removed the top to look and there were more of the same sized circles of splattered blood all located on the right backside of my P.J.'s. I showed Fred the sleeve and front of the P.J.'s. We then checked my body for cuts, or any wounds that might have explained where these blood spots came from. We found nothing to explain the source. I washed my P.J. top and the spots washed out just like blood.

During the night I believe I was abducted with someone I do know, who is a male. The memory is that I woke up in a very dark room, lying on a bed with this male. I thought we were with the Reptilians but I did not see them there. This scenario had happened once before when the Reptilians abducted us. I reached over the male's body and called out to him several times, but he did not answer me. I think he was asleep or something was wrong with him. My vision suddenly went black and I fell back onto the bed.

The next morning when I woke up I felt so tired I did not want to get out of bed. I moved my legs out from under the covers and sat on the side of the bed. I saw that my slippers had been pushed about four feet away from the bed. One slipper was in front of the other by the mirrored closet door. I found my wooden back scratcher (which is always kept under my side of the bed) lying along side of the slippers.

OCTOBER 20, 2004

MORNING

I woke up and sat on the side of the bed feeling out of sorts and very tired. Fred was getting up at the same time. He happened to look toward my back, and he exclaimed in a loud voice, "What is that red line on the back of your neck?" I touched the back of my neck and I felt a sensation of burning skin. I went to the bathroom to look in the mirror at the back of my neck. I saw a red line across my neck that appeared to have been burnt into the skin.

I remember I was up that previous night sitting in the office area in the recliner because I could not sleep. I looked at the clock in that room and it was 3:30 a.m. I happened to glance toward the south side of the room where there are four small glass brick windows. At the top of these windows I saw a large flashing blue light. I thought the flashing blue light was strange looking, as it was reflected on the top wall and below the ceiling where the glass block windows were located; but only on that wall. No other walls reflected the flashing blue lights. For some reason I did not feel compelled to get up from the recliner, open the door, and look outside to investigate the flashing blue light. I stared at the blue light and I don't remember anything else. I'm uncertain if an abduction took place that evening. I do not remember at any point, getting up from the chair, walking back to bed, and placing bed covers over my body. But I found myself in bed next to Fred in the morning.

OCTOBER 26 and 27, 2004

My daughter had invited me to go see the movie, "Forgotten." It was showing at 7:35 p.m. at Century 24, one of Albuquerque's large theaters. The theater was approximately ten miles from our home. (This is a movie I do recommend for those who feel they are under mind control.)

Later, I wondered if something in this movie triggered an unknown memory. Here is the kicker though: walking to my car after the movie with my daughter (I had driven alone to the theatre and met her there) we noticed that a small blue car was parked very close to my car. She continued walking toward her car as I walked sideways between the two cars to unlock and get into my car. I realized there was hardly any room for me to completely open my car door. Noticing two large men in the front seat of this car with the windows down, I immediately felt unsafe, and knew something was not right. The driver of the car was on a cell phone. As I was unlocking the driver's door of my car, intuition told me to get away from my car quickly. I relocked the driver's door, rapidly walked sideways in the narrow path between both cars, then walked to safety where my daughter was entering her car. I asked her to not leave the area until she saw me safely in my car because I felt uncomfortable with the situation of the two men in the small car. As I walked back to my locked car, I turned and looked at the men for identification purposes. I was able to get a good look at the driver because of a light pole nearby. The light from the pole shown down on his face as he turned to look at me; but because of the dim light on the other side of the car I could not see the passenger's face very well and the passenger appeared to be a very large man. I walked sideways again on the narrow path quickly unlocking my door and wondering how I was going to get into my car. I could not open my car door more than several inches from where I was standing. I took a deep breath and squeezed myself into the opening of the car door. I could not squeeze myself into the seat quickly enough. In the process of trying to get into my car, I noticed that the man in the passenger seat was holding up some kind of object and pointing it at me. The object resembled something about the size of a gun except it appeared to be white in color. I quickly locked the car door, feeling very uneasy as both men were now staring at me. My imagination came into play. I wondered if my car was going to explode as I turned the key in the ignition; or what if they had done something to my car? I turned the key and nothing appeared to be wrong. I attempted to back out of the parking space but as I did, another car drove up behind me and stopped me from backing out. My car was blocked by the other car. I shifted into forward gear as there was a space I could squeeze through, but evidently I was too slow because at the very same moment another car drove right in front of my car. I was surrounded and could not move my car either way. Not knowing what was going to transpire, I thought to myself, *"If this other car is going to block my way out, and if anything should occur, I will try to ram my car against either of these cars that block my way out of this unusual situation."* As panic played, I did not think of honking my horn to alert anyone. I saw my daughter had driven away and was about to enter the main street, leaving me alone in this situation. The men who were parked next to me just sat and watched as I saw the car in front of me back up and drive away. I quickly pulled forward and made a left turn, traveling in front of the parked car that had been parked beside me. The light reflected on both men as I passed in front of their car. I was able to see the driver clearly and noticed he was watching me drive past.

"Oh God," I said out loud, "I recognize this man!" I slowed down as I drove past. I was able to get a good look at him. I said to myself, *"Oh My God! Get out of here Gloria! They're going to get you again!"* I recognized the driver as the man I had written about in "Morning Glory" Diary of an Alien Abductee in the chapters about my military and government abductors. The driver of this car appeared to be the very same man that had straddled my body as I kicked and fought him in my bed before being abducted and taken to Washington, D.C. that night!

I drove quickly out of the parking area and did not pay attention to the whereabouts of the other cars that had blocked mine. I pulled out onto the main street and followed it to the busy highway, knowing I would be okay. I kept an eye on the rear view mirror. It appeared

I was not being followed. My thoughts at the time were, *"How silly and stupid I made this situation look. No wonder they were looking at me. The man I thought I recognized could have been any other man who looked like the person who had abducted me."*

I reached the cross street I needed to get home and made a right turn, traveling south. I still had an eerie feeling and felt somewhat uncomfortable. When I turned onto the cross street, I had to slow down as a late model large white car pulled out in front of me coming out of a shopping center. The white car slowed and moved into another lane. When I looked in the rear view mirror, the car was right behind me, driving very close to the back of my car. The driver tailgated me for several blocks. Talking to myself I said, *"Okay, he wants to play games so we will play."* I stepped on the brake so the driver would back off and away from my car. The driver did not back off and I thought he was going to hit me. I repeated the procedure as his car crept even closer to mine and then he did drop back. I moved to the far left lane thinking, if he was following me he would also change lanes. Bad luck. A red light stopped me and I saw that the white car had moved to the far right lane and was even with my car at the red light. I noticed the driver of the white car was "another large man." Just then, a car drove up in the middle lane, blocking my view of the white car. When the light turned green the white car sped up and moved into the lane I was in. Now he was in front of me. I slowed down. For the next several miles, my thoughts were on my safety. I wondered if there was a connection between what had transpired in the parking lot and the car that appeared to be tailing me and was now in front of me. *"Do I take the chance and go home or what?"* I came to the turn bay I needed to get onto the street that led to my home. I made a decision *"If the man in the white car sees me turning and continues to follow me, I will not go home but go to a place of safety."* I made the turn down my street to get home. After arriving home safely, I spoke of these concerns with Fred.

Shortly thereafter, my daughter called to see if I'd gotten home safely. She wanted to know if everything was okay. She lives approximately nineteen or twenty miles away, on the opposite side of town from where we live. Her drive time should have been approximately thirty to thirty-five minutes to arrive home using the freeway. I told her that I had just gotten home about five minutes before she called. My drive home *should* have taken approximately twenty minutes.

I cannot account for the missing minutes. I certainly was not driving ten miles per hour to get home. This was an interesting drive home for me.

Later that evening I just questioned myself about the weird occurrences that transpired that evening. Were the men in the small car in the parking lot, the man I seemingly recognized, one of the men that I remembered as one of my government abductors? What was the object being pointed at me, and why were these two men parked so close to my car in the parking lot? Who was the man in the white car that appeared to be tailing or playing some sort of game with me? I don't know……Perhaps this was all just innocent and I questioned myself again.

Retiring later that night I thought I had a dream. Or had I awakened because Fred was lying almost on top of me? Next to his side of the bed was a strange Being whom I called an "old lady." She was dressed in some type of gold outfit. Evidently, light was shining from somewhere as her outfit glowed and I was able to see an old-looking, wrinkled face. My conscious mind told me that I was looking at an "old lady," but I knew that this was not an old wrinkled lady. "She" spoke to me as she went around the bed doing something to the width and length of the bed. Fred began to make noises as he half-slept through this. The "lady" and I conversed; she stood by the side of our bed while Fred and I remained in bed. Then I must have blacked out. When I woke up she was no longer there. I immediately woke Fred who was now lying next to me instead of on top of my body. I told him what had occurred. He had no knowledge of what had just transpired. I looked at the clock. The time was 3:41 a.m. Feeling a presence nearby, I did not want to leave the bed, but either had to visit the bathroom or wet the bed. I quickly ran to the bathroom. As I ran back to bed, I looked through the open door that leads to the entryway. I saw the large white shadow of a Being. I'd seen this white shadow of a "Being" once before, in the same area, on a different night. Who this Being was, I did not even want to know. I was so afraid I tried to wake Fred, but he would not wake up. I held tightly to his body and waited to see if the Being was going to come into our bedroom. Somehow, I fell asleep. When discussing this incident with Fred the next morning, I could not remember what the conversation was that I'd had with the old lady!

In the past four months, activity had increased in the townhouse where we lived. On some nights I woke up hearing footsteps either walking away from our bed or throughout the house. Whatever entity was wandering through the house at night would bump into something like a piece of furniture, or I would hear them pick up some item from a table.

Several times during the day, I would catch a glimpse of Jack, whom I will discuss later, appearing during daylight. I was able to see him clearly and not as a ghost.

This last incident made me think of some other activities that had occurred while Fred was not at home. Since Fall of that year as daylight was fading, whoever was trying to instill fear in me by scaring me, was taking advantage of that time, once a week, for about one month.

Twice, I was on the telephone when whoever it was, used the river rocks or some type of objects from the outdoor landscaping to scrape the living room window, making a loud scratching sound.

As I sat in the darkened living room speaking on the telephone, a person would come up to the living room window and scratch the window with an object. On the second incident in the lighted living room, I experience the same happening again. I was on the telephone, feeling comfortable and safe. I heard the footsteps outside and the familiar scraping of the window. I thought, ***"This time, I am going to catch whoever is doing this."*** I quickly ran into the adjoining bedroom, and not thinking…turned on the bedroom light and ran to the window…first mistake…I should have known better than to turn on the light……because I heard scrambling outside the window. I thought I'd scared off whoever, until about ten minutes later. I heard someone walking, then a rolling sound on the roof of the house as if whoever was up there fell and perhaps rolled across the roof.

The friend I had been on the telephone with suggested I look around inside the house to see if this person could have gained access to the inside from the roof. Once more, past memories set in. I remembered an incident when two men tried to enter our upstairs bedroom one night in the two-story town home we'd previously lived in. I was alone again during that night's invasion.

Now I cautiously walked from room to room, checking windows and locked doors. My friend insisted on calling the police. I told her "no" that I would run over to one of the neighbors to seek help if the sound of intrusion continued. I slowly walked to the door that led into the garage. Located in the garage was an outside door that we had blocked with shelving. But this shelving could easily be knocked down or pushed aside to gain entry into the garage.

I cautiously opened the door from the hallway that led into the garage. As I did this, I heard a noise. When I opened the hallway door to the garage I looked down at the floor. I noticed that the garage light had been turned on. Suddenly, two black shoes appeared right where I was standing in the doorway. I followed the shoes up to the legs. I saw black pants and as my eyes traveled further up the body, I realized it was a man's body. I saw his shirt then his face, and I was terrified. As the man advanced toward me, I began swinging with my fists and arms hitting and beating him. The man had an astonished look on his face like he could not understand why I was beating on him. When the fear left me, I realized I was beating on my husband! As he grabbed my arms and fists I stared at him and a loud laugh of fear took over my body and I ran back inside the house. I had hung up the telephone. It rang, and my friend on the other end thought I was in pain and that something drastic had happened. I rapidly calmed myself down. With a frightened hush, I explained away the laughter and incident that had led me to beat on my husband so fiercely.

To have someone drastically put fear into one's life such as this incident is quite unacceptable. Whoever was trying to instill fear in me certainly succeeded that night. But they will have to pay one day!

One particular summer evening prior to these invasions, my husband and I found drug apparatus left behind under the seat cover of our patio chairs. Fred contacted our local police department and the police came and picked up the drug apparatus. The policeman made this statement *"**Don't be surprised if whoever left this comes back to take some type of revenge if they find it gone**."* Soon after finding this drug apparatus an intruder seemed to be getting angrier or braver, as evidenced by some attempts to break into our home through the side door while I was at home.

Had I become delusional? Once again I questioned myself, Was this the beginning of activities that had previously stopped? Was the rogue military government still trying to instill fear and intimidate me again?

OCTOBER, 2004

Fred had been abducted on several nights this month but he had no memories of what occurred. On occasion he would awaken me from a deep sleep as he sat up in bed exclaiming, "Something happened!" I tried to remain calm while speaking to him so that any fresh memory could be recalled. With each word that came out of his mouth, the memory faded.

Eventually he would lie down, turn onto his side, and fall into a deep sleep. By morning, he had no memory of the occurrence of the previous night. After so many times of this type of lost memory and his reactions, I began to question if he was being controlled by the Mind Control Effect.

When Fred experienced these disturbing dreams the scenario would be the same. Unable to produce any information, he would shake his head and say that "Something strange happened." He could not remember what it was, but knew it had to do with "my friends" meaning the alien entities.

2002 – 2004
LOS ALAMOS, NEW MEXICO

I was asked by my husband, Fred, to join him on business trips to Los Alamos National Labs on a weekly basis. These trips were made to a highly secured area. Fred had a business contract with Los Alamos National Labs to maintain certain large computers. I did not join him weekly but perhaps every other week, if not once a month. In order to get into the particular area where Fred worked on various computers, a person had to have clearance higher than "Q" Clearance.

The first time I went with Fred, neither of us thought I would be allowed into the area where he worked. Fred planned to drive me into town to a restaurant we frequent in Los Alamos. I would visit the park and various local stores.

We arrived at the first guard shack. Fred would have to wait for someone from the restricted area to come pick him up and take him inside. Normally, that process would take twenty to thirty minutes. That first day, Fred told me to just take the car and go into town. When he finished work he would call me to come pick him up. We waited in the car until his "ride" showed up. The driver was a person we both knew. I was asked to join them. I wondered how this could happen since I have no government or military clearance whatsoever! After that call was made at the guard shack, I was seemingly "cleared" to enter a Top Secret area.

We traveled approximately half a mile in a camouflaged government jeep with a guard and the person we knew. We came to another guard shack where the guards were dressed in camouflage and heavily armed. Again, to my astonishment, I was cleared to proceed into a secured area. At that point, we transferred to another vehicle and were joined by one of the armed guards. I was to remain quiet and not ask questions. We drove down a two-lane road amongst tall pines for about fifteen or twenty minutes. I do not know how many miles we actually traveled. We approached a large white building surrounded by a high electric fence topped with barbed wire. The person we knew and the armed guard telephoned someone inside the building to let them know we had arrived.

The gate opened and we followed a sidewalk to the entrance of the building. To the side of the door was a telephone that was used to place a call verifying that "cleared known visitors" had arrived. Through a loud speaker outside and inside the building, we were announced as cleared visitors to the area. Workers were instructed to please put paperwork and items they were working on in a secured area until the "cleared visitors" have left the building and area of interest. The door was opened electronically. I was told to look straight ahead and follow, which I did for fear of being shot by the guard if I disobeyed. The guard then left the building and we were walked to the refrigeration vault room where the large main computers were located. Before entering the vaulted refrigeration room, another phone call was placed to a person inside who opened the door.

Fred felt quite comfortable with the procedure as he already knew everyone and had worked in that particular area often. On my first visit I did not remember names of the fifteen or twenty people who worked in the area, but I was made to feel comfortable. Everyone in the section greeted Fred and introduced themselves to me. I was then given the grand tour of the vaulted refrigerated room that held many of the large secured computers. On the right side of the door was a secured conference room where dignitaries would meet. Some of the important dignitaries were from Washington, D.C. I encountered such a meeting once while in this room.

Over time, as the years passed, I often went with Fred to Los Alamos. After signing my name twice at both guard shacks, I was readily able to enter without questions being asked. I followed the same procedure to gain entrance to the "unknown building" called Tech Area and was given a number each time. I had no freedom to walk the halls. If I had to use the ladies restroom one of the women would escort me and stay inside with me. After a couple of years I was allowed to be alone in the restroom. My escort would return to the vaulted room leaving me to walk myself back and push a special button to let someone open the door for me. I was given instructions to not look in any direction while walking to the door. There were many cameras and other security objects located in particular areas of the hallways.

Inside the vaulted room was a group of people identified as "Special Forces" for the United States. They were trained to deal with tragedies, nuclear emergencies, attacks on certain parts of the United States, and so forth. Their instructions came from Washington, D.C. Within minutes a helicopter would arrive at the back of the building to pick them up and take them to an airport. A jet from Kirtland/ Sandia Base would then take them to wherever they were needed. I was able to witness this happening once. The team was trained to dress in special clothing within seconds.

Now that I have revealed the above information in this book, I do not ever expect to be put into a situation such as this again in my life. Here though, I am trying to put together the information I acquired as an explanation for an experience I encountered after my husband passed away.

I believe it was during the year 2004, possibly at the end of 2003. I had left the vaulted refrigeration room to use the restroom. The inside of the vaulted door was opened by "the door keeper" which I teasingly called him. On my return trip back to the room, I looked directly forward into another closed area (a hallway that ran horizontally to the one in which the vaulted refrigeration room was located). The area in question was closed off by two large doors that had large windowpanes in each door. I walked down the hallway toward the refrigeration vaulted room and suddenly stopped in my tracks! Staring at me through one of the windows was a Grey Alien! I failed to document whether he spoke telepathically to me. I stood still, in shock, just staring back at him. I was released by the Grey's hold and walked slowly to the vaulted door and pushed the button to get back into the room.

My head was spinning. I tried to make sense out of what I had just seen in the window of the double doors.

Soon after this incident, some men were talking to Fred about a type of system that had been set up at Holloman Air Base, located in Alamogordo, New Mexico. The men wanted to show Fred some pictures and diagrams of the system, which were located in the head official's office. I was invited to go with them and we walked down a long hallway to the head official's office. The official had not cleared off the top of his desk. Lying on his desk was a large schematic (diagram) that I had seen before, onboard one of the alien ships. The large alien ship was being worked on and I had been assigned to help a United States Astronaut and some other men, whom I was told were scientists working with NASA. The Astronaut (who had walked on the moon and who has since passed away) and I were putting some type of square metal pieces onto the outside of a ship the size of a football field. Budd Hopkins hypnotized me about this experience, so there should be a recording of the hypnotherapy session I had with Mr. Hopkins.

Not one of the men said anything to me as I looked at the schematic and realized what it was. For some reason I felt it was left out on the desk for me to see. Once again I asked myself why I had been asked to go to the Director's office.

The unusual day continued. After leaving mid-afternoon and driving back to the guard shacks, our well-known friend asked Fred and me out to lunch. Lunch conversation was the usual "man talk" between Fred and his friend. After lunch, as we walked out of the restaurant, a conversation took place between the two men that I did not pay any attention to. However, when we stopped by the parked cars, my attention was drawn to their conversation. Our friend was telling Fred that yes, he knew what was in the mountain north of the ski area, and if we ever wanted to drive up there we could use the gated, guarded dirt road. The friend said he would go with us and would be able to get us in. The friend made sure I heard his last two statements because he repeated them. Was I to assume that was an area of alien activity? That day was the last time I visited the top secret facility - by my choice. I do not know if Fred went with anyone to that mountain range.

After Fred died, the friend, along with some of the other men, came to my home to pay their respects. A week later when I came home one afternoon, a large brown package was in the doorway from these men and their wives. I opened the package and brought out two large beautiful angel statues. I tried to call the friend, as I had his phone number, but could not reach him or his wife. I also had his address, so I sent a thank you note instead. The note was soon returned. "UNKNOWN" was stamped on the envelope. Trying to contact their family members was also impossible. The family had just simply disappeared from the face of the earth, not to be found!

That situation has left me with many questions. I thought about what I saw and what I was told, what I heard over the years, and wondered what it all meant. Were Fred and this Top Secret unit involved with the Universal Aliens? Did he work with and know them? Are the Universal Aliens still located in the mountain range that is connected to Los Alamos National Labs? What exactly did I stumble upon?

YEARS 2004 - 2005

It is noted that my husband Fred, as well as another abductee, both died of the same rare glioblastoma multiform cancerous brain tumor. The status of the remaining survivor is unknown at this time. Her diagnosis was also this same brain tumor. I find this unusual because of the connection of three families who are involved in this strange phenomenon. This particular, aggressive, fast-growing brain tumor has not been as widely researched or studied as other cancerous tumors. There has not yet been one doctor who could explain to me and answer my questions about how these cells generated or where they came from. How did these rare cells develop in Fred's brain? Is it because of cell phone usage? Or did these cells somehow invade his body through his hands-on work with computers he serviced in his business for so many years? There are many unanswered questions, and no knowledge of what kind of work the other families do for a living. Not knowing, I have no comparisons or answers. But the one answer I *did* get was in the form of the many threats I received from rogue government officials that are involved in this phenomenon.

A researcher told me that it was possible that deep within myself I knew that I had been there with Fred during his experiences with the alien species, or the rogue military government, when they perhaps implanted the cancerous cells into Fred's brain. This statement brought forth a feeling of "knowing" this statement to be true. I do plan to examine this through hypnotherapy and hopefully before this book is published I can share the results. Yes, I will again mention names of humans, and/or the alien species if there is sufficient cause.

There is an analogy used by a friend of ours, who is a medical doctor, to describe this aggressive fast-growing cancerous brain tumor. He used the example of the top of a full branch tree being like the top mass of cells of the tumor. It sends down its roots through the brain. Then the roots of the tumor grow and extend roots to the top of the brain once again with another mass of rare cells (tree tops). Finally, the brain is nothing more than a saturation of these rare cancerous tumor cells.

My husband was diagnosed nine days before his death from glioblastoma multiforme. Two weeks prior to his death the only symptoms we noticed were stress related problems. Day by day he became very sluggish; unusually tired to the point he would come home from teaching around 8:00 p.m. every night, hardly eat dinner, and then quickly retire to bed. Instantly, he would be in a deep sleep. At the end of the first week he began to experience other symptoms. He would forget certain words and how to pronounce them. These were words that he used daily in his conversations. As the second week continued, confusion and more forgetfulness began to present as symptoms.

That following dreadful Monday night, he became lost and could not find his way home from the Technical/Vocational School where he taught. He somehow found his way home after one and one-half hours of being lost. He went directly to bed. Then the seizures began. One day later he had brain surgery. The outcome was not good. The hallucinations, semi-coma and pain remained after surgery. It was as if he became a living vegetable. He remained in this state until he crossed over. The doctors speculated that the growth of this rare tumor began in Fred's brain the previous November of 2004.

Where does all this fit in with the alien species, MILAB control over my life and the threat of "I will pay if I talk?"

Approximately two weeks before any of my husband's symptoms occurred I woke up hearing a voice telling me to enjoy what I have in my husband, as he would not be here long. Twice after this first communication, somehow in my head during the day as I would be pulling into our driveway, I was told he that he was going to die! I did not believe what I was being told and prayed that it would not ever be true. Was this information from "them," the alien species, from MILAB?

Up until this day my heart and soul are heavy with the constant fight within me. This has been the most detrimental trauma that has occurred to my family and myself.

The hurt and rain shower of tears, of loosing him, have not quit on any day. There are tremulous questions I constantly ask myself, "Did I cause my soul mate, my spouse, and the one whom I was "one with" in this life to leave his children and me at an early age? Did I instigate his early unexpected death with the knowledge of the threat made against me by a dark rogue military/government sector? Is it because I followed through and took it upon myself to speak out with regard to alien species who are allowed to abduct humans? Have I informed the many people in attendance at conferences where I speak? Has my telephone been tapped so that whoever is listening to my conversations has knowledge of my involvement in this phenomenon? Was it a mandatory decision to carry out their threat against me for identifying top government people and the rogue military/government's involvement in this phenomenon?"

There are even more questions I continually to ask myself, like: "Why did you have to do this in such a way, to take my husband in death, hurt my family and myself in such a manner? You left *me,* the "defiant one," to rebel against you and to let the populace know even more. Yes, I am dearly paying, every moment of my days, for "talking." But you know what? You have *not* shut me up because you have given me more to speak about. And because I am alive, I am going to continue to inform people about what has happened, not only to my family and myself, but to many other humans. You left the wrong human on this planet earth and took away in death a loving, kindhearted, supportive, God given human being, just to make me pay for *"talking"?*

If the truth of this last paragraph is correct, then I am so heavy with my burden of causing the death of my loved one by publishing <u>Morning Glory</u>. By speaking out at conferences about my secret life story, by agreeing to be filmed in a documentary that is being edited at this writing, perhaps the involved government sector cannot accept the outreach I have for other alien abductees who need guidance and knowledge that they are not insane or alone in this phenomenon.

Or....was it the selected time from the "One Above," the "Higher Power" (familiar and known to the alien entities) for Fred and this other abductee to leave us? Was it just their time to cross over?

With my husband's passing I know that he is more thoroughly aware of the truth with regard to the alien abduction phenomenon. I believe he is now able to be with all these universal creations, knowing and learning more about them because my husband is now in heaven.

Are the persons in charge of these "life threatening" events still working to end my life now? I cannot help but wonder about this. Since the last week of October, 2005 until November 2005 I caught the "bug" that was going around here in Albuquerque and this "bug" (viral or bacterial) caused immediate pneumonia in both lungs. Because of the interstitial lung disease and pulmonary fibrosis that I spoke of in <u>Morning Glory</u> I normally get a worse case of any type of respiratory illness.

On February 17, 2006 I was getting over a worse case of "pneumonia" once again in both lungs. The lungs were in severe stress and completely full, causing the pulmonary fibrosis to take over. It is unknown what damage was done to my lungs this time. Since October/November (the beginning of these illnesses for me) I've only had approximately seven days of not being ill with pneumonia. This last "bout" showed a high unknown infection within the lungs and throughout my body. I noticed the serious concern exhibited by my doctors as they shared information on my illness. I was sent home with strict orders to remain in bed until both of my doctors conferred and made a decision. The fatigue incurred was awful as it was difficult to do anything other than lay in bed and sleep. The only symptoms I had the day before this happened were fatigue and horrific coughing "attacks." That Monday evening I had a bad coughing attack that took my breath away frequently during one hour. The more I coughed the more listless I became. I don't really know how I made it to my bed. I decided it would either be to fall and stay on the floor or get to the bed. Once on the bed, I could not reach the phone to dial 911 or to call my daughter for help. As I lay there, after the hour, I was able to maintain control and calm myself down. I had never experienced fatigue like this before. I fell asleep. The next morning I contacted the doctor. I was afraid of the outcome.

One night a couple of nights later, after having had friends to help take care of me during the day, I experienced a "Knowing" that I would not be on this earth much longer. I was on medication that drugged me, rendering my body much weaker in a state of deep sleep. While in this state, the thought or perhaps a voice told me, "This is it. Go and be with Fred." But I was given a choice. I could remain here and live or I could join Fred in death. Though it was not my time yet, I would be welcomed just the same.

Not knowing how ill I was, twice I chose to go with Fred. I missed him so much! I just wanted to be where he was - in a place of love, joy, peace, light and happiness. I never knew about the powerful loneliness widows experience without their soul mates. I had been married to one person for over forty years. What did I really have to loose? I spoke with Fred, my deceased mother and Mother Mary continually during this time.

Surprisingly, when I would wake up for meals that were served to me, I had a flash back memory. I realized I was in a darker, quieter room. There was a familiar soft silky blanket over my cold body. What I was lying on was not that comfortable and I experienced some pain in my chest above my breasts, a different kind of pain, I thought to myself. I felt as if I was lying on a table in this darkened room. I was suspicious that I was on an alien ship! Looking around at the environment I recognized light shining from a distance. I experienced coldness. I saw no one. I heard no movements. Unexplainably, as I am able to do this, I left my body and looked down toward a not-shiny larger silver table. I saw myself lying against a tall Grey who did not move his body. He appeared to be dead. His thin lips were parted and his large, pear shaped head was turned toward his left shoulder. His body appeared to be very lifeless. His thin left arm seemed to be turned and somehow twisted outward, away from his body, in such a manner that he would be in pain if he were not so limp and listless. His left leg was turned inward toward the other leg.

The vision of this memory soon faded when people began speaking to me as I lay ill in my own bed. I did not have the will to get pen and paper. I hoped to rely on my memory of this flashback. Curiously, until most recently, I was thinking when did this happen? Was it the night I woke up to a strong punch in my chest where my lungs are located? The "punch" was so strong it woke me from a drugged sleep. The pain felt as if I had been punched very hard in the chest. The pain radiated out in a large circle above my breasts, from the inside to the outside of my body. I really thought I was having a heart attack! I waited before turning on the lamp, waited for pain to go down my chest, arms or perhaps to quit breathing again. I laid there waiting for other occurrences of pain which never happened. There was only the pain in my chest.

Someone had placed the telephone near me in case I needed to call 911 or the person designated to help me. Either because of the drugs, or perhaps that was the night of abduction, I was in a deep sleep mode. When the "entities" bring you home and place you in your own bed, they touch the side of your head and put you into deep sleep. My chest was painfully sore for the next four days. When either of my two cockatiels walked over my chest, it felt as if someone had indeed socked me very hard.

I was not made aware of how close to death I was in that last week. When I was taken to an appointment with my doctor, he put his arms around me tightly stating they all thought they were going to loose me that week. They were very frightened for me. I also did not realize how ill I had been until family and friends began to tell me how pale and sickly I looked, and that it was good to see color in my face! After two weeks, still somewhat bedridden because of the fatigue, the concern was now about pulmonary fibrosis. Would the fibrosis take me in death or cause me severe disabilities? This was another rock in my road of life. I was told the reason for not putting me in the hospital was because of the possibility of hospital acquired infection. Such an infection would attack my already weakened body, possibly resulting in death.

I did not feel as ill as I had been a week earlier. I remembered when in past months my pulmonary doctor upon seeing recent x-rays of my lungs shouting, "This is bad!" Your lungs are really bad!" I was not shown the most recent lung x-rays, but my doctors said they were far worse! I was not out of the woods yet. I was waiting until I could be tested to determine my current state of health.

Many researchers and friends within this phenomenon who had called me during this last illness, (as well as my "normal" friends who have no experience or knowledge of my alien abductions) thought my illness might be caused by having lost four close family members in less than two years. Fred was taken from me three months after my mother died. She died a year and four months after my Dad passed away. Then a close male cousin also died within that two year period. The shock of loosing my husband and long time friend devastated my whole inner being that year. That kind of grief is unexplainable to anyone who has not lived through it as I have. Many times during that year and a half, I would reflect on the hard life Fred and I shared. Yet we had an unending love and made many wonderful memories during our life together. Fred understood me, knew me and believed in what was occurring in "Our Secret Life" of strange alien phenomena. Fred too, was being abducted by these alien species!

FEBRUARY, 2005

During this time, three things happened in my life that did not make things any easier for me.

First. While living everyday through different and difficult emotions and the constant hard crying from the trauma of losing my husband, my immune system "flatted out" (the words the doctor used). I became ill even before my husband died.

Second. The first day I was allowed to drive to a meeting (before the funeral) I was involved in a car accident. The lady that hit my car as I was slowing to stop at a red light, admitted that she was not paying attention to driving but talking on her cell phone. She rear-ended my car, throwing me violently forward. I was hurt and the car was damaged.

Third. Late one afternoon in early April, after leaving my daughter's home, I had another car accident. The young lady was late for her prom night, leaving the beauty shop and speeding. I was at the end of the street, a block away from her oncoming car, making a left turn onto the main street. Suddenly, there was large Bronco at my driver's door! It appeared to be less than a half foot away from my car. I felt my leg being forcefully pushed onto the gas pedal, speeding into the eastbound lane I was originally headed for. This put me out of harm's way as I quickly swerved out of the Bronco's path. Hearing a loud crash, I thought she had hit the driver's side of my car. The young lady had over-corrected her Bronco, sending it into a large cinder block wall and garage. We both survived. At the accident scene a policewoman came to me and told me, "Someone above is surely taking care of you!" All indications from the street markings and the damages from the accident showed that this young lady's car should have connected with the driver's side of my car. Because of the excessive speed the Bronco was traveling, I should have been killed! The officers were amazed by the fact that this did not happen. I told the officers that I had just lost my husband in death. The officers exclaimed that "He (meaning my husband) protected you from death on this day!"

On a Thursday in October of 2011, I once again eluded death by car. After leaving my volunteer position I drove to the nearest Chevron station to fill the car's gas tank. I next went to a fruit and vegetable stand where I normally buy seasonal goods. Walking back to my parked car, I saw a large white truck traveling at a fast pace going south in the parking area, heading directly toward my parked car. The truck, which had been traveling south on the main street, had jumped across northbound traffic to avoid an oncoming car carrying a family. The truck jumped the curb once again into the parking lot and smashed right into the passenger side of my car.

Witnesses came running. I did not realize how close I was to my car as I walked toward it, yelling at the driver of the truck. The witnesses said I was just a couple of feet away from my car and they thought I had also been hit. They grabbed me and pulled me out of harm's way while holding me tightly. They were crying. I let go of their hold as I saw the white truck pull away from my car, backing up to flee the scene. A woman employee saw what I saw and we both ran to the back of the truck. Luckily the driver stopped. It took the man what seemed like five minutes to open the truck door. He looked at us, said something incoherent, then quickly closed his door. He began to pull forward again in order to flee. The employee yelled that he was drunk, while she quickly wrote down his license plate number.

The man stopped his truck and got out, explaining to us that he had "blacked out." I did not experience the shock of this incident until firemen, ambulances and about four police cars arrived on the scene. They came to me immediately, asking if I was the owner of the Hybrid Honda. They asked if I was okay or did they need to transport me to the hospital. I told them I was fine.

Eventually both vehicles were towed away. The next morning I received a phone call from the towing company. I had to sign papers that would allow my insurance company and investigators to examine my totaled car. I knew after hanging up the phone that the man from Mexico who had no car insurance or driver's license, who had been driving his sister's white truck, was *not* going to be in the state of New Mexico. And I was fairly certain the truck was *not* going to be at the towing company where both vehicles had been taken after the wreck.

On arrival at the auto wreckage place, as the owner walked us to the back lot where they had my car I said to the lady, "I'll bet that white truck with the large black gate on the front is no longer here." She stopped walking and turned toward me and said, "I'm not supposed to tell you this but the man showed up early this morning." After speaking with his sister, the auto wreckage place had to release the truck, which was drivable. The man told her he was fleeing to Mexico!

Approximately seventeen months after the accident the insurance company was still receiving phone calls from the police. They have not located this man or his family. I have been told there is an arrest warrant out for this man. Okay…. I was involved in three car accidents. Is this just a freak of nature? Or is there something behind all of this related to the phenomenon in my life? This thought is unknown. I have a life to live. And I need to let go.

On a warm summer evening in 2005 at 10:30 P.M. a couple of months after my second car accident, I had the TV on, watching the local news while lying in bed. I heard a hard thumping noise that seemed to cause some vibrations in the walls of my home. I turned the TV off and the thumping noise became louder. I got out of bed to investigate, and followed the noise. The noise led me to the guest bedroom where someone evidently was pounding on the guest bedroom outside door that connects to a small, enclosed, gated patio. I stood in the doorway for about ten minutes. The pounding stopped. I rushed to a window thinking I could see someone leave the area. I saw no one. I went back to bed, thinking, everything is okay. I must say, those strong prescription sleeping pills certainly did help to relax me. I had no fear and went to sleep. The next morning I asked the man who lives next door to me (knowing his bedroom is downstairs facing my guest bedroom) if he had heard the banging noise last night. We walked around to the enclosed, gated, patio out back and went inside. We found California red roof tiles below the bedroom door. The door had some damage, as if someone had been trying to get in. They'd hit the guest bedroom door with some red roof tiles. Okay, fear set in right then, and I called the police. I was strongly reprimanded (not just once, but by both of the officers) for not calling 911! I had thought this incident would just be a one-time occurrence. Previously, late in the evenings, I would hear what I thought were the sounds of someone walking on the roof of the house. Eventually the walking steps would stop.

One evening a week later, at exactly the same time as the previous occurrences, this incident was noted. On that night I turned off the TV after watching the evening news. The night was hot, so I had opened the connecting sitting room back door to the outside. I got up and went to brush my teeth. I stopped midway in the brushing process. I heard metal hitting metal and metal that sounded as if it were being ground into metal. Once again, I followed up with the noise, and it led me to the bedroom archway that connects the sitting room. I heard "him" breathe as he worked intently to get the security double bolted door opened! I hollered as loud as I could, "NO!" and found extra strength coming from where, I don't know, but I slammed the door shut on him as hard as I could. (I was surprised I had not broken the door, slamming it with such force). I locked the door and turned on the outside light. I ran to the bedroom phone and dialed 911. The officer kept me on the phone for safety. I heard the sound of a heavy truck that had a loud motor, pulling away from my home.

The police arrived within ten minutes. They searched in the dark but no one was found outside. During the interview with the officers I was told that a certain type of tool could be purchased which opens double security locks. After examining the door knobs and some scratches to the area, this was what the officers suspected may have been used on the locks. The police stayed around in a hidden area near my home for the night. To have to contend with added stressors such as these, and other minor happenings, I sometimes wondered, *"WHO IS IT OUT TO GET TO ME AND WHY?"* Or was I just a victim of circumstance?

During the following year of 2006, I moved from that house into a brand new home and new area where I thought I would be safe. It would be a place where I could begin my "NEW LIFE!" WRONG AGAIN!

The first three years were beautiful in my life as a widowed woman. I finally had peace and quiet and no evidence of the universal beings or military/government around me. My question to myself was, "Where did they all go?" and "Why did they all disappear from me?" But leading a new life of normalcy was very much welcomed.

I have a memory and some discoveries that occurred within the last six months of 2008. Though I believe this ridiculous memory was caused by me. For some unknown reason, in my "normal state of mind," I often questioned if perhaps my husband did not die at all and was living on a mother ship. Was this "real life dream" confirmed? Since the death of my husband Fred, to my knowledge I had not been abducted.

Speaking of "real life dreams," what I used to call my abductions had not occurred and normal nighttime dreaming had completely stopped. Until I had this "real life dream."

Why was I having these strange and repetitive "real life dreams?" I needed to interrupt the sequence of the year's experiences. I did not document the date of this dream that I had either in late July or early August 2009. However, I made note of it on the computer and was quite surprised by these repetitive experiences. Who was trying to relate a message to me with these "Real Life Dreams?"

THE REPETITIVE DREAM

It was a rather warm summer evening. I was very tired because of having had no sleep the previous nights, so I took a sleeping pill on this particular evening. Sometime during the night I awoke in a familiar place. I was looking upward at a "chilling" (but very familiar looking) face. The face was staring back at me with huge almond shaped black eyes and a pear shaped head. His telepathic mind was welcoming me aboard the ship. In my "dream's view" I also saw the most 'infamous doctor' who is also a Grey, standing at the end of this table. To my left were a couple of other Grey's who looked familiar to me. I don't really know how I can recognize the different Greys (their names and who they are) that have abducted me throughout the years and whom I have come to know. Yet I seem to know who they are and I no longer fear them as I had at the very beginning of my awaking in 1988.

The Grey I am most familiar with and know well is Raytheon. It was Raytheon who came into this dream experience as he pushed himself in front of the other two alien Greys. He stood by my head and extended his long thin arm, placing it under my back. With his other arm he pulled me up and forward as he took a sideways step toward the end of the bed. As I turned my body toward Raytheon, I realized I was on the familiar silver bed that I always found myself on when I awoke on board ship. Raytheon told me they had a surprise for me and at that moment, I think my heart fell to the floor. I was wary of the surprise they had for me. I could not imagine. As soon as Raytheon made this statement a sliding door opened in front of me. Just a few feet away who should walk through the doorway but my husband Fred! I stood up from the bed but could not walk toward him. I felt my body go rigid, as if frozen. Fred was not dressed in any type of uniform or different looking clothes. He had on a light blue cotton shirt and dark pants. This type of clothing was normal dress for Fred. Standing there, I felt this was another one of those experiments I was being subjected to so the Greys could study my emotions and reactions to the situation. The reaction I had was shock at seeing my husband who had died but was now alive! I think I said to myself, (and I don't know if I said it out loud) "What a dirty trick to play on me. This is nothing but a hologram! Fred is dead! He died, and he was cremated!"

The room was deathly quiet as I heard his footsteps coming closer. I stared at Fred as he walked toward me. If this was a hologram of Fred this procedure put my mind in a tizzy. I thought to myself, *"He looks healthy and not like the ill person who had an aggressive cancerous brain tumor."* Glioblastoma multiforme and a stroke had caused his death. Fred slowly and cautiously walked toward me with his usual smirk. This man *looked* just like Fred. He had the same height, weight and graying hair as when he'd left me. I was in shock. I saw him come closer to me. Raytheon moved to the other side of the table, and then Fred was suddenly standing right in front of me! I could not talk. I was in disbelief. My mind was whirling around with so many questions. I knew he had died and was cremated, but how could he be here? Fred reached out for me and

held me as I stood in this frozen state. "It's me, Gloria." I think he repeated this twice to me. I felt faint, and my body seemed to fall right into his arms. Yes, it was his voice I heard speaking to me, and yes, his arms and body felt strong and warm. All I could say was, "You're dead. You died!"

I was thinking inside my head, "If this is not a hologram then it is a Reptilian who shape shifted into Fred." Then these words came out of my mouth and I screamed, "You are a Reptilian and you have turned into my husband! Quit playing this game with me!" I cried out loud. "Why, are you doing this to me?"

Fred was staring back at me with his hazel eyes, and told me that he did **not** die. He was close to death and they switched him out with a look-alike clone that **did** die. "They" (the extraterrestrials) needed to save him (Fred). Apparently they did and were able to heal his brain of the cancerous tumor and restore his body. "No. This is just a nasty game." I said.

That is all that I remembered when I woke up in the darkness of my bedroom. There were tears streaming down my face. My body was limp lying on top of the covers. "This cannot be true." I said to myself. Then I was "out" for the duration of the night.

Waking the next morning, while lying in bed with this memory, I tried to keep my body from shaking. I wanted to quiet my mind from the memory of the night. I could not do this. The thoughts of my dream kept racing around with so many questions. I was striving to make some kind of sense of it in my mind. I began to pray to my God for answers.

Even though I remembered this "real life dream," I've come to the conclusion that perhaps it was just a dream...a normal dream, a dream I created by my very own mind. Perhaps I was hoping in the back of my mind that this could be true. Yes, that the Greys (or whatever extraterrestrials) had taken Fred for whatever reason or purpose and kept him alive. Perhaps one day I would see him in person, if not in heaven. I wanted to see and be with Fred for the moment. I wanted him back alive, healthy and here with me. But if this dream was/is the truth then one day perhaps when I am taken again, I *will* see him, and hopefully be strong enough to realize the truth of this dream.

APRIL 20, 2007

I had been having severe back problems so I made an appointment with a friend of mine who is a massage therapist. He worked on the front part of my body first then I was to turn onto my stomach so that he could work on my back. In turning onto my stomach and as he pulled down the sheet to work on my spine he hollered out to me "What is this on your back?" I did not know what he was talking about so he collected his camera and took several pictures of my back. I immediately was able to see the large scratches on my back. As he touched the scratches on my back they burned and the area reddened. I have no idea who made the several scratches on the right side of my back. The scratches began to disappear within three to four days.

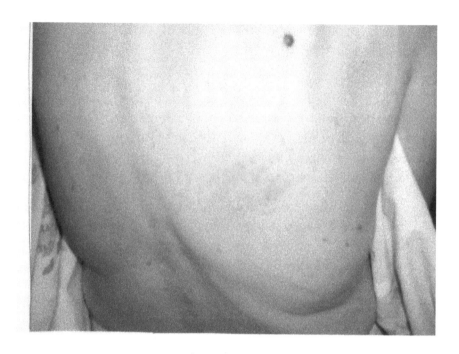

DECEMBER, 2008

Reflecting back to the end of 2008 where much concentration was spent on my declining health. The first of December, I ended up in the hospital for a long stay with pneumonia and other complications. Upon being admitted to the hospital via emergency room, I was asked to donate to the "Dracula" blood department. Vials of my blood were taken by a technician who told me that it would take around seventy-two hours to find out what type of pneumonia I had and any other information they could get from my blood work. After twenty four hours, a male technician from the lab came into my room with a report. (This report was not due yet, as the blood samples needed least forty-eight hours more to grow in the lab). The technician woke me up to tell me what they found in my blood. He said he wanted to tell me before going to the nurse's desk to give the paperwork to them. The technician told me they had found an unknown staph and chemical in my blood.

Some hours later, I was awakened by two nurses with a very large, clear plastic bag filled with antibiotic. This is where confusion comes into play. I told the nurses that a technician had come into my room earlier and woke me up with a report of an unknown staph infection that was found in my blood. The nurses said no one had delivered any report of that nature to the nurses' station. So why had the hospital doctor ordered antibiotic therapy before any report was delivered with a diagnosis?

The next morning when the head nurse came into my room, I questioned her about the technician who had previously come into my room with a report of my blood test. The head nurse was quite curious about this because no one had been to the nurse's desk with a report on my diagnosis. The head nurse was going to check to see who might have delivered this information. Maybe the report had been misplaced. Later that morning, I was told that no one could find the report or the person who had come into my room the previous day. This information was not documented on any of my medical files. Once again, I experienced another happening concerning my blood, as I have described in <u>Morning Glory</u>.

I was released from the hospital. Many tests and doctors later (including home health care three times a week until the end of April, 2009) I began to experience some other entities or humans invading my home. I believe they were using either holograms, or some other technique to locate themselves in my home. I felt a distinct presence. I would turn around quickly to see if someone had somehow gotten into my home without my knowledge of how they had gotten inside. I would see an arm or part of a human body avoiding or rushing away from me. I would feel someone touch me on the shoulder and not be able to see who it was. I could not identify these persons. I didn't know if they were there to take care of me or harm me however I did not feel threatened.

I've had this type of experience periodically until fairly recently (2012). During a period of two weeks for example, I encountered at nighttime, (being fully awake and with lights on) some men and a couple of women who appeared out of thin air. These happenings occurred approximately three to four times during a two week period. Their entire bodies were visible to me and they were dressed in dark clothing.

The next experience I had was on board an alien space ship in a darkened room where I encountered these same women and men. I recognized their faces. They were the same women and men who had appeared in my home. Behind them on a wall, was an opening like a large window. It had white or aluminum slats that covered the opening of the window. I don't know what the opening was used for. I was not lying down on any type of bed. I was standing up, staring into their human faces. I am unaware of what transpired next because I blacked out.

A couple of these experiences were daytime happenings that involved pets we had at the time. One was our pet Cairn Terrier dog named Queenie. The other was a Gray Persian cat named Dutchess. I spoke of Queenie and Dutchess in "Morning Glory" Diary of an Alien Abductee. The following is what I saw and felt at two different times and on different days. I was walking, looking directly toward the area I was headed for when I felt a presence and a swift rush of air past my lower left leg. I looked down at the floor. I almost tripped over Queenie as she ran by my left side and just disappeared into thin air. On another day, same scenario, but I saw our Gray Persian cat walking by my side until she too, disappeared into thin air. So what was going on here? I don't know.

THE THIRD YEAR IN MY NEW HOME

During the third year of living peacefully and quietly in my new home, life took on a new change to old frightening circumstances. At the beginning of 2009, I would be awakened from a deep sleep, not knowing why or how I was awakened. I would be staring out my east window looking over the city, or opening my door to the balcony. Walking outside, I would see someone being brought back by a large silver space ship with a very long, bright light extending to the ground in the southeast quadrant of Albuquerque. I had hoped to hear "reports" of sightings of an early morning encounter from someone who had witnessed the same event. But no I never saw or heard anything while reading the newspaper or watching TV. There was nothing on the internet, where items such as this could be reported on Paranormal Sighting sites, if someone witnessed such an incident.

JUNE, 2009

Again I did not document the date. This occurred the last week of June. After showering that morning, drying my left leg with the towel, I noticed some red markings on my left leg. Upon examining the area I found these new markings were located in the same original area where I had been needle marked some years ago. These original "needle marks" are identification from the Greys or another entity that has abducted me. The original four needle marks are in a pattern to indicate the Orion grouping that I spoke of in "Morning Glory" Diary of an Alien Abductee. I noticed I had been re-marked again during that night in June, 2009. I now have a triangle shaped marking once again! I have no memory of being abducted during the night. This marking has remained on my leg.

SEPTEMBER, 2009

Recently, on many a night in September, I would awaken to the noise of a train traveling fast, somewhere in close proximity to my home. I would then hear the squealing of the train's brakes as it stopped. I thought it might be a semi (truck) making the noise of a traveling train, as I live close to the I-40 freeway. Eventually, I got up to investigate the sound. I wanted to see where it may be coming from as I live many miles from train tracks. I remember thinking, "Gee, the wind must be blowing in the direction of my home carrying the sound of a train traveling in the night." So I ventured out onto my balcony to see if the wind was blowing in the

85

direction of my home. To my amazement, there was no wind. No heavy traffic of cars or semi trucks could be seen or heard that night. Only the sound of a train traveling on tracks and the squealing of brakes could be heard, but not seen. After forty-five minutes of hearing a "train" stopping and starting in a repetitive pattern, I was able to pace the "train" traveling from south of Albuquerque to the north side of Albuquerque, ending near the Sandia Casino. Then the train seemed to travel to the south of Albuquerque, stopping, and going north again. "How strange." I thought.

The following week I was awakened again to the sound of a train. Lying awake in bed around 1:00 a.m., I realized my bed was shaking! This same occurrence happened many times with the train sound and the shaking of my bed. I had no answers for the cause of these events. Many months prior, at a meeting, I'd heard that there was underground drilling of large tunnels leading out of the base here in Albuquerque. The tunnels were being drilled underground to Arizona with the goal of ending in California. Two tunnels would branch off of the main tunnel, going north to Los Alamos, NM and eventually to Dulce, NM. *Dulce?* I can understand Los Alamos, but *Dulce?* I wished there was truth to this instead of speculation. I was *definitely* experiencing *something*. And at presence time, (2012) my south bedroom wall will *still* vibrate on occasion.

ONCE AGAIN ANOTHER SIGHTING

At 2:00 a.m. one morning, I was awake and stood at the closed bedroom window looking outside. I was once again investigating the train sound, which had become quite noisy. It shook my bed. I did *not* want to remain in a shaking bed!

Once again to my surprise in the southeast quadrant of the city, I witnessed an oval alien ship. There was an elongated downward, bright light coming from the middle of the ship. I stared in amazement. I thought to grab my binoculars. Too late. When I got back to the window the ship had left the area! My summation was either someone was being abducted or being brought home. This was the third time I had encountered this scenario in the southeast quadrant of the city. The city lights outlined the ship's form, making the outer skin of the alien craft glow.

OCTOBER 28, 2009

After showering and drying off, I noticed more red markings on my right leg! Upon closer examination, I found the same identification marking of the Orion Grouping. But this marking was laid out differently. The almost half-moon shape across my right leg had the addition of a triangle after the three round needle marks. Again, I have no memory of an abduction.

NOVEMBER 25, 2009

MONDAY EVENING 11:00 P.M.

I hadn't fallen asleep. I felt as if something was wrong, as if something was going to happen. The lights were out and I was lying in a dark room. Suddenly a blue flash of light lit up the southeast corner of my bedroom. Not thinking anything of it, I think I fell asleep.

The following event I failed to document right away. Either late Monday evening or Tuesday morning I was awakened by the noise of a "shuttering" sound like someone going through the wall. This is a sound that I am familiar with. This left me with the question of who just left me? Was I abducted but don't have the memory? What was "their" purpose for this unknown visit and by whom? What was done to me? Yes, I was fully awake.

JUNE, 2010

After this military abduction I came back with these names: Deborah or Dorothy Holt or Holte. I do not know which is the correct spelling of this person's name. Also the name "Matthew Lopez."

SPRING, 2012
CONFUSION

Another similar dream experience occurred. Was I being confused with a past memory? I don't know. But did the previous dream of 2008 and 2009 that was still so fresh in my memory, occur again?

It felt like a repeat dream occurred just like it happened again…but why? In the third or second experience seeing Fred once again, I found myself in a state of shock. The memory of what I subsequently did was to check his lower back hip, as he had special birth mark markings on his body. In the second or third memory, I had Fred turn around and face away from me as I told him what I was going to look for. He did as I asked. He pulled down his pants to expose the area in question. To my surprise, there were the same birthmarks on his backside! The confusion here is with my memory. Did I have him do this in the memory of 2009 or did I in fact, experience a new abduction in 2012 as stated? Is Fred really alive and working with these universal entities? Or are the universal entities performing yet another emotional test on me? Are they using a clone or is a Reptilian shape shifting into Fred for this emotional test?

I do have some concrete evidence that I cannot reveal for my safety but perhaps the Grey's have told the truth about taking Fred before he passed over into heaven. Some recent evidence has been pointed out to me about involvement Fred had between Los Alamos, NM and Sandia Base here in Albuquerque regarding knowledge of universal entities.

The question I have is, when someone is cloned, how accurate are details such as the birthmarks on Fred's body? If Reptilians are shape shifting, how accurate are they in their detail of humans?

If this previous scenario of psychological emotional testing is the plan of the Reptilians and the Grey's for their studies, may they be damned for doing this to me! They will one day have to "meet their maker" in Hell!

AUGUST 4, 2012

Somewhere along my lifelines I had been told of other alien abductees who experienced life threatening medical issues. An example would be a lack of "potassium" in their bodies that would cause instant death or severe illness. I bring up this topic because on August 4, 2012 I experienced a harrowing situation of this sort. How life can change in an instant!

I woke up that particular morning feeling great. Then, as I made my bed, I felt a horrible sock of pain in my chest, in the right side of my body and in my legs and feet. The pain was accompanied by numbness and tingling on that side of my body including face, jaw and neck. Ten minutes later, after taking an aspirin, I waited to see if I was having a heart attack. I called my dear friend, questioning him about heart attacks, and he immediately said, "I'll be there." The pain became stronger. I dialed 911. I was taken to the hospital and was told I had a clot in my heart. I was given the wrong diagnosis. Blood testing revealed that my body was quite low in potassium and that I was going into a heart attack. This situation was remedied after a three day stay in the hospital.

While in the hospital, I experienced a same situation that has occurred many times before having to do with blood withdrawal. My blood was taken every hour. But in a couple of situations a technician (normally at night) would come into my hospital room well before the hour was up, to take even more blood. This was done without the knowledge of the real technicians who showed up later and on time. I did mention to these "real" techs that their department had already been in my room to draw my blood. Who are these unknown people who take my blood unexpectedly and for what purpose? What are they doing with my blood? Was this medical situation planned once again by **OUR GOVERNMENT?** Am I still under their control and considered to be a military/government abductee?

AUGUST 2012

I did document the following information on paper right away. Later when I looked for the paper, where I normally put work I need to attend to, it was gone. I readily typed my memory of this incident into the computer, and I remembered the incident very vividly.

One evening in August, I went swimming with my friend at the gym we normally go to. We normally swim for one hour. Half way through our lap swimming and just before we began to snorkel, my left nostril was so clogged that I could not breathe through it. I was thinking I had taken water in on that side of my nose, which had clogged the sinus cavity. I felt a strange pressure in the left side of the sinus cavity so I stopped swimming and began blowing my nose profusely to get the water out. To my surprise no water came out of my nostrils. I blew and blew to no avail. Still nothing but pressure as if something was stuck way up in my nose. We decided to start our snorkeling anyway. I thought perhaps the "water" would eventually come out of my nose.

The left side of the sinus cavity and nostril stayed clogged until we finished swimming and visiting the steam room. Then I went to shower. As I was showering I felt "pressure" traveling down from the sinus area to the left nostril. I began to blow, holding the right nostril closed, so that whatever was in my left nostril would come out. To my surprise, something came out! At first I thought I was holding a large black bug! I was immediately ready to let this "bug" go down the drain. Thank goodness I did not do that, realizing as I looked closer, it was not a bug at all! I was standing in the shower looking at a black sponge about one inch long and half an inch wide. I stood there in a stupor wondering how and where this thing had gotten into my nostril! Who placed it there? Bringing the rectangular black sponge closer into view, I saw on the top or bottom of this item, three copper circles. These copper circles were a sort of wire. Within the copper circles were dark holes. I was thinking *female* now, so what was the male counterpart to this thing? Was the male counterpart located someplace else other than my body? Who did this black sponge belong to? I began to squeeze it tightly to see

what it would do. In playing with it, I found out I could get the sponge to be quite "tiny" and thin enough to be put up my nostrils by whomever. I tried to tear it apart but the sponge would not tear. I twisted it very tightly as well. No matter what I did, it always went back into the perfect shape it was when it came out of my nostril. What exactly was the information they were looking for? My immediate thought was whether this sponge could somehow connect to my brain, eyes, nerves or muscles. What was it used for in my body? I felt so violated! Then I was "told" to drop it! I followed the command and watched it go down the drain. "How stupid of me!" I said out loud, "How very stupid!" But I let it go and with it went confirmation and information for me.

OCTOBER 2012

I was traveling east on a far northeast main street in Albuquerque around 7:15 a.m. I was so excited to see many hot air balloons landing just north of the highway near the vacant land that abuts the highway. Yes, the Balloon Fiesta, which is one of Albuquerque's yearly features, was putting on quite a show that morning. The weather was warm with clear blue skies. It was a perfect day for the balloonist. As I drove closer to the west side of the Sandia Mountains, a reflection caught my eye. To my surprise, straight in front of me, in a canyon below the crest of the mountain, on a large ridge overlooking the area, were two long silver rectangular objects! Many recent sightings during the last year had been reported on the Sandias but I had not seen anything unusual until this particular day. I thought I could keep an "eye" on the two objects because I was traveling to a home that was located just a few blocks away, to the north of them. To my disappointment, larger homes, just across the arroyo, blocked my view of the two silver objects.

I attended a paranormal meeting the following Saturday and during an open discussion with many people in attendance, one woman stood up and spoke of the sighting she had the previous Wednesday at approximately the same time I saw the two silver objects. What a confirmation for me!

Two weeks later I walked upstairs to the master bedroom that has a window facing east. The time was around 4:30 p.m. With shorter days now and the sun setting earlier, I quickly looked outside this particular window. Something shining caught my eye. Again, located on the west side of the Sandia Mountains but further north than the other objects I had previously seen, the sun was hitting a reflective object just right to catch my attention. I quickly grabbed my binoculars and to my amazement, there were two round silver ships sitting on the long ridge of a lower part of the mountain. In back of this ridge is a large canyon that I can see from my home. There were other silver objects located on a higher ridge within the canyon. I could not see what the activity was in the canyon. The sun set around 5:15 p.m. and I thought I might be able to see some kind of lights in the area that evening. I did not. I searched the same area the next morning but saw nothing.

DECEMBER-MARCH 2012-2013
I'VE STUMPED MY DOCTORS AGAIN!

I started feeling ill about three days after Christmas. A good friend had come to visit during the holidays. Florence and her husband had lived in Albuquerque many years ago. She too found herself widowed over the past few years. When Florence comes for a visit we try to get to the places she would like to visit. I did not want to complain about not feeling up to par. I just wanted to make her Christmas holidays perfect. She left Albuquerque before New Year's Eve.

After Florence left, whatever was afflicting me hit quite powerfully. I was plagued with fever, stomach problems, sleeping my days away and visiting my porcelain friend "the commode" with vomiting and diarrhea. I made an appointment with my primary doctor and was given some prescriptions to help with the symptoms. I was told I should feel better in the next couple of days. Not so. For the next couple of days and nights, I lived next to the commode. I sat on the *floor* next to the commode because I could not leave the vicinity. I grew weaker with nothing more to vomit aside from bile and green liquid. I argued with my doctor's nurse about getting myself to the hospital emergency room. Sick as I was, the last thing I wanted to do was wait long hours just to see a doctor. After a few more hours of misery at home, I finally gave in. I was only getting worse.

My friend, Max came and picked me up and drove me to the emergency room where we waited for many hours. I was admitted to the hospital that evening and put into quarantine. I was diagnosed with one of the three flu viruses going around Albuquerque at that time. I was also extremely dehydrated which did not help the other drastic symptoms. During the next few days in quarantine it was determined that the virus was affecting my heart. I was then moved to the cardiac floor. The same doctor followed me to the cardiac unit and this is where the puzzle of my illness began to unfold.

The Cardiologist came in the second evening after I was transferred to the cardiac floor. The results of the heart tests I had been given showed quite clearly that there was nothing wrong with my heart, even though ultrasound and other tests indicated otherwise. The cultures of the green substance that came out of my body were not growing properly. As a result of this, my doctors could not give me any indication of what was ailing me. For several more days I was given potassium, magnesium, many bags of antibiotics, fluid, and shots. Though I finally got better, there were still no results on the cultures they had taken. I was released with final diagnoses of the flu, but my doctors were in a dilemma and not satisfied with their diagnoses.

It took me over a month to recuperate at home. March first, I had another bout of whatever was going on with my body. This time I was diagnosed with the "other flu" that was going around. I fought against being readmitted to the hospital because of my experience with a previous negative "roommate." Private hospital rooms were scarce because of the rapid spread of these two different flu viruses. There was also a third bad virus - the H3N2 virus - that was rapidly spreading throughout the United States and New Mexico. People were dying from it. I certainly did not want to end up in a hospital hallway as a result of the epidemic. Therefore, my primary doctor ordered more prescriptions and allowed me to stay at home. I followed his directions faithfully. It was approximately two weeks before the "new flu virus" went away. I did not start feeling "human" and healthy again until the first weeks of May.

I had been vaccinated the previous October for these viruses. I wondered if the two different encounters (abductions) with two different men who wore white lab coats and the woman I had written about had anything to do with my illnesses. Had they done something to me? For what purpose? Who were they? I never was able to see the human or alien who stood at the head of the bed they had me lying on. Had these been military or alien abductions? Or had I merely just contracted two different flu viruses?

FEBRUARY 2013

I did not document the date of this occurrence. The first part of February I awoke around 6:00 a.m. I went downstairs and followed my morning ritual. When I pulled opened the shade on the front window I thought I was seeing a very large fire on the west mesa, which is not too far from where I live. I saw a great massive fire that had a huge circular ball of fire in the center of it! The flames on both sides of the circular ball extended (I thought) at least a mile or so to the south and north. I called out to my guest who stayed the night, to come and look. We both went outside to determine the direction of the fire. If it was coming my way I would have to evacuate as well as warn my neighbors. We smelled no smoke. We heard no sirens or

emergency equipment. Nor did we see any activity in the area. My guest had to leave and drive through that area to get to the freeway.

After my guest left I received a telepathic message to get inside the house, lock the door and go sit in a particular chair. I felt compelled to do this. I was under whoever's control as I tried to fight against this message. The telephone rang. Strangely enough I was able to get to the telephone. It was my guest calling. He was able to get through the street. He was excited as he told me what he had seen. He said that it looked as if the sun was on the ground! There were some kind of rays that extended from the ground and what looked like fire, which extended for over a mile to the south and north. This was what we had seen from my home. Something kept my guest from stopping to investigate and he found himself traveling east on the freeway far away from the area.

Around 7:00 a.m. I felt a release from whatever had held me in the chair. I immediately went to the west window and looked out. Whatever it had been was gone! Everything looked normal again. I later drove to the area in question. There were no burnt grasses or fields, nothing out of order, everything normal. I had thought, living close to the freeway, that early morning drivers, or at least other early risers in my area would have reported seeing what we had witnessed. I listened to the T.V., car radio, and even looked in the paper the next morning, but nothing! We were stumped and didn't know what we saw or who controlled us the way they did.

APRIL 14, 2013
SUNDAY

What is going on? I don't understand! I woke up with a clear and vivid memory on this morning. I laid in bed trying to make sense of it. I woke up thinking, "I am lying in my own bed." The smell was horrific, worse than sulfur! I thought to myself, "Something is wrong in my house. I need to get up immediately. Is the house on fire or what?" I realized I could not get up. "Why can't I see? What is going on here? I can't see! I can't breathe! The smell is getting worse. I *need* to get up. What is holding me down?" (I heard men talking ... not in English.) "Where am I? I heard the lady say, "She's awake."

Did I get sick during the night? Am I in the hospital? What's happening to me? "Finger tips." Yes, I see fingertips. Something was sliding across my face. I can see a little bit now. Yes, I see light. But what was covering my eyes, and my head? Who moved this object that slid across my face? Where is the lady that I heard speaking? I looked forward and saw two men wearing the familiar white lab coats, standing several feet away from me. They had their backs opposite from me and working at a white counter top that seems to be connected to three large windows. I didn't know what these men were working with. I saw microscopes then I looked out the windows … blue skies … sunshine. But it was supposed to be nighttime. The two men were conversing again, in a language I could not understand. The woman's voice then told me the men were two Russian scientists. Further messages that I heard got somewhat confusing here. The lady told me the scientists were or had something to do with "Adrian Russian Scientist?" I felt weird about hearing the words "Adrian and Russia."

The two men turned to face me and told the woman something. I felt someone lifting me up from a lying down position and turning my body to the side of the table or bed. Why can't I see the lady? I know it is a lady who is helping me down from the table or bed. I felt strong, small hands (unlike a man's hold). I was walked away from the two men and noticed I could not walk correctly. I was walking stiff and

could not turn my body, therefore I believe the lady had to support my body.

I saw a large crib ahead of us that appeared to look like a baby crib. I was taken to this crib. Lying in the crib sideways were three baby girls around five or six months old. They appeared to be triplets and looked quite healthy. They appeared to be human and Caucasian. They had chubby faces, their dark eyes were open and they had shorter than shoulder length brown hair. But something was wrong. I saw black stripes. What were these three black stripes on their foreheads, going down to their naked bodies? The black stripes were about 1½ inches wide. The stripes appeared to be part of their bodies. Or were they painted onto their bodies? Do the black stripes have some kind of medical purpose that connects them to a type of electrical conduit?

After this episode, I went online just out of curiosity and typed in "Adrian Russian Scientist." I was quite astonished to find information on this subject. I could not pinpoint any of the descriptive information I found. And yes, I did find much. I was looking for medical information. Perhaps I was looking for the *wrong* information.

NOVEMBER 25, 2013
MONDAY EVENING 6:30 P.M.

For the last two weeks I had been having unusual looking stools that apparently were dark with blood. I also experienced pain in my lower abdomen. I would have to use the facilities many times during the day. When I flushed the toilet the water would become red. I was concerned but did not make a doctor's appointment. I was actually afraid to make an appointment because of what I might find out was medically wrong with me. A shocking conclusion came that evening which *did* prompt me to make that appointment.

After dinner with my guest I had the painful discomfort of having to use the facilities. I had grown accustomed to checking the commode after I made a deposit. I looked down into the commode and what I saw shocked me. Actually, I did not know what I was looking at! Standing there in a state of delirium, I thought, "What is this object that came out of me?" I mentally gathered myself for a moment, wanting to examine this thing. I was afraid to even touch the object in the commode. I did not know what would result if I brought the object out of the water. But I could not just flush it away without knowing what it was and whether it had somehow been living inside my colon! Was it alive? Who in God's name put this object inside me? Just what is it? "How do I quietly bring the object out of the water to examine it?" I wondered.

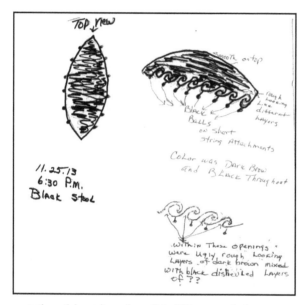

I could not find anything readily available to put the object into to examine it. I stood there looking at it from different sides of the commode; it did not move but just remained in place. I did not realize how large the thing was. I thought of using the trash container to put the object into but felt if it crawled or moved I might not be able to control it. The trash container was made out of straw and I felt I might lose the object if I put it into the container.

I thought, "How do I quietly exit the bathroom, go to the kitchen to get a covered container and find some sort of utensil I can use to grab the object?" I just knew that if I left the bathroom, my guest would come and use the facilities as well, and he would flush the toilet. What could I do? My head was spinning.

I wound a tight roll of toilet paper to make it thick and strong so that I could move and perhaps bring this object up and out of the water. The object felt hard, and I could not move it with the wound up tissue. I stood at the side of the commode staring at it realizing it was even more "scarier looking but kind of fascinating." What a weird thought to have!

Then I heard the loud voice in my head. It was a demanding electronic voice telling me to *flush the toilet!* The command was repeated over and over again, until I flushed the thing into the sewer. "It's gone." I said. Then I became so angry at myself for obeying that demanding voice! My confirmation was gone! **"Why** did I have to listen to that controlling voice and follow the instructions?" I hollered at myself mentally, "Why didn't I get the object out of the commode?" I was so angry with myself!

I walked out of the bathroom with an unexplained feeling that I cannot describe. Yes, my guest **did** go into the bathroom to use the facility as we were preparing to go to Wal-Mart. When we returned to my home an hour later, I went into the bathroom and was stopped in my tracks! I called out to my guest loudly and he came quickly. I insinuated that he had urinated on the floor. He looked down and quickly let me know that he could not have had that much water in him. I felt so bad for making that statement as we both stared at the amount of water that surrounded the commode. There was about a foot of water that surrounded the commode! We both thought there was a water leak so I began feeling the outside of the bowl of the commode, which was dry, then trying to track down the water leak to no avail. To our surprise we found no water leak. My guest brought paper towels to clean up the water mess, and yes, it was just "water." The question is, how did that amount of water come out of the commode? Did this object come out and was it hiding some place in my home? Did someone enter my home to get this mysterious object out of the commode? So many strange thoughts!

When my guest left that evening I drew on paper exactly what I saw. I did make a doctor's appointment for the following day. I found it quite hard to explain to my primary care doctor the incident and what I saw in the commode. I began with the unusual bloody stools that led up the incident. He asked if I could draw the object, and I pulled out the picture that I'd brought with me to the appointment. My doctor was in shock when he saw the picture and stated he had never seen anything like it before. He ordered blood, urine and stool tests. As I had mentioned in Morning Glory, Mr. Budd Hopkins asked me many years ago to make sure I had a doctor that I could trust because one day I might need a doctor to medically treat me for injuries or illnesses connected to this phenomenon. I had been with this primary care doctor for many years and yes, he was aware of my alien/military abductions of many years.

My doctor was shocked as he listened and viewed the picture. His eyes opened wide and he covered his mouth. Then he stood up and walked out of the examining room saying, "I don't know how to treat you, Gloria!" I thought I might no longer have a primary doctor.

A few weeks later I received the results of the medical tests and everything was negative. Below the written results was a note from my doctor asking how was I doing and if I needed to talk or if I had any questions to please contact him.

The story continues. For the last year and a half I'd had a periodically sick cat who had been hospitalized on two occasions. The veterinary doctors could never decide on a diagnosis as to what was ailing my cat. A couple of weeks after my "incident," the cat once again fell ill. She was violently throwing up pink foaming liquid and not eating. She became quite lethargic. I made an appointment with her veterinarian. The tests were once again not giving us any answers until the doctor x-rayed her digestive system. This time the x-ray did show something large and round in her stomach. My cat was hospitalized and the doctor wanted to put an IV into her to be able to "wash" the object out of her stomach and into the colon. Perhaps then my cat would expel this object. The procedure did not work. The Veterinarians decided the next step would be to do an endoscope on my cat to remove the item. If this process failed then the doctors would perform immediate surgery.

The appointed time of the endoscope was 3:00 p.m. the following day. I received a phone call from the doctor who could not understand what had just happened. The object was in my cat's stomach as they watched the procedure on their screen. As the doctor reached with his tools to grab the unusual object, the object suddenly disappeared into thin air! Yes, both doctors were quite stumped and could not explain this. I was told this had never happened to them before. They kept my cat another day to watch her and to see if she would excrete something out but my cat never did. I brought her home and she has been doing fine. This past incident brought forth known knowledge. I had also been told by different people within this phenomenon that military government (who have been involved in my life) or the extraterrestrials will at times put their technologies (objects) into the abductee's body and also into their pet's bodies. The purpose for doing this is unknown. I would like identification of this object and what it is used for. I would also like identification of what was found in my cat. If the reader of this book has experienced something like these events, would you please come forward and contact me?

Alien Manipulation And The Love Bite
By Eve Lorgen

Alien manipulation covers a wide spectrum of observed "effects" in the abductee population and the public at large. The more obvious aspects of alien manipulation are the suppression of memory, or falsely implanted screen memories after an abduction event takes place. Not only the abductee in question becomes affected by memory loss but those surrounding them may be affected in such a way as to become distracted from paying attention that an anomalous event has transpired. For example, in an abduction case in Oklahoma investigated by Barbara Bartholic—a UFO investigator and therapist of 30 years, a woman was taken on her way to work one evening as she was driving her car. The woman was directly removed from the car and examined for over an hour. When she returned, and proceeded to go to work, she had confusing thoughts implanted in her mind about a confabulated story as to the reason she would be late for work. She arrived over one and a half hours late to work. The strangeness was that her boss and fellow employees didn't even notice, or say anything regarding her tardiness. Mental perceptions are being manipulated, such that the person(s) do not notice the alien visitation. Obviously surrounding people interacting with the abductee don't even have to have physical alien contact to be manipulated. This is only a fraction of the things aliens do to their human guinea pigs.

Other varieties of ET/alien manipulation involve conditioning of a person's beliefs about religion. In a case referred to me, a woman at age 4 was contacted by an alien who put her in a euphoric state and was told of a beautiful place "beyond" and that Christianity was a false religion that needed to be eradicated from the planet. In this particular case, the abductee developed great animosity towards her very Christian grandmother, and rebelled to such an extent that she later became involved in Gothic Dungeons and Dragons games, and developed a negative arrogant attitude of superiority towards others. If they were benevolent aliens, this abductee wouldn't have a negative and arrogant attitude towards others. It is a mask of deep trauma.

Many abductees are conditioned to maintain a positivist New Age belief system, in ways that activate their ego or cooperation with what the aliens want to do with them. In a Milab case, a female abductee was trained to operate alien spacecraft through a mind-body interface. All the while she is given positive reinforcement as if she was "an equal" with the Grey aliens, as long as she did what they want. This woman later believed that the Greys and human secret government factions programmed her in New Age ideologies, such as aliens being here to raise human awareness and psychic development. When she challenged these views, she found what she believed to be technology held by humans who are dead set on destroying the human race. Is the Secret Government taking orders from the aliens to carry out their agenda?

Other cases involve a more complex set of "tasks" on what their alien handlers want them to do. These tasks may have nothing to do with what happens during an abduction event, but what the person does for a living, or who they interact with. In one case, a woman was instructed to teach others with latent alien DNA (mostly other abductees) a certain color therapy exercise, which the hypnotherapist/investigator later discovered to be a triggering system for those with part alien DNA. (This was based on the testimony given by the abductee under hypnosis as to her "job" with the aliens) This unique exercise would create a shift in their DNA programming, making them more susceptible to alien mind control programs. In yet another case with a reptilian overseer, the abductee would be continuously set in a life of chaos, until a specific project they wanted her to complete was done. All other activities were derailed—along with the persons she associated with, until she finished this project. She reluctantly described herself as being a "Typhoid Mary", when others she interacted with started having bizarre events in their lives. The net effect was very isolating, not to mention the guilt she felt about what would happen to the other persons she came into contact with. In fact, this type of activity can happen to investigators as well , if they happen to put their noses in places the aliens or secret government don't want them to go!

Contrarily, in a private case shared through discussions with two separate reptilian contacts, one contactee told another "reptilian contactee" to just do the jobs and assignments she was told to do— then "you can have anything you want". In other words, in this particular person's case, they received positive perks when they simply did the job the reptilian handler asked them to. No questions asked. Does this sound scary to you? It should!

Milabs

A Milab is a genuine alien abductee who also has abductions by human secret government or military agents. The main defining characteristic of Milabs is that they are taken involuntarily by military/secret government agents for purposes of interrogation about their alien visitations, or they are sheep dipped into deep black operations as a "secret agent" with specific abilities of use to the intelligence agencies. Some Milabs are a type of Manchurian Candidate who works for the aliens or secret government under mind control. It is my supposition that Milabs are of particular interest to the intelligence agencies because of latent alien DNA and unique abilities that others do not have. A type of real life X-men and women, super warriors and astral spies. Many Milabs are very talented with extra sensory perception, remote viewing, martial arts, etc. Some have compartmentalized abilities to read and write alien script or speak in alien languages. Some are simply used for medical experimentation, while others have photographic memories, and can be employed as scientists and medical assistants to the aliens or secret government activities in underground facilities.

Thus far it appears that Milabs are an American and its allies phenomenon. It is my contention that the intelligence agencies who track specific abductees will use these persons in deep black military operations and covert programs. The Milab memories oftentimes involve working with aliens, interdimensional time travel, remote viewing, weapons training, escape and evasion training and leadership roles in an uncertain global apocalyptic future.

Types of Alien Manipulation

In general the alien manipulation games are primarily focused on "truth detracting" efforts towards the abductees and general population regarding alien/ET influence on humanity—or what the true alien agenda is. The manipulation spans a very vast degree in terms of the aliens' long term plans for humanity. There are individual levels of manipulation and collective efforts, as in media representation to distort and deny the evidence of alien visitations. A large-scale effort can be described as " The Alien Civil Affairs Program". This is basically a pacification program that can be best quoted in a paper by James Bartley called The Alien Civil Affairs and Pacification Program.

"The first thing an abductee must understand is that the aliens work on us during our sleep and abductions under mind control. They create "stage managed" dreams filled with images of UFO's and heavily laden with symbolic meaning. During these stage- managed dreams, abductees are given pabulum in the form of spiritual teachings and warnings about global ecological catastrophe. The abductee is given to understand that not only are they responsible for these calamities but they also have a responsibility to undo all the damage wrought by their spiritually degenerate fellow humans and "governments". During this phase of manipulation the abductee is steered toward the acceptance of belief systems (i.e. New Age "false light") the aliens want them to have. In a parallel exercise the ego of the abductee is being activated in order to better control and manipulate the individual. Eventually through a seemingly endless series of synchronicities, UFO sightings, stage-managed dreams, etc., the abductee will begin to see themselves at the center of this effort to raise the spiritual awareness of the rest of the human race. They will become an activist and be compelled to find others of a similar mindset. All along the abductee believes that it is through their own process of self-education that has led them to this stage of their journey. The abductee may be led unwittingly to a number of books that will further solidify this belief. Some of these books may come from channeled sources, which is often deceptive material coming from the reptilian beings—as in the Ted Rice case of Dr. Karla Turner in Masquerade of Angels. As the abductee meets more experiencers and researchers who are only having what they perceive to be positive contacts, whilst ignoring other sinister abduction reports, they become more enmeshed in a web of deception and intrigue at many levels of consciousness. At the same time they will be steered clear from the "Fear Based" writings of other researchers."

Pacification works by guiding one away from "true awareness" and evidence of mind control conditioning, and steering the individual to an overly positivist (and ego activated) mindset. Some have gone so far as to claim that any and all negative alien/ ET reports must be done by our own secret government or military, and no malevolence exists at all with the aliens. This sets up black and white belief systems aimed at more chaos and infighting within the UFO research community, thus disrupting and marginalizing the more "malevolent" abduction reports. Sure, there are neutral and even positive visitations reported by people. But this doesn't change the fact that some very unpleasant and deceptive alien encounters are happening also. What is unnerving is the amount of deception some of these aliens carry out in the name of "love and light".

The truth detracting efforts are made manifest when certain abductees start behaving "triggered" when confronted with information that could lead to their healing and recovery. For example, they are warned in dreams by their handlers to stay away from a particular researcher or therapist. Or if at a support group or discussion they suddenly fall asleep or have to leave the room to smoke when sensitive alien information will be shared.

It is important to know that truth-detracting efforts occur whether or not a person is an abductee seeking the truth about their experiences. These efforts appear to act in a manner akin to a Hive Alien Mind, working in an intelligent and synchronistic fashion to accomplish its goals—human mind control, ignorance and a continued source of misery and chaos to feed upon. One wonders whether this " Alien Hive Mind" is in actuality the collective unconscious of humanity's ignorance. I believe it is not so simple, and those who inflict guilt upon the aware truth seeker are themselves being manipulated by their own darkness. Compassion must be present or else those claiming "positivist ET contacts" ("spiritually evolved")are simply pawns in a larger game of multidimensional spiritual warfare and delusion.

There are levels to the alien manipulation game, from subtle feelings to overt harassment and even death threats. The first levels of manipulation can be seen with sudden chaos and infighting at home instigated by a person other than the abductee seeking information or going to a support group, conference, therapist, etc. The abductee may get a telepathic, beamed in psychic message not to see a particular person, or else….their kids will get hurt or any number of fears. If the abductee is strong and seeks out help, then the detracting efforts will find a route through a family member, spouse, work buddy or whoever is closest and available to be an unwitting agent of disruption.

Other detractors can be sudden health problems, auto accidents, computer crashes, phone disruptions, or power outages. Abductees-- especially Milabs and researchers-- may be followed by unmarked vehicles, or strangers being seen near the home of the individual taking pictures or obvious spying. Psychological operations of various kinds can be perpetrated upon the "truth seeking" individual.

Second level manipulations occur to truth seekers who were determined to continue their searches despite the first level disruptions. Reprisals often occurred after public speaking, radio shows, or support groups where taboo information regarding UFO's aliens, abductions, reptilians or Milabs, were discusses. In general, the more sensitive the information is, the greater the tendency for reprisals. In a case described in "The Love Bite: Alien Interference in Human Love Relationships", an abductee named Sophia was threatened by military in a vivid lucid dream resembling a Milab encounter. In this case, Sophia sought out to visit a well-known abductions therapist for a hypnotic regression. Sophia was threatened to not visit this therapist and told to not say anything about her orchestrated love relationship, or she and her family would be assassinated. Sophia became too ill following the "Milab warning dream" and had to cancel her trip.

The Love Bite
By Eve Lorgen

The Love Bite

Aliens can manipulate the emotions of people in such a way as to orchestrate love obsessions, or sudden switching off from a relationship. These dramas may range from simple break ups of love relationships to elaborate love obsessions between two targeted abductee partners. At first glance, one may infer that the purpose of alien matchmaking would be for breeding purposes. Perhaps a bloodline studies of specific genetic combinations to engineer the human race in ways favorable to the alien agenda. But this is not always the case, as many of the love bite reports do not involve pregnancy and childbirth. The love obsession follows a pattern that tends to create maximum emotional tension between the couple. The entire bonding process may take years, as early as childhood when two abductees meet in playtime bonding scenarios. This type of case is best demonstrated in Budd Hopkins' Linda Cortile case, and also recounted in detail in The Love Bite. Usually the couple bonds several times before meeting later in life. These events are sometimes recalled as vivid dreams, such that at least one partner has a stronger sense of recognition and chemical attraction to the targeted partner. When the couple finally does meet, it is often described as an instant attraction, de ja vu, a profoundly powerful magnetic attraction. These are not normal "falling in love" types of relationships. A love bite usually includes a number of bizarre synchronicities, vivid dreams, "astral sex", and paranormal phenomena. During this phase of bonding, the alien visitations increase. The emotional, passionate and even telepathic connection between the individuals is remarkable. Usually one partner will fall in love more than the other, and may be the only one who recalls being previously abducted and "bonded".

Many of the love matches take place between two abductees who are already married or involved with another partner. This causes even more distress, as the tension to not be able to consummate the passion is a pressing issue, especially for the abductee who is obsessed and already emotionally plugged into the other partner. Of

109

course the temptations are great, and many have affairs or fantasize about the other person for years! In at least two cases, when the abductee did not bite back and fall for the sexual temptation, they received telepathic messages (from their aliens) that "they passed the test." According to these love bite experiencers, the match was done to test their emotional reactions.

In the Ted Rice case, (recounted in The Love Bite) Ted is matched with a schoolmate at 14 years old. In his bonding procedure he recalled a Grey alien perform an energy movement in his heart "chakra" where luminescent energy fibers were literally weaved into Jill's heart with a wand like instrument. In Ted's case he had a "one sided" love obsession. His partner Jill had little, if any feelings for him. One of the characteristic features of the alien orchestrated love obsession is the switching off of one partner from the other, leaving the love stricken one pining away in unrequited love. The chosen partner either has no attraction or an initial attraction, which suddenly turns off—usually after an alien abduction. Again, the alien abductions are usually remembered as dreams, if at all. Some abductees report spontaneous remote viewing images of the intended partner in such a way as to elicit emotions such as jealousy, obsessive love, yearning and grievous unrequited love pangs. The alien manipulated love obsession process is akin to a carrot being dangled just enough to get the obsessed lover into a constant cycle of love and unrequited love. This can extend from one relationship to another—unless the abductee becomes aware and spiritually empowered. Please note again that these love obsessions do not always result in an offspring, which begs the question as to the real "motivation" of alien orchestrated love obsessions. They want something else. What is this? Human emotional "prana". The creative energy generated from unrequited love is probably one of the most painful and powerful experiences a person must go through. The sexual energy—which is our most sacred and primal power—is of great interest to the aliens.

One very aware abductee was told by her " Tall White" alien handlers, that the love match was done to generate a powerful delicacy of great value to them. It is postulated to be related to kundalini sexual energy. One interesting topic this abductee brought up was why " such and such" a person has to be matched and not others? The Tall Whites responded that they were more successful in creating love obsessions when there were "tendrils of past life connections" in the energy fields of both partners. The aliens would then watch and see—which matches gave birth to strong love attractions. They stated that if a person didn't have a strong enough past life connection to that person, then the love match would fizzle. In another case, the female love obsessed partner was told by the aliens "your bonding is no longer useful to us". In this event her male partner was switched off and matched to another female abductee on board a craft—which created jealousy and grievance to the love bitten woman.

Milabs also experience love bite relationships. In these cases, the partner is often another abductee or Milab. If the partner is not very aware, they tend to act as controlling and disrupting influences upon the Milab. In fact, they themselves are often mind controlled by secret agencies being set up as a kind of Romeo Agent. I cannot tell you how many female Milabs have had controlling partners sent into their lives to neutralize them. The late Leonard Stringfield, an expert UFO crash retrieval and abductions researcher, had reported this anomaly after investigating several female milab cases. The disruption tends to happen as a countermeasure to awareness, healing and recovery of the Milab. After all, many Milabs are being used as black op agents under mind control and security measures must be taken by the agencies who use these people. Even if the MILAB is on the path to self-empowerment, they often are set up time and time again by military/intelligence agents or another abductee under the control of their own alien handlers. You would think the usual relationship problems are bad enough to deal with! But with alien abductees and Milabs, it is compounded beyond most people's comprehension.

The types of aliens involved in abductions are myriad. Most of my cases involve the Greys, both tall and short, tans, browns, insectoids, cloaked hooded beings, reptilians, tall whites, human Nordic looking ET's and human military/secret government and medical personnel. Milabs report humans working alongside aliens in underground bases, for example, and other times it is only military contacts for long periods of time. Many Milabs will have a human and reptilian handler, of which the latter has higher authority. The experiences can be quite physical, and other times they only recall experiences as lucid dreams. A characteristic pattern of Milabs with reptilian handlers is to have some kind of "reptilian sexual" contact where the kundalini of the Milab is activated. On the tail end of these sexual arousals is a military abduction where the Milab is then tasked with some kind of astral op, remote viewing or other paranormal "black op". From the military's standpoint this would be the ideal time to exploit the woman's psychic abilities. If one understands how the kundalini affects the human mind and bio energy, this is a good method to amplify the phi factor.

In the hard core love bite cases, a Draco or reptilian being was involved, as in the "Sex Dragon" case of Wiz and the Viper girl. This is a case discussed on "http//:www.alienlovebite.com". In this love bite case, the Viper girl was believed to be a reptilian hosted shape shifter who vampirized Wiz of his life energy. Barbara Bartholic has a number of cases where the alien shape-shifted from a Nordic human looking being right into a reptilian. In the case of "Kundra", a love bite experiencer interviewed on my web site, was set up with a male sorcerer who had reptilian handlers. The man was involved in black magic and was sent in on Kundra because she had the ability to transmit "shakti energy" as a healer. At the time of her love bite set up, Kundra was involved in using her shakti energy to heal, and had published a newsletter to help others empower themselves. In my opinion, Kundra was set up to be "neutralized" and used by the dark side because of her unique ability. After all— as Barbara Bartholic sarcastically chides, "No good deed goes unpunished!"

In The Love Bite book, the motivations for aliens and human orchestration of love relationships is thoroughly discussed. A new, curious, repetitive theme in alien love bite relationships has been recognized. The aliens seem to know ahead of time if a person will have a soul mate in the future. They then will seek to sabotage the "real" soul mate partner from finding their mate, and instead set up a cookie cutter counterfeit to the abductee—which turns out a disaster. (A love bite) The counterfeit love bite set up serves to keep the abductee disempowered and distracted from finding the true soul mate that is destined for them. When they do find the "real partner", they often have an uncanny resemblence to the former love bite partners that they were set up with before. If they do meet the real soul mate, the dark forces seek to either control and manipulate the relationship to their agenda, or try to break it up. This has been reported many times, especially by milabs. (See the case of T Cell and Rebecca on http://www.alienlovebite.com) True love connections have a tantric soul emersion quality to them, are very powerful and can literally change the world.

The solution for those who are experiencing the dark side of the alien equation is to stay present and compassionate. If the aliens are truly looking to "feed" off negative energy and life force, then the best way to stop them is to not react to them at all. Aliens play mind games and appear to seek to engage us in our reactions to their machinations. What other choice do we have other than to learn from these experiences? Let go of ego, and maintain the presence of our Divine Being. It is said in the story of the Buddah, that before he became enlightened, "Mara" sought and attacked him from all directions. Mara is another name for the forces of illusion and ignorance. If it took 40 years for Guatama Buddha to become enlightened under the Bodhi tree, how long do you think it will take each one of us?

FEBRUARY 23, 2004
AM I INVOLVED IN A "LOVE-BITE"?

I realized something was not quite right. This extremely bothered me even though I'd had several alien abductees who had experienced the "Love-Bite" phenomenon. I saw how it had changed their lives completely. I myself fought against the idea of this happening in my life but the memories were there. I repeatedly told myself, "No way" until it got the best of me. I had worked with other researchers who had studied the "Love Bite" effect and had worked with many clients through hypnotherapy on this subject. I finally opened up to two dear friends, one of which was a well known researcher and hypnotherapist Barbara Bartholic. After speaking with Barbara many times about my memories and telling her about what was now occurring, she confirmed that indeed I was in the middle of a Love-Bite experience. She followed along with me on this until her death.

One other dear friend whom I initially contacted first also did confirm my suspicions and suggested I also open up to Barbara. I pleaded that my male friend involved and my family were not ever to know. I never dreamed I would be caught up in a "Love-Bite" experience. I found myself thinking that these experiences I was having were just hallucinations. At this time of writing the only reason I feel I was (or still am) put through this one-sided heart wrenching love affair is because I needed to learn and better understand these unusual life experiences. Possibly I did not have enough compassion or belief in three of my clients' stories that these experiences (Love Bite) can and do, in fact happen. The result of these experiences causes major trauma in a woman's or a man's life here on earth. In my case, what ungodly species but the Reptilians would have the HONOR of these experimentations for their studies or demonic pleasures?

My personal viewpoint of the species "Reptilian," is that they are a very sexual species that uses humans as their "lab rat" specimens. They conduct experiential studies of humans beginning in early childhood when they connect a small female child to a male child as playmates. These children are abducted many times during their childhood years and into adulthood. As adults they find each other and fall in love, leaving their married partners to make a "normal" life together in a new married relationship. In some cases when an abducted couple is brought together, one has no interest in the other. This leaves the childhood partner in a forlorn, distraught stage, as Eve described in the previous chapter. My understanding is when both male and female reach puberty, sexual relations will begin with these humans who have known each other since childhood. When they become adults they begin to seek each other out, wanting to know each other outside of any "abduction scenarios." However in some cases the Reptilians "quick wipe" the couple's memories. Normally, one or the other will have their memories wiped clean. Usually it is the female who maintains the memory of her childhood sweetheart. Thus, as an adult she wants to find her male "Soul Mate" whom she has "been with" for many years.

Let me first explain MY experience of what possibly led up to what is known as the "Love-Bite affair." I will then attempt to compare my experiences with those of three female clients I have guided through this "Love-Bite" experience.

Just a couple of years ago, my husband Fred and I realized that our marriage had taken a turn for the worse. I blamed it on "Male PMS syndrome." A couple of our children had noticed this as well and commented on the changes in their dad. Fred never put blame onto me. Time passed and many crucial problems arose between us that seemed to be destroying our marriage. Neither of us understood what was transpiring. It took 100% from each of us to find our love for each other again. As a result our love became much more solid between us.

During the past years I had been guiding alien/military/government abductees through hypnotherapy. I have had three clients who survived the horrific "Love Bite" experience that had threatened to destroy their lives. Each person had already lived through their own alien abduction and all the horror that I was hearing. These stories involved the Reptilians, an uncouth, demonic species that experiments on male and female humans.

When I guided my first client through her "Love-Bite" experience I acknowledged her story. I thought to myself, "What a story!" not realizing I was about to fall into the depths of a "Love Bite" syndrome myself. My own "Love Bite Story" began with past life regressions in hypnotherapy school. I never believed that what I learned in past life regressions would have an effect on me that would result in a "Love Bite" experience. Thus, I will tell you about my "Love-Bite" experiences beginning with three past life regressions, which provided evidence of an indicator spoken of by Eve Lorgen.

PAST LIFE #1

I found myself in a large rocking wooden boat, with what I believed to have been several French men. A bad storm had been upon us, ripping the sails and tilting the boat sideways causing men to fall into a raging sea of large waves. I grabbed onto a nearby small wooden boat, and as another large wave came aboard I was washed away into the sea in this small boat for many days and nights. The hot sun blistered my lips and swelled my face. I was so thirsty and death was upon me, when suddenly as if I was having an out of body experience I found myself above the boat and looking into the boat. I saw a man with black hair, and somewhat rounded sun burnt face. His blue eyes caught my attention....and I said to my guide, "this is not me in this boat" and I was told by my guide "to go with what I was living then." So I followed through with the given instructions but continued saying "this is not me in this boat" as the boat rocked with fury caught in yet another storm. The storm carried this young almost lifeless man upon to a barren beach. Seconds later, in the darkness of night men from another culture appeared wearing headdresses made of feathers and colorful decorated animal skins around their midriffs. Holding pointed wood spears and sharpened rocks in their hands, they began to pierce the body of the young man in the boat. Suddenly, a man of authority who wore a larger headdress with many more feathers stopped the killing of the man in the boat. The man of authority commanded the others to put down their spears, pick up the wounded man and carry him to a fire in the middle of animal skin covered teepees. The unconscious man had no strength to fight the men who picked him up.

He was carried to the fire and offered some kind of drink to quench his thirst. He could hardly swallow, feeling that death was upon him. Suddenly he opened his eyes. Standing there was a female native. He looked at the female, and it was myself that he was looking at. I was the native woman who summoned the medicine man who had ordered the others to go into the forest and bring him some particular healing herbs.

When they returned, the young man had been moved into a tent of sorts for his protection, where the young native woman gave him more drink. The medicine man and young woman made tea out of the herbs and gave the warm tea to the young man.

After many days of drinking tea and having a paste made from herbs rubbed over his body by the young native woman, the young man's strength and health were restored. This young, dark haired, slender man wanted to remain in camp learning the ways of the natives, as he now felt like one of them. He and the young native lady were soon married.

PAST LIFE #2

I found myself in a long-ago century. I was living in a bungalow that had a thatched roof. I had a loving husband, two small daughters and a son. The place was Scotland or Ireland. The year was somewhere in the 1440's. There was much upheaval in this land.

My husband of this time was slender, tall, blue eyed, and had long blond hair. His face, body and personality resembled that of the French man in the last past-life induction. I recognized myself as the wife, also with fair blond hair. I wore my hair up in braids mostly, but would take them out in the evening and let the hair fall into beautiful tresses.

Our children had blond hair as well. I was a typical woman of this place. I found myself braiding strands of long blond hair to squeals of protest from my daughters. I found myself weaving fabric that I would sew into dresses for the girls and shirts and short pants for my son and husband. My husband tended the small yard with a vegetable garden and fruit trees. My husband also looked after our chickens, a cow and a goat. I did the cooking and baking on a hearth. We did not own our land. A king ruled this country and many wars were fought.

When nighttime fell, music entertained the family. My husband made up songs while he played his stringed instrument. His voice was so tender in song. There was much laughter and joy as our children and my husband played games on the floor together.

The king's castle sat high on a grassy green hill above the small town below. The country was once again in turmoil. Many wives lost their husbands in the upheaval of the king's quest for land he thought was his. The king's men often rode down into the town gathering up more warriors to fight for him, taking men away against their will. One beautiful warm day the king's men rode up to our bungalow and beckoned my husband outside. As I followed my husband outside, I saw the king's men on their tall stocky horses. The bodies and heads of the men were covered in metal to protect them. They carried swords and knives at their side to fight the opponent. One of the king's men read my husband's name from a scroll. He was being called forth to battle to service the king. My husband had no choice but to go. He would either leave with them, or die on the spot. My husband, with tears in his eyes, kissed me good-bye, then kissed his children and told each one to be strong. With tears in my eyes, I watched him climb up on a horse and wave goodbye, feeling I would never see him again. They rode down the dirt road far away into the country.

Summer, fall and winter passed with no news of my husband. Life was difficult being both mother and father to our children. I listened to their cries for the whereabouts of their father. Harvesting the vegetables and fruits and tending to the animals, life was different now for all of us. Instead of hearing the joy of laughter and tenderly made up songs of the night, the nights were full of prayer for the safety and return of our loved one.

One spring day, a messenger rode up on his horse and beckoned me outside to tell me the unhappy news of my husband's demise. I listened twice to the news that my husband had been killed in battle although he fought hard. The tears were unending as my widowed neighbors gathered, with arms around me, and food in their baskets. Our town grew small with hardly any men in sight.

I "awoke" to the words, "I don't believe in past lives." But this man, who once again was my husband, was the same man I saw in my first past-life regression. "How could this be?" I asked.

PAST LIFE #3

The third hypnotherapy induction began and I found myself as a six-year-old child running and laughing in a beautiful meadow. As I kept running, I instantly found myself as a young lady, running and still laughing in a meadow at a different time and place. The time and place was in the 1770's in Paris, France. I wore a long cotton dress with petticoats underneath. The dress had a white top with puffy sleeves to it. The bottom of the dress was ruffled and blue. A young man was chasing after me as if in play. I ran swiftly, holding up my dress, to lead him to the front door of our home.

We lived in a quaint two story home along a street with other similar homes. The newly married couple were so much in love and very happy. The husband spoiled his wife with any of the riches that she wanted.

I looked upon my young husband who had lucid blue eyes and dark hair. He presented himself as a slender, tall, well dressed young man. He was a concert pianist and played his music every day for me, as I sat and listened intently to the pieces he composed especially for me. He played his beautiful compositions on the grandest of concert pianos made. As days, months and years went by no children were born into this union. The man worked tirelessly everyday of composing and playing his music in the grandest of concert halls.

Overtime he grew away from his wife and began to have secret affairs with other women, as he felt his wife no longer satisfied him. As the betrayed wife I had no knowledge of the extra-marital affairs my handsome husband was secretly involved in.

I had maids and a lady-in-waiting to help me with expected social duties. My lady-in-waiting and I formed a close relationship. I would tell her my deepest secrets and the wishes of my life. She was a lady whom I grew to trust and valued so very much in my life. Yes, my lady-in-waiting was a tall, beautiful lady with long blond hair. I envied her beautiful shapely body.

I loved dressing in the expensive bouffant dresses and wearing my hair up in long brown curls. I then began to dress my lady-in-waiting in beautiful bouffant dresses as well. She lived in our home and kept me company when my husband was away on his concert travels. My husband traveled all over Europe, leaving me alone to tend to social daily life. Rumors began to trickle in of his affairs, but I did not believe these rumors. I felt it was something for the rich of the richest ladies to speak about. I did attend many of his concerts.

Over time, I found myself too embarrassed because of the rumors and stopped attending his concerts. I believed my husband's word that he would never do such a thing to me, us, or our marriage.

Not until one day when I returned from a trip earlier than expected. I found my lady-in-waiting sexually intimate with my husband in her bed. My lady-in-waiting left soon after I found her and my husband together and she was never heard of again... until one day in the twentieth century.

Once again, I was brought out of this past life regression, not telling the whole story of what I lived through during this time. And once again I said, "I do not believe."

During the time in hypnotherapy school many other classmates could see a correlation between their past lives and to their way of life now, in the present and between people in their lives now who were also part of their past lives. On many occasions I questioned myself as to what had transpired during the three regression sessions I explored with my teacher and other students who guided me to my memories of past lives. I had never met any man who looked like the one in my three regressions sessions. He always seemed to be my husband in those past lives. Unlike my classmates, no present connections had occurred to me. I wondered where those memories came from and why. In some sense, I had believed that we, as humans, only lived one life, not two or three. We are just given one life to live.

The years went by quickly after those days of being in hypnotherapy school. I gave no further thought to *my* past lives, but I **did** believe in the process of guiding my hypnotherapy clients into *their* past lives. I saw them realize their present day lives as connected to their past lives.

The awakening of a realization of my own past life history was acknowledged. The year was 1995. Some friends had told me about a lady around the same age as myself, who was also an alien abductee. The subject of this lady came up when I described a particular lady I had seen on several occasions while experiencing alien abductions with the various universal entities. This lady had been invited to a party given by friends, Richard and Marie Rowlette, who also knew of her alien abductions.

When I walked into their home there was the lady who looked so familiar to me. It was as if I had known her from some time other than meeting on board an alien ship. We were introduced and I immediately felt I had always known her. Strange as it may seem, I also felt close to her and I did not know why (other than having shared alien abduction experiences with her).

Chris told me that she too secretly had the same feelings I did. We began calling and visiting each other often, getting to know one other and talking about our memories of shared alien abductions. Quite surprisingly, Chris also came back with total memories of our shared abductions.

Our friendship grew close and as time passed, more memories invaded my conscious mind of a particular past life experience that included my new friend. I could not believe what I had re-lived in the last hypnotherapy regression experience was true. Those memories constantly replayed for me. Now I wondered if perhaps in this present life, Chris and I were once again together. I questioned the memories. Chris looked like the lady in my last past life and had the same type of personality as my "lady-in-waiting." But intuition was telling me differently and perhaps one day, I would ask her if she believed in past lives. I knew how wrong I could be but over time, just observing her, I soon felt that perhaps she could be my lady-in-waiting from that past lifetime.

I kept this "silliness" to myself until confirmation of those memories came to me. One day she said she wanted to talk to me about something important. We sat down to talk. Chris immediately asked me if I believed in past life experiences. I felt that she was the stronger of the two of us, as she came forward first to speak of the past life memory that involved both of us. She shared the same feelings and emotions that I also felt about these memories. She began telling me about being a lady-in-waiting to a woman in Paris, France, in the 1770's. Every detail that I remembered in the hypnotherapy regression session as well as memories that came back to me after the hypnotherapy regression session was over were the same memories she was telling me about now!

I sat in awe and was astonished as she told the story of her/our past life together in Paris, France in the 1770's. She also could not remember what year in the 1770's we lived our past lives in the beautiful house.

CHRIS' PAST LIFE

A man who was a concert pianist and his lovely wife took her into their beautiful French style two-story home to be the wife's Lady-in-Waiting. She spoke of the beautiful dresses the wife dressed her in, described her bedroom, and the beautiful home they lived in. She described the husband as being slender and tall, with black hair and blue eyes, and that he was a concert pianist. He would write music and practice his music at home.

We both laughed when we could not remember our names, or my husband's name.

Chris' story continues.

She, as my "lady-in-waiting," lived with my husband and me for several years. We enjoyed a closeness that was almost like being sisters, sharing secrets and laughing. We supported each other, especially when the ritzy ladies of the time would come for tea, and knowingly hurt me with stories of my husband's extra marital affairs. Chris spoke of my husband and his extra-marital affairs and her private affair with my husband.

Chris apologized to me and I felt she too had fallen in love with my husband of that past lifetime.

Chris told me that she immediately recognized me at our friend's party that night. She knew I was the lady in her past life of that era when I walked through the door that evening. She said I looked the same as I did in the 1770's.

Reliving her memories that afternoon over tea together, Chris also mentioned:

The daily routine for all of us would be to sit in the large living area while my husband serenaded us on the grand piano.

Staring at her I recognized the little perks of her personality that were so familiar to me. Soon I too, believed she was my lady-in-waiting, in that past life.

I was shocked and astonished when I realized that I *did* have a past life; and not *one*, but *three* that I had re-lived through hypnotherapy. I was now ready to believe and accept the other two past life scenarios.

That same afternoon over tea as we shared knowledge of our past life together, I began to tell her about my memories of the other two past lives I had re-lived through hypnotherapy. I also told her about the memories that came to me after I experienced the regression. We re-lived an era that afternoon having tea, as we shared our memories with each other.

We both felt different and strange, meeting once again in this future time and finding that we also share past and current memories of alien abductions. Chris, being the positive person she is, kept saying that one day I would meet the man who had been in my three past lives. I felt I never would, of course.

THE YEAR 2003
REALIZATION COMES FORTH

A New York Film company had contacted me with regard to being in a segment of a film by Steven Spielberg. They were interviewing several alien abductees about their alien experiences. Out of several abductees one or two would be chosen. I was not chosen. I was grateful for that because I selfishly thought that having my book published, "Morning Glory" Diary of an Alien Abductee was the only medium I wanted to use to reach out to help other abductees. I never dreamed that film companies would be contacting me because of sharing my secret life experiences through my first book. Thankfully, this proposition did not pan out. I had never thought about using the medium of film to reach out to other abductees or other interested parties within this phenomenon. Another thing I had heard was that some film producers turn the truth of UFO/abduction experiences into a lie or a horrible tale. My book was out and that was all I wanted.

A month later I received a phone call from another film company based in New York City. This man was referred to me through a friend of mine who recommended that he contact me about a film documentary on alien abductions. My friend did not tell me that someone might be calling from this other film company. I was surprised when I received this particular phone call. The man introduced himself over the phone as "Jack Carter" (*Not his real name. I am not allowed to publish Mr. Carter's real name or the name of his company in this book*).

During the phone call Mr. Carter told me of his plans to make a documentary. The friend had told him that I had written my personal story of alien/milab abductions. He thought perhaps I might be the person to be in this documentary. As he spoke on the phone, I muttered under my breath to myself, "Not again. Just go away. This is not what I want to do. I am just not interested in this."

After listening to Jack's introduction and spiel he asked if I would be interested in being in a film documentary. He wanted to know if I would be willing to talk about some of my abduction experiences with him over the phone. He asked me questions about my alien and MILAB abductions, which I grudgingly answered while trying to find a way out of the conversation. Finally, I asked him if he had read "Morning Glory" Diary of an Alien Abductee and his answer was no. So I said, "Go buy my book and read it. Then call me." I was thinking he would not ever do this and that would be the end of a documentary film offer.

Over a two week period, I had some time to think about further resources that might be available to help me "reach that one alien abductee" that I had initially sought to reach. I thought I would never hear from Mr. Carter again. To my surprise, on the second weekend, Mr. Carter called me again. He told me he had bought my book and read it. He said he could not put the book down until he finished it.

I felt differently about this second phone conversation with Mr. Carter and listened to him. He questioned me on certain subjects I had written about, which confirmed that he *had* read my book. I felt grateful when he asked me to consider the possibility of being in his documentary. Jack asked if he could come to Albuquerque to meet and do an interview with me. I was somewhat intrigued by the idea but also I still had negative feelings. We spoke on the phone a couple more times before he came to Albuquerque. Mr. Carter arrived in Albuquerque on March 13th.

I planned to meet Mr. Carter at the airport on the designated afternoon. I arrived twenty minutes early but his flight was on time. We had previously talked about how we would recognize each other. He said he would be the one to recognize me since my picture was on the back cover of my book. I had no idea what he looked like. Nervously, I waited by the escalators standing off to the right side, looking at each man who came down on the escalators and wondering if that was "Jack." I did not want him to miss me as he would be the one to identify himself first.

I had negative feelings yet about this process. I thought, "Suppose this was just a trick and there really *was* no Mr. Carter who worked in film and wanted to make a documentary? Suppose Mr. Carter was part of the government?" I went through so many negative thoughts while waiting. I thought he might be able to see me better if I stood to the right of the escalator instead of in front of it. Many people rode down the escalator at different times, indicating that a plane had just landed. I knew his flight was on time but he was not in any of the groups that descended. I stood back from the escalator and looked around intently; men who had arrived had someone waiting for them. This increased the negative thoughts and feelings that swirled in my head. "What do I do, just leave because this was a big joke on me?"

Another large group of mostly men came down on the escalator and one young man stood out in the crowd. "Oh my gosh, I know that man! But who is he?" I asked myself. I followed the man down the escalator with my eyes trying to identify him. Who is that man and where have I met him? The man exited the escalator and began to look around. Then he looked right in my direction and began to walk toward me. I was thinking, "This man knows me" and "I know him. But who is he? His face, his eyes, his body movements are so familiar."

Jack seemed to recognize me and I was asking myself, "Do we know each other?" At that moment I did not think *this* man was Jack. I watched a slender, tall man walk toward me. "I *do* know this man. I recognize the way he walks and holds his body." As he got closer I remembered those lucid blue eyes belonging to someone of long ago. I quickly snapped out of this...*whatever.* I heard him calling my name. "Gloria." And I answered, "Yes."

Like magic, hearing his voice, I knew where I had known this man before. Jack stood in front of me. As he kissed me on the cheek and then introduced himself as Jack, my head went into a tizzy. I tried to stay calm and grounded. Calm and grounded was not working for me. I felt even more nervous and as I spoke to him, I stumbled over my words.

When I initially saw Jack walking in my direction, after he got off the escalator, a memory suddenly flashed into my head. I was immediately taken back to a year in the 1770's. A little voice in my brain kept repeating, "It can't be.......but how can it be?......It is......He is from my past lives." And the sarcastic voice within me argued back, "No he is not......You don't believe in past lives...... Remember?" The little voice again, "This man's voice.....I *do* know the voice and his face. The *same* voice.....It *is* him!"

Over the course of the weekend I fought off and on in my mind trying to reason within myself if this could be the same man in my past lives. I made an agreement with the voices in my head. That agreement was to watch Jack's personality, his body movements, everything about him that I remembered. Then we, the voices within me, and I would decide if this was a true happening in today's life. I could not understand how this could be happening; a man of long ago reappears in my present life. I was secretly crying inside of myself.

Jack stayed with Fred and me in our home over the long weekend. Jack continued to interview and observe me and I kept observing *him.* Some of his movements and personality traits would throw me back into a past life memory of him.

One day we traveled to the Jemez Pueblo, as this is something he said he wanted to do. We found the weekend full and exciting. If this was *not* the same man of my past life, he certainly spoiled me in the same way my husband did in a long ago life. For example, he bought me a large gift of bath items to just enjoy. I had said before that my husband of that era of the 1770's spoiled me with anything I wanted, just to spoil me.

When it was time for Jack to leave Albuquerque on that rainy Sunday evening, I drove him to the airport. We both got out of the car and he kissed me on the cheek goodbye, telling me that he would not be back in Albuquerque. He had to interview some other people for his film. I was disheartened and thrown back because I would never see him again; this man whom I thought lived with me in three past lives. I was so certain of this fact. Overall though, the occasion gave me food for thought to help other abductees, and to reconsider being in a film regarding my family and my alien/milab experiences.

The week after he left, I fought with the idea of how wrong I could be if Jack was or was not the man who was my husband of long ago. I kept reviewing memories and the weekend with Jack. His voice..... the same voice I had thought....his height.....just everything about the man was correct. I was so sad that I would never know if this was the man from a past life so long ago.

I called Kathryn, a fellow hypnotherapist and dear friend who had knowledge of my past lives and who also, knew of this venture of the "weekend." The next call placed was to Chris. Both ladies were eagerly awaiting my phone call and they listened intently to what I had to say. Then we discussed the reality of Jack. Kathryn has more knowledge in past lives than I have. Listening to Kathryn's words that day, the possibility was great that Jack and I could meet now in present time for some unknown reason. Perhaps something in our past lives had not been finished, thus promoting a meeting in this life. Because our lives are so different now we are meeting under different circumstances. He is younger and I am older. Our life situations are different now than they were then. The possibilities to consider are many.

Chris and I spoke about that weekend and Jack. My description of Jack she felt, was so correct. The excitement between the three of us (Kathryn, Chris and myself) was great. The negative voice within me returned, saying "Forget it, Gloria! This cannot be true. Get on with your life. You have much to contend with." Since Jack had said he would never be back in Albuquerque, I knew there would not be another chance of meeting with him or being in his film.

Approximately one week later Jack called me and asked if I wanted to be in his documentary. I said "Yes." He said he would be back in touch with me. Jack scheduled another visit to Albuquerque, and interviewed me on camera. Another long weekend we shared. I observed him with different and open eyes as well as putting puzzle pieces together from a time long ago. I felt surer of sharing a past with this man of long ago. At that point I was embarrassed to even speak with him on the topic about past lives. The negative voice started up again. "I don't believe in past lives. How can this be?" Even though I felt this could be the same man from three past life regressions, I still had doubts.

The shoot was scheduled and I was to fly to Manhattan. Jack prepared the areas where the filming was to take place. The other UFO investigator who was also in the film was apparently ready as well. My expenses were paid. Just the excitement of being in a documentary able to tell my story, led me to question, "Where is this going to lead? Am I doing the right thing?" Within my excited heart I knew so, and I knew Jack believed in my "secret life" story.

A couple of days before I was to leave for Manhattan, Jack called, sounding discouraged. He told me that the investigator had suddenly changed his mind about the documentary and was not going to participate. Jack needed some time to find someone else he had asked to take the investigator's place. Everything fell though on this project.

Several weeks passed and Jack stayed in contact with me as he always did. He scheduled another trip out to Albuquerque. He had come up with a new plan. The plan was to film his documentary in Albuquerque and other parts of New Mexico. This was the beginning of a year and so many months of frequent visits to look for filming sites. During this time Jack and I spent many hours together traveling throughout New Mexico, scanning off-road bumpy trails and looking for the perfect places.

Getting to know Jack as a person once again, deep inside of myself, I knew this was the man of long ago. Did he know this too, I wondered?

He spoiled me on our travels with gifts of special chocolates that I liked or different fruits I had never had eaten before. As we drove through different areas of New Mexico he would compose and sing songs to me. His songs were either about me or the particular area we were in. Jack had his cameras with him and sometimes it seemed we would travel only a short distance when he would find another beautiful site to take the perfect picture. On our journey in the farming country or mountainous areas, if people were standing outside and near the fences of their property, he would stop and get out of the car to visit with them. We met many people on our travels. We spent many hours talking and laughing. He eventually told me that he too, was an alien abductee. His abductors were the Reptilians (which will lead into my story of shared abductions with the Reptilians).

We got to know one another during these journeys throughout New Mexico. He told me about his past lives and of one in particular that he was presently "investigating." I could not tell him about my past life which occurred in 1770 in Paris, France, or the past life in Scotland/Ireland or of the small boat where I first "met" him. I kept waiting to see if he would reflect on those memories, some of which he touched upon vaguely. I felt like this was *my* secret. If I revealed my own secret past life that included him....what a "heel" I would feel like if he did not remember being a part of it.

While driving through the El Malpias area of western New Mexico, I took him to meet a very special man who had come to me for guidance through hypnotherapy. This man was a Native American and a Shaman, as well as an alien abductee. He was a well taught and learned man. I knew Jack would be thrilled to meet him. I was right, and a friendship developed between Jack and this "mountain man" as I used to call him.

Jack and I were honored when we were invited by the Native American man and his wife to participate in a four day Sundance festival. There were many other Native Americans from North and South Dakota and from other areas of the United States as well as New Mexico. It rained hard every day of the festival. We were washed out of our tent on the first night, so we slept in the car the rest of the nights. We woke up early each morning to the call of drums and a beautiful sunrise. We enjoyed the opportunity to get away from our normal busy lives. We felt privileged to be included in a beautiful time of celebration with the Native Americans, sharing their beliefs and culture. To be able to experience those festive days was so over powering. As we danced and supported our Native American friends, we felt truly blessed to have been a part of their celebration.

Jack and I made many memories traveling through New Mexico in his search for perfect places to film his documentary. While we were in Chaco Canyon he wanted to hike up to a plateau that overlooks the pueblo ruins below. I've written a poem that explains the memory we shared there.

WIND SPIRIT

The young Man traveled far with a quest in mind
A Woman from the Southwest was at his side.......

After many attempts to a region of many Ancient Ones
The dream He sought was realized.
But not before a climb to reach for.

The high Mesa above and below the bluest of sky
held the hidden secrets of those of many a year ago

The Woman feared the climb and height they had to reach,
With the helping hand of the young Man over the large rocks
They conquered the wind tunnel where Wind Spirit sang them a song
As Wind Spirit gathered them both up to guide them on their trek
to the highest mesa above the skeletal remains of an ancient pueblo below.

They walked with Wind Spirit at their backs until the Man found
The place of rest to sit and ponder, to reflect, to meditate on the gifts
He found and shared with the Woman.

They sat at the perfect spot overlooking the canyon below
The vastness of the walls of the opposite canyon and the indention
Of perhaps a long ago river that flowed below
Whilst Wind Spirit remained with them

The Woman meditating and reflecting on the Ancient Ones
Wondered if the Man was in same meditative reflection
As quiet was theirs' except for Wind Spirit's song

Listen closely she whispered....Can you hear...the Children at
Play.....Can you hear the Men working their crops...
                    Oh no!....
Can you hear the tearful cry of the Women as the Men
Fight for their protection against the ensuing force against them
.........The Woman asked the Man....
Black Birds above them flew.
As the Man shared with the Woman the sweet fruits
Of the land, and they drank of the purest liquid to quest

Their thirst in this land of the Ancient Ones

The Man said yes, this is where I will soon meet my dream quest
As they stood up to descend the high Mesa that held
Many a secret of the Ancient Ones.

The Woman thanks the Man for sharing in such a
Memory made that she was able to share in his dream quest.

During Jack's visits to Albuquerque we were invited guests at two dinners at Nathan Twinning's home, and there Jack found the grand piano and entertained the guests by playing the piano.

Was this a coincidence of past life and present day? Jack loves to play the piano and guitar. He would sit down at my piano and play pieces he knew from memory. He played as beautifully as I remembered. I would dance by myself as he played, once again remembering times of long ago. We spent one day at guitar stores. He played the guitar just as beautifully. He still loves his music and is very musical in this present life.

During our times together I was able to get a picture of Jack. I had a purpose for this photo. The purpose was to show his picture to Chris and Kathryn, who had already gone to Jack's website. When Chris saw Jack's picture, along with some others I had, she excitedly picked out the one of Jack. Jumping with joy, she identified him as being the man from long ago!

WHO IS RESPONSIBLE?

Over the years, Jack would appear in different situations inside my home. These many different scenarios had to have been done with a hologram system. Many times I felt a presence either while alone in my home or with other people around me. Fred could be home when Jack would suddenly appear. I could be cleaning house or working on the computer, any time of the day or night and he would just show up.

For instance, one Christmas Eve, while cleaning up after our traditional tamales and posole dinner with many guests, I was at the kitchen sink washing dishes. My mom was in a wheelchair at the time. I wrung out the wash cloth to clean tables. As I turned around, facing my mother, there was Jack standing right behind her with a smile on his face. I stopped and stared at him, in shock. My mind was in turmoil. ***"How could he be here? Where did he come from? How could this happen?"*** He looked as if he was real. I could touch his body and it felt solid. My hand did not go through his body but was stopped by the consistency of human material.

Later, during a phone conversation, I asked Jack about his Christmas visit. I asked him how he was able to make his appearance in my kitchen. I described the clothes he was wearing. He made light of the situation with laughter and said he'd come home without his brown sweater and asked if I knew where it was.

BACK TO THE FILMING PROJECT:

The Jemez Pueblo area was special to Jack, so that was where he chose to do some of the filming.

The filming began. The other person whose story was being told was Al Bielek. Filming also took place in several other locations throughout New Mexico. A very famous Native American from Taos and a Shaman from Mexico were also in the film.

During the two weeks of filming, I began to hear stories from the other camera men about Jack and his camera *woman* and about their love/sexual affair. One night while the other camera people were packing up, I found this lady in Jack's arms enjoying a passionate kiss. Sudden flashes of past life number three invaded my mind. Jack had apparently carried his love of women over from the past. It broke my heart but I had to remember I was now a married woman with a loving husband - a man I loved dearly. Every night I returned home to my husband who surrounded me with safety and love during filming. In present time, I did not understand why seeing Jack with another woman who was free with herself, would bother me. But it did. Every day and night while filming, I listened to the negative blasts coming from Al about this situation. The "affair" should have been less public and more private and personal. Because of this situation, filming was an unpleasant experience.

Jack and I remained friends through this ordeal. The documentary was filmed over a two week period. During the years after filming we stayed in contact with each other. Jack gave me support during my husband's death, calling me every evening to find out how I was doing. Jack and I have come through many trials in our different lives and have remained friends.

At present time though, our friendship is nonexistent. I was coerced by mutual friends to avoid Jack because of other film work he was involved in. Some time ago, I had discovered this and could not believe it. The type of work he was doing went against my values. These mutual friends were concerned about how easy it would be for Jack to take my face or voice and put it into one of these other films. I was concerned about my safety, so I did not renew my contract with Jack. Knowing Jack, I felt that he would never have done such a thing. He was just not that type of person. I had found him to be quite respectful, intelligent, caring and loving. I miss his friendship and everything he gave to me during those years of friendship.

REPTILIAN EXPERIENCE

During the times apart, when Jack was in New York, or traveling abroad, I began experiencing abductions by the Reptilians. In the past I had only been with the Reptilians a few times, seemingly working with them observing a room full of men of different ages lying on the familiar silvered colored tables. It did not matter to the Reptilians if it was a male child, adolescent, young man, or an older adult. All these males were in a type of distress situation that was somewhat sickening to me. As an example, I was led into a big room by two "lizard looking" Reptilians who were quite large in stature. I was between both of them and I was not walking on my own. I questioned them as to why I was there with a Being I detested. I wanted to know why they were taking me into this room.

We entered the large room through a dark hallway on a ship where different aged males were naked or half dressed. Most of the males were moaning or crying. I still do not know why I was taken into this disgusting room and shown what I saw. We walked up to a table surrounded by at least four Reptilians. On top of the silver table lay a young man. What appeared to be a younger Reptilian was raping this young man. My heart fell when I saw the fractured face of the young man screaming. I too cried as I stood there and just wanted to blast out with vulgar words or grab something to kill these dammed Reptilians! In my memory, I tried kicking at one of them, but was stopped by the other with their wide horrific hands on my leg. There was no use in my trying to throw the Reptilian off of the young man, as the Reptilian was heavier and stronger than I was. I looked around the room at some of the other tables. The same thing was going on with other human males. I saw human males tied down with a type of black restraints or males just not moving as if they were asleep. I don't know why I was taken into this room to witness such things. I often wondered if this is what they also do to females. I would like to know the reason why I was shown this.

LOVE BITE: THE BEGINNING

Through research by investigators/researchers, and studies, abductees are "pulled" into what is called the "Love Bite" which is orchestrated by the Reptilians. I have no love for these beings, and I feel that they are a spin off of (or in fact) Satan, himself. I had just a few experiences with the creatures known as the Reptilians. I did not have full knowledge of these Beings before the Reptilians "pulled" me into a "Love Bite" affair with Jack. "Past Lives" play a major factor with two people who are involved with the Reptilians in a "Love-Bite affair." Thus, this explains my experiences in the three past lives that included Jack.

2003 DATE UNKNOWN
REPTILIANS

I recognized the symptoms of an apparent abduction this particular night. I was experiencing the anxiety that something was wrong. Tossing and turning, feeling very restless, sleep did not come to me until late that night. I woke up in a small, very well-lit room, lying on a table that protruded from a curved wall. I turned my head to the left where I saw a lady with blond hair sitting in a chair. I'm not sure but I thought I recognized this lady. She did not speak but just stared at me, then looked downward. My vision was somewhat fuzzy, but became clear after a short while. I could not move my body as I

had been paralyzed. I thought, *"Why fight it? Whatever is going to happen, will happen."* I wondered, *"Why won't this lady talk to me?"*

After what seemed like a long time (but in reality was just a short while), a door swung open to the left of where the lady was sitting. I gasped, as what looked like a large lizard or snake Reptilian walked through the door. He stopped and gazed at the lady, then walked over to me and touched me on my stomach. I wanted to just spit on his face, especially his orange slit eyes. I was telepathically told not to do this. The door opened again and another Reptilian entered who was holding onto a very dazed, incoherent Jack, supported by another Reptilian. Jack looked at the lady with blond hair and said "Hi" to her as if he knew her. Jack's incoherent mental state quickly went away when he saw me lying on the table. He stared at me in dismay, as if he did not believe it was me lying on the table. Jack said, "Gloria" and I said, "Yes." The Reptilian who was standing by me sat me up as if I were a rag doll. It appeared I was free to move about, though I chose to remain on the table, staring at Jack. Many thoughts were going through my mind and I could not comprehend what was about to transpire. *"What was their plan,"* I wondered, *"and why was Jack brought into this same room? Why do I recognize the lady, but cannot put a name to her yet?"*

A Reptilian pulled me by my underarms and dragged me down from the table. I felt the strength of his strong ugly arms. All three Reptilians looked at each other as they communicated telepathically. One Reptilian walked me toward Jack, and then turned both of us around facing the doorway. Two of the Reptilians went through the doorway. Jack and I were instructed to follow and not speak to each other. We did as instructed, but Jack took hold of my hand and we walked hand in hand following the two Reptilians with a third Reptilian following behind. We walked down a dimly lit hallway until we reached a door on my right. One of the two Reptilians opened the door. They went through and we followed them. I thought my eyes were playing tricks on me because of what I was seeing. I was in a bedroom. There was a double bed with night stands on either side. The walls were painted in what I thought was a dark avocado color. The night stands held two dimly lit lights. We were told that this was going to be our bedroom for exploration and experimentation purposes. We were told they were going to study us. Now I was shaking and Jack held my hand tighter. I had an idea of what might transpire in this room and hoped I was wrong. Perhaps the lady with the blond hair was going to show up any minute, and I would observe what took place. Wrong thought to have! One of the Reptilians led me to the bed and forced me onto it. *"Oh God! That bastard is going to rape me!"* I thought.

I turned around and sat up quickly. Jack was led to the bed as well. My memory goes blank and dark here. My conscious mind came into play to protect me from what happened next.

My mind did not stay in that state for long I guess. When I woke up Jack and I were nude, lying in bed. Jack was on top of me apologizing for what was taking place and telling me he was under "their" control to do this. I glanced around the room and saw the Reptilians watching us perform for them! They would look at one another as if telepathically communicating with each other. For sure they did not get the response of emotion I believe they were looking for out of Jack and myself.

The next morning when I awoke it was hard to look at my own husband, knowing what had happened to me during the night. I knew he would not understand or accept what had happened, so I could not tell him. My emotions were so hurt that I felt as if I had betrayed my husband and our marriage. I was very distraught and needed confirmation of the validity of this experience. Sexual intercourse was very sacred between my husband and me. And now I felt as if I had betrayed that sacredness. I never dreamed I would be put into this particular situation. Again I questioned "Why?"

I found bruising on my upper thighs - an indication of force having been used. I felt I could not speak to Jack about this and had hopes he would call about this experience we'd both shared. I could not even talk with my husband about this experience. I felt I had to deal with it myself. I felt those Reptilians got the information they were looking for, so I would not have to endure this again. Many unanswered questions continually went through my mind. *"Why me? Why with Jack, he is younger."* I had many "whys" to my questions and no answers. Did Jack have the memory of what transpired? I felt so angry that I had to live with another secret that was forced upon me and that I could never tell anyone about. Not even Jack.

I had thought those disgusting Reptilians had whatever answers they needed. I was wrong. Approximately two weeks later, I found myself waking up in the same "motel" room by myself. A Reptilian entered. Then another one came in leading a sleepy, dazed Jack who seemed to wake up quickly when he saw me. The Reptilians undressed us as we were in "paralyzed mode." They had us lay on the bed next to each other. Somehow Jack was on top of me. He and I were made to perform for the Reptilians once again. Jack continually apologized quietly to me saying, "I'm sorry. I'm not in control of this."

I do not know how long they kept us there. My mind eventually blanked out. I woke up and found myself on top of Jack, "performing," while we were continually studied by the Reptilians.

JUNE 5, 2004

I woke up in the familiar lit room sitting in a chair. When I opened my eyes I saw that Jack was already there in the room standing close to the chair I was sitting in. He appeared to be more awake and alert than I was. There were two Reptilians in the room with us. The Reptilians appeared to have a stern expression on their faces as they paced in front of us. They glanced at me, then at Jack. They quickly gave Jack a piece of white paper and went to stand in the back of the room. Jack turned to face me after having looked at the Reptilians. He asked, "Howse it going?" This was a phrase he often used when he called on the phone or came for a visit. I did not answer him. We just looked at each other.

I thought, *"How can this abduction be taking place at this time? Jack is in Germany and I am in the United States in New Mexico. The question is, how do they compensate for the time difference? Perhaps Jack has not left for Germany yet and he is in New York City. If Jack is in Germany though, I am told the time (hour) difference does not matter to any of the known universal species. They are able to abduct anyone on either side of the planet no matter how much time difference there is between countries.*

I could not see what was written on the paper. Jack quickly glanced at the paper. He began asking me strange questions about certain abduction experiences with the United States high profile government people who had abducted me in 1996. Jack gave me a firm look when I refused to answer the questions he was reading off the white paper. I wondered now, when I noticed the expressions on the Reptilian's faces, if they had threatened Jack to get the answers out of me. I questioned myself of the validity of these questions. Was this why Jack seemed to have a firm face and stern voice while asking the questions? Was this a test devised by the Reptilians? I know they have the history of my abductions by the U. S. Government military personnel. Jack knew what my answers would be. We had discussed this many times because of the documentary he had filmed that I was in. Jack knew exactly what my answers would be. So, in his stern voice, he would repeatedly ask me "If I was sure." I would not say a word but nodded my head to the questions. Further interrogation continued with questions about the type of work I was involved in at the laboratory and about being transferred to certain places of government interest.

Some other Reptilians came into the room after several minutes. With their orange slit eyes they looked directly at Jack, apparently communicating with him as he gazed into their eyes. Perhaps Jack was under "mind control" by the Reptilians to conduct this interrogation. One of the Reptilians came and touched me on both sides of my head and in the middle of my forehead. I blacked out.

When I awoke the next morning, I remembered the experience and the exact questions Jack had asked me. As the day went on, I continually put off writing down the questions. "I'll remember and get to it later," I thought. I never got to the questions but did write down the abduction experience. Thinking I would remember and be able to write down the questions, I found I was unable to attend to the task, as I was preparing to leave for a trip to Massachusetts. The Reptilians use mind control, but they also control your mind to forget the memory of abductions and what transpired during those abductions.

TUESDAY, JANUARY 24, 2006
INVOLVEMENT WITH THE REPTIALIANS ONCE AGAIN?

Jack C. and I stayed in telephone contact through most of 2005. The last time I spoke with him on the telephone was around the first of November. He e-mailed me a Christmas card and I called him to wish him a Merry Christmas. Usually he would call me back if he did not answer the telephone but he did not.

This particular Tuesday evening thoughts of Jack were far from my mind. I was focused on healing myself and staying well. I had slept a lot for three days, yet my body was still craving healing sleep. I experienced no symptoms of an oncoming abduction that night. In fact I had no problem closing my eyes around 10:30 p.m. I fell into a deep sleep, only to be awakened sometime during the night. I opened my eyes and saw a dark form standing above me while I lay in my bed. The form bent over me and I recognized it as a human male. A dim light behind him reflected a familiar face, it was Jack's face. He greeted me with a huge smile and spoke to me. I got out of bed or sat up in my bed and came face to face with him. I don't believe I said anything to him as I was in shock at seeing him on my bed and above me!

"How did he get into my house and my bedroom? Is this a dream?" I asked myself. I knew I was awake and in my bedroom. I looked around to see where the light was coming from. I immediately thought of and remembered the involvement of Reptilians. This thought suddenly brought to mind a past memory. It was the memory of Chaco Canyon and I was re-living it exactly as it had happened that day. It appeared to be happening again, right at that moment, as I sat on my bed with Jack in front of me. I was re-living the time when we sat together above Chaco Canyon that particular day. The memory was very vivid.

Jack and I were on top of a plateau above the old Indian ruins of Chaco Canyon. We were sitting on the hard, light brown colored ground facing east, looking over a canyon. We had shared some oranges, apples, water and conversation. Jack was tired as he had not slept well the previous night in his motel room. He would not discuss with me what had occurred to make him feel so uncomfortable during the night. These feelings had remained with him until mid-morning. He arose earlier than the time we had set to get up and was anxious to begin the day. He knocked on the door of my room until I woke up and answered his wake up summons.

Lying on the hardened ground, Jack enjoyed the hot sun on his back while he rested. I reflected on the day. My thoughts turned to the Ancient Ones' past history. As I reflected I thought I could hear the ancient Indian women talking amongst themselves and children playing, while the men worked the crops. Then I saw another tribe viciously attacked the pueblo and many lives were lost in the fight.

At this point into the memory, I was interrupted by a male voice that began questioning me about my present trust and belief in Jack. The voice repeatedly "instructed me" about Jack needing my trust and belief in him at this time in his life. I asked this "voice" the "why"

142

questions and in particular, "Why me? Certainly there are other more important people in Jack's life than myself." The "voice" then showed this part of the memory of Jack and myself.

We were down at the bottom of the plateau in back of the Indian ruins. We were looking up toward the small opening of huge rocks that we would eventually climb through to reach the top of the plateau. I was told by the voice that I had trusted Jack in the past and I needed to trust and believe in him now. The masculine voice used that experience of Jack helping me climb over large and jagged, misshapen rocks. I *do* have a fear of climbing such rocky upward terrain with nothing to hold onto. I also have a fear of falling and slipping or losing my balance and being hurt and thoroughly embarrassed. I re-lived the conversations Jack and I had as he held tightly onto my wrists and arms, guiding and pulling me up the rocky terrain, through the opening between the large rocks that appeared to be a wind tunnel. We climbed through the wind tunnel high above the Indian Ruins and onto the plateau.

Again, like the "re-run" of a movie, I once again experienced Jack holding my arm and wrist tightly as he had on that day. As I re-lived the climb, I was told to remember and believe in the trust I had in Jack that day. Now Jack needed and wanted that same trust and belief in *him* from me. That statement was repeated to me two or three times during the memory.

As quickly as that memory had appeared, it was gone and I was back in the present moment. I found myself in bed with Jack on top of me, having sexual intercourse. It was like many times before when the Reptilians put us together. When he was finished, two other forms that appeared to be human took Jack by the arm and led him away through the dark bedroom into the office area. Then the three of them left through the light of the east wall of that room.

Who is in control of "scenarios" such as this? Was this another example of Reptilian control and for what purpose? I am concerned about Jack's life and safety. Before this book is published, I pray that what he may be experiencing in his life will be made known to me. I also want to know why Jack needs my belief and trust in him.

143

I would like to point out at this time too, that in real present life, I would not be the woman chosen by Jack to have sexual relations with. He has his choice of many younger beautiful women in his life.

Once again, is this an example of Reptilian "love bite" control involving shape shifting, and mind control of Jack and myself by these sex-obsessed creatures? The Reptilians are known for this type of behavior and they force many human male and female abductees into these scenarios. It is just another form of being a "Lab Rat"! Jack and I have been used in this manner over and over again as a study of our emotions and feelings during the experience. I really don't know if Jack is aware of these many "Love Bite" affairs with me. I believe he would be repulsed. Where is all of this leading?

LOVE BITE ABDUCTIONS
MY UNDERSTANDING

If my understanding is correct, other alien abductees I've worked with have also been brought together in the scenario of a "Love Bite." Through hypnotherapy and/or past released memories, they too, have experienced past lives and are currently involved in romantic relationships within a "Love Bite" affair. Are these "Love Bite" affairs produced and directed by "satanic" Reptilians who use the information for their own sadistic studies on humans?

The "Love Bite" study by these demonic creatures is certainly no "Love Bite Affair" between Jack and myself in *this* life. On Jack's part, there is no love or need to be with me forever. Nor does Jack seem to be attracted to me. I believe he has his own very different life. I am not his soul mate. As I said my life was made more difficult with this happening, as I had found my soul mate in Fred, my husband. But I had and still have feelings for Jack, remembering him in my three past lives and getting to know the man in my present life. The question is, did the *Reptilians* put Jack and I together on this filming venture in New Mexico? Was it their plan for us to get to know each other very deeply through sharing of our families? There seemed to be so many variables for me in this situation. It hurts because I believe that Jack is not aware of these occurrences. I know that he does not care for me like the true "Love-

144

Bite" scenario dictates. Jack's and my good mutual friend, Barbara Bartholic helped me throughout this "Love Bite" scenario from the start. Before her sudden death, she had planned to have me meet Jack at her home to reveal these abduction experiences between the two of us. She felt Jack knew what had occurred between the two of us. I don't know if that statement is correct.

The Reptilians are shape shifters. An example of their shape shifting ideologies can be seen in repeated scenarios that I have heard from many of my "Love Bite" clients. The scenario can begin while lying in bed by yourself. You feel full of anxiety and not resting comfortably. You are agitated and you feel a presence in the same room with you. You cannot see the presence yet. Your mind is being controlled by a Reptilian. You are directed to think of your favorite singer, actor, or famous person; a man you are dating, or the handsome man down the street. As you shift or turn over and look down at the end of the bed, there is the person you are envisioning. You are controlled not to scream, run, hide, or have fear. The person is actually there undressing him or herself. Next, he or she comes near you and begins to undress you, caress and kiss you. You feel as if this is the best moment you have ever experienced in your whole life. You then have the most wonderful sex you have ever experienced. As soon as the sex is over, while your sex partner is still on top of you, he or she shape shifts into one of the most disgusting beings. A Reptilian! A Reptilian, who calmly gets off you while you are in shock and dismay, walks away and simply disappears through a wall, ceiling, or hallway.

I cannot describe the feelings and emotions an abductee experiences. I've heard the shocked cries of male and female humans who have had or are experiencing, one of these "real life" moments. I've also heard the opposite reaction from abductees who say they have never experienced such happiness and wonderful sex in their lives. These abductees seem to be able to handle the realization that the Reptilians will eventually show themselves. These abductees experience no shock or disbelief and can accept what has transpired. They feel they have much better, exciting sex than their soul mate or partner can ever give them. These humans who are a combination of alien/

milab (military/government) abductees can be any age, single, married, happy or not happy in their current relationship.

Returning to the subject of a "normal" "Love Bite" affair, the human subjects involved can first be brought together by the Reptilians as small children, teenagers, young adults, or older adults who are alien/milab abductees. They have been put together physically with the opposite sex at some point in their lives, to be observed in specific situations. These human subjects can be abducted by the Reptilians many times a month, or many times a year. They can be put into different scenarios to discover the mannerisms and personality of the other person. Eventually they get to know their "partner" intimately and eventually fall in love with that person. If the abductee is a young child, the Reptilians will wait until the teenage years to allow sex to happen between the two. The abductee, when returned home, can hardly wait until the next abduction when they can be with the other person whom they have grown to "love."

In the majority of cases, the abductee is normally left with a conscious mind that cannot remember what occurred, who was involved, and at what age the whole scenario began to play out with another human being. However, some abductees need to have answers to the questions of "What, When and Where."

The Reptilians will, at some point in this unfolding scenario, take the abductees away from the long term situation and let them lead a normal life with or without knowledge of the other person they are involved with in abductions. They grow older, perhaps get married, or have a partner in their life. They feel that something is dramatically missing in their life. They have the feelings and inclinations about someone else, feelings of loss of someone else in their life. One day their paths might cross and the two humans involved may recognize each other. But the question is, "From where?" The abductees are automatically drawn to each other and find themselves quickly in love.

Do I need to heed my own words here in my own situation? I am tired of having many a tear falling. I should say very sarcastically and hatefully, Thank you Reps! Go to hell for destroying my life!

But you know, I am leading a wonderful normal life now, **without** their presence in my current life!

At present date (2015) Jack is not in my life anymore. I **do** regret that, as I did have feelings for him (feelings that were constructed by these demonic creatures). Sadly, I have lost those feelings.

Jack. You wanted me to reveal my past life stories and that was hard for me until I thought of writing them as a poem to you. Believe in my heart and soul for these are true. Thank you, my friend, for your understanding of my feelings. Perhaps you can understand me now. God's love be always with you, Jack. Perhaps there will be no more future "past lives" – only this present life for me to include you.

MAY 12, 2004
JUST SOME MISPLACED THOUGHTS AND NOTES

The following is hard for me to write about. I have worked with Jack for one year now because of the documentary he is making on time travel, including the knowledge of the Philadelphia experience and Montauk and alien abduction phenomena.

The other male person who was involved in this documentary was a well-known older man from Florida who had and lived with these phenomena. We worked on the documentary using our combined experiences. Sadly Al Bielek passed away on October 10, 2011.

I have lived three past lives with Jack and perhaps on a fourth "life" experience in the present time when we met in 2003 and 2004. I felt an immediate closeness to him when we met. That ended today when certain information was revealed and confirmed with regard to his being a "ladies man." Even though I knew this from the last past life experience in Paris, France, this information was revealed to me when the lady-in-waiting and I met in this present life. Apparently, Jack has not changed his sexual promiscuous activities in this lifetime. This tendency seems to have carried over into this lifetime for him. He is not married so I guess in this present lifetime his sexual promiscuity is accepted by most humans in today's society.

Because of Jack's and my three past lives and the confirmation from an investigator, my feelings for him have grown. I feel as if he is more than just a close friend, even though I am older in this life than Jack. It is hard for me to accept this and I blame the dammed Reptilians for involving me in this "love bite" situation with Jack.

(The Story Continues)

MORE UNANSWERED QUESTIONS

Where does all this fit in with the alien species, MILAB control over my life and the threat of "I will pay if I talk"? Approximately two weeks before any of my husband's symptoms occurred I woke up hearing a voice tell me to enjoy what I have in my husband, as he would not be here long. Twice after this first communication in my head during the day, as I pulled into our driveway, I was told that he was going to die! I did not believe what I was being told and prayed that it would not ever be true. Was the information from "them" the alien species or MILAB or because I am psychic?

JUST SOME AFTER THOUGHTS...

I wrote about this experience in "Morning Glory Diary" of an Alien Abductee.

I was chasing after a small Grey and choking him, hearing his squeals. To this day I am unsure if I indeed killed him or not. From that evening in question, a majority of abductions apparently stopped for me with regard to both the aliens species and rogue military/government. At least I had thought so because I no longer experienced symptoms of pre-abduction or post-abduction.

About six months after this particular experience, I once again found the unusual bruises and needle marks on my body but had no memory of abductions. Then my unconscious brain began to release some memory of abductions.

For some unknown reason, I felt the need to not document any of these memories. I just did not care to do so. Why I experienced these feelings of not wanting to document is suspect of an abductee being controlled by the alien species or MILAB to not produce given information. An abductee has the stored memory and thinks it will remain with them, which it does in the unconscious mind. But in the meantime the abductee begins to experience disbelief about a particular abduction and wonders if it ever did occur. Yes, it is common to make abductees feel somewhat "crazy" until they pretend to face the fact that "nothing" occurred. But the in-depth feelings eat away at them constantly.

Memories would come back to me when working through hypnotherapy with my clients. A word or scenario would trigger a memory in me. I had to realize this was *their* story and not mine.

Normally, I would wait for a safe time to reflect on that particular word or scenario. I would question and try to reason out certain memories. I wanted to know *why* a particular word or scenario could throw me back into an abduction experience. In a sense, my clients were helping me, through their stories, to confirm and be aware of my own previous abductions that were "secretly" stored and protected in my unconscious mind.

Many times over the years, abductees would call on the telephone or during guidance into their abduction experiences would excitedly tell me their stories of how they had "seen me" last night or the week before. I seemed to be accompanying them on a space ship with the aliens or in the underground bases with the aliens and military. To dissuade me of my disbelief of these abduction happenings, my clients would then correctly describe what I had been wearing or what reactions we shared at that time. Thus, is this the real answer to my body markings, bruises, cuts, and needle marks?

I felt ready to accept these unknown abductions that had been covered up by the abductors. The gnawing feeling that eats away at your soul because of the "knowing" of your unconscious mind will at times reveal memories in spurts. I felt a sense of relief. I needed to stay "grounded" in order to further my work with alien abductees, guiding and helping them to deal with the phenomenon of alien and rogue military/government abductions.

My unconscious mind soon released more information of some of these memories. But do I document them? No. I feel the veil of mind control playing out its part within me. It has been a tough fight to work through and document, to get this further diary written. Memories are coming forth as I write. The release of some memories occur, if I have paper and pen close by, I will jot down the memory. I am learning that I need to carry paper and pen with me wherever I go. I should follow the advice that I give to my clients.

JULY 15, 2013
SUNDAY
BLOOMFIELD, NM
APPROXIMATELY 4:00 P.M.

I was riding in the back seat of my daughter's Toyota van with my young granddaughter snuggled in her car seat. We were about ten to fifteen miles out of Bloomfield, NM traveling south on state road 550. I glanced out the window of the van and scanned the sky, noticing a few white clouds here and there. Looking slightly backward I thought I saw a half-shaped moon, but something was wrong with this moon. The moon had two circular round rings within its circumference. These black rings were different sizes. The larger ring circled the outer circumference within the moon and the smaller ring was closer to the center of the moon. I made the comment to my daughter who was driving, "The moon is already out." She quickly glanced out the window and said, "Mom, I don't think that is the moon. I think it is your 'friends'!" I then made the comment that I had not seen my "friends" for some time now. I looked out again to make sure it was just the moon. To my surprise, the moon was gone! Vanished! I searched and did not find the "moon" I had just seen. This led me to believe I may have just seen a space ship.

ROSWELL
THE BEGINNING OF MANY CONFIRMATIONS'

In the year 2002, "Morning Glory" Diary of an Alien Abductee was published. A new and busy life was opening up for me. I began guiding other alien abductees through hypnotherapy. I approached local book stores around the United States and New Mexico to get my book onto their shelves and was quite successful. This became a full time job and I met many different people within this phenomenon who are open-minded and who accept this phenomena.

I traveled to Roswell, New Mexico to the International UFO Museum and Research Center where my book was on display and selling quite well. I met Julie Shuster who, along with her father, was the proprietor there. I also met Sandy, who ran the gift shop as well as helped Julie. I could say that Sandy was the center's manager as well.

These two wonderful ladies made possible numerous book signings during the many yearly UFO Festivals, and would also have me come to the Center for "private" book signings. Yes, this is the first place I was able to tell my story verbally to a crowd of people. This experience was the beginning of being asked to many other UFO conventions and UFO meetings. Originally I had a lot of fear when speaking about my abductions with the universal aliens, and of the government abductions. I was afraid because of not knowing how I would be received in a room full of people. I would read from hand written notes and show my drawings on a large white screen which was always provided for me. I soon gained confidence because so many people understood and knew of these two different entities (Reptilians and the Greys) that affected my family, my life and yes, many of their lives as well. After the first talk at Roswell with the warm reception of hugs and love that was shown to me, I was ready to take off on my own and talk from my head and heart. I found many people who were so hungry for this truth to be known and confirmed for them.

I'd already had several national radio experiences even before the book was published. I found that speaking on the radio was easier than speaking to an actual room full of people whose eyes were constantly on me. I did get used to this type of communication because a whole new community was there for me, as I was for them.

After the book had been out for about three months, my engagements for both radio and invited speaker grew in number. I received wonderful tangible gifts and letters that meant so much to me because I was finally reaching out and touching those who needed information. I found that many people were experiencing the same insanity that I also had experienced throughout my "awakening." I would have people come to speak with me privately about their experiences on these occasions. During this time it was quite hard for me to put my own abductions aside but I had to because these people needed help in finding the truth for themselves.

With the knowledge I gained from my own abductions by the various universal aliens and in the military abductions, I was able to help other people. Yes, I am grateful I can and still am helping other people who are just discovering their own awakenings. I have had other people come from all over the United States to work with me in hopes of finding their truth using the tools of hypnotherapy.

This previous thought brings me to Coeur d'Alene, Idaho. When I met Ms. Joy French I found her to be a beautiful, warm, loving lady who also had universal alien experiences in her past. This lady is well known in Coeur d'Alene. In past years she had privately spoken of her alien abductions in quiet conversations to many people in Coeur d'Alene. She was taken by surprise when many people in Coeur d'Alene told her of *their* abduction experiences or encounters within this phenomenon. I was informed that the people in Coeur d'Alene were very afraid that someone would retaliate against them or that they would be harassed if "their secret" was known. I found that this information was true as I met many people who were being retaliated against and harassed.

Ms. French had purchased my book "Morning Glory" Diary of an Alien Abductee. After she read my book she told me that she felt compelled to contact me. She wanted to make a change for these people within the alien abduction phenomenon in her town. She was quite upset about how people were being treated because of their ongoing alien abduction experiences.

Many phone calls and letters later a plan was devised. She contacted the Coeur d'Alene radio stations and newspaper. She was on her way with her plan. Radio stations as far south as Wyoming and as near as the Pacific Northwest in Washington State carried her outreach information. The newspaper and radio interviews led to hundreds of phone calls from people who were experiencing this phenomenon in these geographic areas. Her plan also included me. I found myself on my way to Coeur d'Alene on May 16, 2007 as her guest. She made reservations at the Coeur d'Alene Inn for my presentation and talk. In the four days prior I met many people who were experiencing abductions from the universal aliens and the military rogue government. I listened intently to their fears and cries for help and for someone to just believe them and to understand. I found such an upset town.

Nearing the evening of my presentation, Ms. French and the other people who had invested in her plan were quite concerned about the opposition stemming from political sources. Not having support from these people and non believers might cause severe problems on that evening. Ms. French had received some threats prior to the presentation. These political sources had the capability of preventing a turnout for this occasion. I said to her, "If only one person shows, then it is worthwhile. We have not lost. Even if 10 people show, don't be disappointed. We are here to help those ten people!"

We left early for the Inn to make sure everything was running smoothly. While sharing a dinner that we thought was going to be just the two of us, surprisingly, there were many people already there who had planned to share a meal with us. We could not finish our meal as the manager came and took us to the entry way of a large meeting room. We were met with a double line of people and the management needed to know if they should let them in to the large meeting room. I went into the meeting room to make sure the microphone and other items were working. The manager came in and told the men who were setting up the hall to open the partition to the other room and set up more chairs. As our 7:00 p.m. start time drew near, the ladies who were to collect monies for this event stationed at an assigned table were overwhelmed. The doors were opened and people rushed in to find a seat. I was overwhelmed as well! In the meantime, I walked around and spoke with many of the attendees while extra chairs were being set up. I found that people had traveled from the states of Washington and Wyoming to attend this event. When all extra chairs were full there was standing room only and people were asked to stand in the back of the room. Double doors were opened and to my amazement there was a crowd of people standing in the hallway. Ms. Joy French's work paid off! I was still answering questions at 10:30 p.m. and I was told this event could have lasted a lot longer, but because of time constraints it could not happen. Yes, people hungry for their truth! Some people stayed after the event hoping they could speak with me. I did not deny them, but collected e-mail addresses and promised that Ms. French and her helpers were going to find a place to have local and hopefully weekly meetings. A week later when I got home from visiting my daughter and family in Seattle, my e-mail box was full of messages from many of the people in Coeur d'Alene. Ms. French and her UFO helpers did locate a place to have future meetings and I heard these meetings were a success!

While we were at Ms. French's home her telephone rang constantly for me. I gathered information from the phone calls and from people who spoke privately to me while Ms. French and I walked the hallway prior to the presentation. Family secrets about the phenomenon were never discussed among family members or friends in Coeur d'Alene. If a person spoke out about their alien abductions that person might very well face a diagnosis of mental health problems. Many people were put into mental health institutions because they were considered to be "insane." I found this statement to be true one evening when a psychiatric nurse contacted me about several of their patients who were institutionalized because of this phenomenon. They did not know how to treat those patients other than keeping them sedated with heavy drugs. I could not believe how closed minded these psychiatric doctors and nurses were, especially working in the medical field in this day and age. I spoke with this nurse for awhile one evening and did refer her and the psychiatrist she worked for, to investigators and researchers that I worked with within the phenomenon. Unfortunately I could not stay in Coeur d'Alene as requested by the nurse and doctor to interview their patients. Several of the people I met at the presentation and while walking with Ms. French told me they were being treated by a psychiatric doctor and that they too were under heavy medication.

I don't know how true or accurate the following information is, but several people I met told me that Coeur d'Alene is/was a white supremacist town. Therefore people never spoke to one another about this phenomenon until now; and then, only in secrecy to people they thought they could trust.

AUGUST 9, 2013

MS. JOY FRENCH

I spoke with Ms. Joy French today. It took me awhile to locate her after I left Coeur d'Alene in 2007. We had initially stayed in contact but her life became very active as she began interacting with people experiencing the phenomenon. She had been traveling to Washington State and throughout Idaho organizing meetings, talking and helping people who had contacted her. Her research has also put her into contact with Washington, D.C. working with a particular person there with regard to this phenomenon. She would not identify the person. Ms. French is currently disabled from a recent fall resulting in a broken leg and now because of her age she has had to stop working within this phenomenon.

Another memory that has come forth at this time concerns a couple in Phoenix, AZ who heard me on a radio show and contacted me. I found this case quite interesting.

MARCH 2006

Once again I found myself on the way to Phoenix, Arizona as the guest of a family who are alien abductees. We had spoken many times on the phone with regard to what had been occurring. The woman was a surgical nurse, the husband worked in insurance and their son was a chef working at a local restaurant.

After the initial interview on the telephone and many calls later I put them in touch with Derrel W. Sims CM., HT., R.H.A. for further help. The husband had a suspected alien implant on his leg below the knee. This suspected leg implant would rise to where it could almost be seen through his skin. It would become quite painful for him to walk on the leg. This alleged leg implant was more painful than the other implant located on his back. Mr. Sims was quite interested in the case and would have liked to work with this couple and especially the husband to remove the suspect leg implant. The husband became quite agitated with the amount of paper work that Mr. Sims requested and chose not to invest the time or effort.

The man's wife attempted to remove the item in her husband's leg but to no avail. When she opened the suspected area on her

157

husband's leg she could see a black nondescript metal. As soon as she tried to grab or cut into it in order to remove it, the item would sink deeper into her husband's tissue.

Because of the many abductions and paranormal happenings occurring in their home, they decided they would all like to go through hypnotherapy.

When I arrived at the airport in Phoenix, Karen and her son Karl were there to greet me and drive me to their home. I would meet Alan later that evening. I was able to view the suspected implant in his leg and was able to maneuver it around myself.

My work was rapidly cut out for me during the three or four days I spent with the family in their home. I had a good friend who also lived in Phoenix at the time. James Bartley was so very gracious to lend me a room in his home to work with the tools of hypnotherapy with this family. Hypnotherapy was quite successful and answered many of their questions as they relived the experiences of their alien abductions.

On the third night while in their home, I was awakened suddenly to scratching on the walls and the door of the bedroom I was staying in. I heard an unusual sound and then someone began to whisper to me. I could not understand who was whispering to me or what was being said. I sat up quickly and saw the bedroom door open to the dark hallway. There was no human opening that door! I had been informed of such happenings within this house but to experience it was something else! The incident was discussed the next morning.

When I left this family, I could not convince Alan to finish filling out Mr. Sims' questionnaires so he could travel to Houston, Texas and have the implant situation resolved. I did stay in contact with the family for several more months. I felt so hopeless because this family was not working as a family unit to resolve and accept what was/is occurring with them. They were continually and severely upset with one another. It is hard to realize that the experience of universal aliens can and *will* have a negative effect on families and individuals. Thus, the situation never gets resolved.

My memory now brings me back to situations I have heard of many times while guiding young children and one or two teenagers.

My first encounter with such a situation was written about in <u>Morning Glory</u>. It concerns a young boy whom I had never met while in Manhattan, New York in 1997. I stated that I had spent two weeks in New York while Mr. Hopkins guided me through hypnotherapy. While in New York, I stayed at the home of Mr. Hopkins' assistant. On the evening of March 2, 1997, after a day of exploring New York, I arrived at Karen's home. I experienced an unusual occurrence as I unlocked the door and stepped inside Karen's apartment. I felt a very strong presence. My attention was immediately drawn to a large mirror that covered most of one of the walls in her apartment. My attention was drawn to this mirror for one hour. During that time I heard "They're coming. They're coming!"

I had symptoms that I normally experience before abductions. I originally thought someone was or had been in Karen's apartment. I discussed this occurrence with Karen when she arrived home. I told her about the voice I had heard and how my attention was drawn to the large mirror.

The next day when I was getting ready to go to Mr. Hopkins' home, a lady called twice for Karen. That evening when Karen came home from work she called the lady back. Karen had worked with this lady and her family and knew them well, as they are also abductees.

The four year old who was the youngest son of the lady was the reason for the phone call. This young boy would be abducted every night by his "teacher" (whom I suspected at the time, was a Nordic). On board an alien ship he attended "school" along with other children.

The lady's son told his mother that Sunday, that he wanted to go to New York to visit Karen. When the young boy's teacher arrived that evening the youngster told his teacher that he wanted to go to New York to see Karen. The teacher complied with the young boy's request and brought him to Karen's apartment in New York. They were transported through the mirror and remained behind the large mirror so they would not be seen by whoever entered into the room. They thought that Karen would be home but found that she was not so they waited and hoped she would be the person to open the door to her apartment. Instead, I was the one who opened the door and entered the room. The young boy and his teacher soon left but returned later that evening while we were asleep.

The young child told his mother that he tickled Karen on her face and arms as she slept but she did not wake up. He saw another lady sleeping on a couch and walked over to her. He said he looked at her face for awhile before lifting up her soft hands. He noticed a pretty ring on one of her fingers. The next evening the mother of this young child called Karen and told us what her son told her about going to Karen's apartment with his teacher. The boy described exactly what I looked like. He described my pretty ring in detail. He also described some rocks that Karen had in her living area. He was correct in all of his descriptions!

Before leaving New York, I stayed in contact with the mother and remained in phone contact for some time. Through our conversations I learned from the mother what her son told her about being taught in a special classroom. It was quite amazing to hear these stories of how he was being taught by the Grey's and Nordics.

I never dreamed I would one day encounter such a situation as when a young man contacted me for guidance through hypnotherapy in 2002. This young man had moved to New Mexico from another state.

The procedure I follow when contacted by a potential client is to interview the person over the telephone first before bringing them in for a hypnotherapy session. Sometimes it takes two interviews over the telephone because I am not sure if this is a true abductee who has had experiences within the phenomenon or a person who is just fooling around with misguided information and wanting notoriety.

The young man told me he was working with a former client I had guided many times. This former client was the person who recommended the young man call me. In fact, during this former client's last session, he had told me about the young man and asked if I would see him. My client told me what he knew of the younger man and his paranormal experiences within the phenomenon.

The evening this young man called me, information began spilling out of him as we talked on the phone. It was very difficult for him to tell his story. By this time in my life's work, I had grown used to hearing men cry. I had learned that there are "points" to look for and recognize even during a telephone call. This man exhibited what I look for as verification that there is certainly something going on in his life regarding the phenomenon.

We made an appointment for him for guidance through hypnotherapy. He showed up early on the appointed morning. After another "in person" interview I then guided him into his first hypnosis session.

I will call this man "Rick," as I do not have his permission to use his real name.

Rick was quite sure that his "abductions" began at age five, so this was where he wanted to begin his hypnosis. He relaxed quite readily and was immediately drawn into his unconscious mind (the hidden part of the mind containing memories, thoughts, feelings, and ideas that a person is not generally aware of but that manifest in dreams and dissociated acts).

Through the relaxed state of hypnotherapy Rick found himself not at age five, but around three years old, sitting in a high chair by himself as his mother had left the kitchen for a period of time. While in the high chair, a little "grey toy thing" comes directly to him and looks at the small child, then disappears. The little boy does not cry and he is not afraid. Instead, he finds this toy fascinating.

These scenarios of introduction from an alien species (usually the first visit to a baby or small child) normally come from a Grey who is literally "getting to know a prospective child for a specific reason. This "Grey toy" would eventually come at night and take Rick to an unknown place where there were other babies and small children to play with. This situation would eventually happen nightly as he would be awakened in his crib. As he grew older and could speak fluently he would tell his mom about "his Grey toy" that would come in the night and take him away. Mom felt her son had a great imagination for such a young age. This scenario occurred many times; as it had with the young child I'd met in New York.

Time passed and Rick grew older. At age five Rick would be playing outside in his back yard, or awakened at night time, or just inside his house playing by himself when he began to experience missing time.

One experience Rick remembers is when his brother was babysitting him one evening and Rick's brother sent him up to bed. After awhile he heard his brother hollering out to him to listen to a strange noise. Rick heard a strange whirring noise that seemed to come from their backyard. He also saw an orange light with several other lights revolving around. The lights seemed to move in waves. Rick experienced missing time after that episode. The incident was actually documented in the local newspaper the next day as many other people also witnessed the event.

Rick would be sitting outside on an early summer day, feeling compelled to look up at the cloudy sky, noticing a separation in the clouds. The clouds would part and he would see two silver silhouettes sitting across from each other. In his ears he heard whispering. That would be his last sense of awareness until he woke up much later that evening in a different place from where he had been. These incidents would occur often as Rick grew older.

He had vague memories of a Grey who would appear and take him to a place up in the night sky where he was introduced to his "teacher" who looked human. As Rick grew older he had many teachers. His teachers were not all human but included various extraterrestrials.

This is Rick's story of extraordinary learning.

Rick would "wake up" while lying on a table in a small room. He is then walked to his school room (wherever it was located) where he meets up with just a few other children.

Rick is soon introduced to a nice tall man who looks human. (Rick later learns that this tall man is called a Nordic.) The Nordic has gained

Rick's trust over the years and Rick knows he is in a safe environment.

Rick sees that there are no black boards for the teacher(s) to write on. There are no normal looking desks that he would eventually find at "real" schools here on earth. He is taught three-dimensional drawings. Many of the mathematical teachings he describes are drawn by the alien teacher or his Nordic teacher in the atmosphere of the enclosed space within the school room. Just hanging in the air are neon green equations, pictures and writings as the teachers telepathically speak to him. He is learning new technologies within a new science.

I must make note here that Rick's mother never seemed to know of his disappearances. Rick does not know where his mother was or what she was doing at the times of his abductions.

While Budd Hopkins was guiding me through hypnosis sessions (that I previously discussed) I realized some of Rick's stories and those of the small boy I'd met in Manhattan, New York were similar. I compared the stories and experiences of Rick and the small boy concerning their abductions by the Greys and Nordic teachers. The information I got from both Rick and the small boy was similar. I wondered if the young man I originally met over the phone in New York had done anything (as an adult) with the knowledge of sciences he had been taught as a child.

During many hypnosis sessions, Rick described his life from babyhood to his present adult age. Guiding him through those endeavors had become quite frightening for both of us. Having heard a similar story from the other child in New York, I now had confirmation of the experiences Rick was living through.

Rick looked forward to those evenings when he would be taken on board the ship and into the unusual "school room." Rick grew older and more intelligent in his lessons and learning because of the way his "Nordic teacher" was teaching him. Rick found the new sciences along with new technologies quite intriguing. This new "intelligence" caused problems here on earth for Rick especially when attending public school. In his public school science classes

Rick was never taught the "new" sciences that he was currently learning with his universal teachers. He found the situation quite confusing and hard to understand. Rick had very few friends in public school. However, those he had were close friends in whom he could confide his experiences with "unusual teachers" and the space ship.

As Rick entered his teen age years he felt very different from his human friends. His friends seemed to disappear when he would try to establish a relationship with them. Rick considered himself "different" and more intellectual than anyone within his sphere of friends and family.

At age fifteen and another summer vacation, Rick was riding his bicycle home from a friend's house late at night. The roads were deserted. He recalled a dreadful feeling of being watched. He felt compelled to pedal faster and at one point, he looked over his shoulder and saw the constellation, Cassiopeia "the throne." Suddenly he became overwhelmed with fear. The feeling of being watched and pursued intensified. He felt as if the stars were descending upon him. He was about halfway home. The next morning when he awoke in his bed, he had no memory of how he had gotten home or into his bed.

Many years later, when Rick would watch movies like "The X-Files" or other related episodes of this type, his mind would be filled with violent, blinding flashes of that particular night.

Through extensive hypnotherapy sessions many questions were answered for Rick. His knowledge and understanding grew and developed over the years with regard to his learning of the new sciences and technologies. These sciences and technologies became quite frightening, and sadly amazing, during the time when he was expected to begin to demonstrate/exhibit on board ship what he had learned since the age of five. What was learned by this child as he grew older, and his understanding of what the experiences and training entailed, terrified him. Rick's story is shocking and unbelievable to the "normal human mind."

Graduation Day arrives on board ship. Rick is taken into a large room where he finds items made out of metal and steel products. Rick is expected to show his entourage of Universal alien teachers what he has learned these many years. He is unaware of what he is to do until he receives his instructions. Rick feels he is in a stupor and thinks to himself, *"No". **I cannot do this because I don't want to do this. But it might be fun.** "* He does not know what is expected of him or how to follow the instructions that are given to him.

Before leaving the room and following his disgruntled "teachers," he hears a horrific sound and turns around. Rick sees distorted metal. He is unaware of how this damage has occurred. Rick is given more training.

From that day onward, the understanding of what his teachers had taught him became quite clear to Rick. He was to focus on the training and development of a part of his brain that humans normally do not have the capability to use.

More time passes with repetitive mental concentrations in what he is expected to do. Rick finds the instructions are intolerable as well as the exhibitions that he is to perform. At first it was fun and amusing to discover what he was able to do. But now it frightens him. He is able to manipulate physical environments (substantial material), nonliving things and if necessary, to deconstruct molecular substances which are changed beyond recognition. He learns to penetrate substances including metals, and/or relating to a type of radiation, with great mental concentration. Also what is learned by him is that he is able to get into humans heads (their minds) quite easily.

To make a long story short (perhaps one day Rick will be able to write his own story) let us skip ahead to the years in which he finds himself in the state of New Mexico.

Rick does not know why he is directed to come and work in New Mexico but soon finds an answer to that question. He finds himself in western New Mexico at a ranch. At the ranch he finds another person who is also an abductee. This intrigues him. Now he can share his story and listen to his new friend's stories of abductions by one of the universal aliens.

His new home is a small trailer and he is happy. He likes his new job. He is thinking the past is over. He has a new life, a future, a chance to start over and become a normal human being. But this is short lived. One dark night after retiring, bright lights appear, the motor of a helicopter wakes him. This same scenario repeats at least three times a week.

There is a black military helicopter. Many times there is also a small craft that is "boxy" in shape and gun metal gray in color. This craft is approximately 20 to 30 feet long. It is there to pick him up on the darkest nights with either military men or the Greys, who are the abductors. He fights the men but has no control over the Greys. The Greys paralyze him. He is then put aboard the space ship for a few minutes or a helicopter for fifteen minutes.

When he arrives at the secured area and is walked out of either vehicle he begins to scan for a memory of this environment. Somewhere in the forest of tall pine trees is an area secured by a tall electrified fence. Military guards surround the electrified fence and are armed with M16's and sub automatic–standard issue artillery. He sees a couple of camouflaged tents. There are a couple of military jeeps. Approximately twenty-five men and some women in military wear are there. There are also Reptilians and other Nordic beings there as well. He is walked into one of the tents and introduced to a well known scientist from the United States. I do not remember the man's name, which is good for my well being! Rick will be working with this scientist and many others, for many months to come.

Rick was put to many tests during the many abductions he experienced and realized this secured base continually moved throughout the mountain range. One test that Rick was trained to do is to manipulate one of the military jeeps. Rick knows how to accomplish this and does it quickly as he walked by the jeep. Where the jeep once stood is now a pile of melting metal. Everyone is quite happy at Rick's accomplishment.

This is the time when Rick needs help with memories. He needs someone to understand him and help him. Through word of mouth he learned about me.

During our interviews and hypnotherapy sessions Rick told me about the severity of the headaches he experiences. He says that the pain is always there. The intense pain in his lower leg creates problems when he walks. Rick tells me that he has some large bumps on his leg and several on his head. As a hypnotherapist working in this phenomenon, I was taught to look for implants on a person's body. Upon examining his leg, I found the suspected implants. On the right side of his head and right below his ear and neck there were more suspected implants. When these are touched, Rick experiences excruciating pain.

Gabe Valdez happened to call me about another case one afternoon to see if I had time to watch a video recording he made. I took the opportunity to discuss this client with him. Gabe asked if he could meet my client and check out his implants. I contacted Rick and he was agreeable to meeting Gabe Valdez at his next appointment with me the following week.

Rick arrived early for his appointment eager to meet Gabe Valdez and to have him look at the suspect implants. Rick was not having a good week because of the recurring pain he was experiencing. Gabe arrived soon afterward and the meeting got off to a good start. Gabe interviewed Rick for the first hour as he wanted to hear Rick's story from Rick himself. Gabe then proceeded to investigate the suspect implants on Rick's body. Gabe felt sure there were "implants" or definitely something strange located on Rick's leg and head. Gabe excused himself and went out to his car. He brought in some strange equipment explaining to us that "his friend" from Washington, D.C. allowed him to have this equipment for investigation purposes. The two units Gabe brought into the house would detect foreign bodies such as "foreign implants." When Gabe ran either of the two units over the suspected areas the suspect implants began to vibrate and move deeper within Rick's body causing him horrific pain. When Gabe ran the units over Rick's head he had to quit. The pain became unbearable for Rick. Gabe and I both felt these were alien or military implants. Rick wanted them removed but had to think about what this kind of surgery would entail.

Several weeks passed and Rick was unsure if he wanted me to contact the medical source who does this type of surgical procedures. So in the meantime, further hypnotherapy sessions were conducted. One morning Rick showed up very tired and disoriented. He said, "They took me again last night." He made some drawings of the abduction that he wanted me to see and copy for his files. He reached into the black bag he carried to every session. In the black bag he would have drawings and written documentation of what had transpired during the week.

As Rick reached into the bag, he made a weird loud sound. He said, "There is something strange in my bag." He pulled out approximately ten small, misshapen, shiny red rocks. He looked very puzzled and astounded at what he had pulled out of the bag. He knew nothing about these rocks and assured me that he had never seen anything like this before. He did not know where the rocks had come from.

Rick placed the red rocks on the end table and before we knew it, the rocks began to jump everywhere on the table. It was shocking and amazing to see the rocks come alive! One rock jumped off the table. When this happened, Rick collected the rocks and immediately felt energy from them. He handed me a few of the rocks and they began to move in my hand. We picked up several of the rocks and began to examine them. We held the rocks up toward the morning sun and they began to produce a bluish color within.

Gabe Valdez called right at that moment and I answered the phone. He wanted to come speak with Rick again. When he arrived, he was just as astonished as we were over these unusual red rocks. Rick divided up the rocks between Gabe and myself and leaving some for himself. Gabe was going to examine the rocks to see what was causing them to have such "energy." He also wanted to identify the rocks. I had put my rocks in a sealed glass jar and Rick did the same. After two weeks, I pulled out the glass jar and to my surprise; I found *more* red rocks in the glass jar. I called Rick and he too discovered that his rocks had multiplied. Gabe had stored his rocks in a vial and they too had multiplied.

Gabe had no information for us about what the rocks were or where they might have come from. So over time, the three of us watched our rocks grow larger and produce "baby" energized red rocks! I have a friend who is a chemist and she traveled from out of state to examine these rocks. She conducted many chemical tests with no results as to exactly what they were or where they had come from. We relayed the test results to Gabe. Hopefully, his person out of Washington, D.C. could resolve this for us. That turned out to be a bad move on our part. The few rocks Gabe gave to this person, suddenly disappeared.

One day the boss of the ranch where Rick works hired on three other people, two males and one female. One male was to live in the small trailer with Rick. After a time of getting to know each other, the new man began to realize that something was going on that did not seem right. He realized that things were happening, especially in the evening. He questioned whether he was awake or just asleep and dreaming such weirdness was going on in his new home. The new man thought he was just dreaming of strange occurrences and brought up the topic with Rick. Rick felt he could trust "Bob" and revealed to him what was actually going on and told Bob that he was not dreaming all these strange occurrences.

Bob became quite curious about the phenomenon and wanted to be included. The phenomenon presented itself in a frightening way to Bob but he was still interested and wanted to learn more. The abductors (meaning the universal aliens and military) who invaded their space at night, stopped paralyzing Bob. Then Bob found he could move around inside the small trailer as the extraterrestrials or the military men took Rick either in a small space craft or a silent black helicopter. Bob never knew when Rick would be returned. Bob would simply wake up in his bed in the front part of the trailer and notice that Rick was home. When Bob looked in on Rick, he appeared to be a disheveled shape on his bed.

Rick begins to realize that the encampment moves monthly to different areas in western New Mexico. The younger man eventually begins to experience abductions within this encampment as well but not as often as Rick. Bob has no memory of what they are doing with him or to him. The memories he retains are of witnessing Rick's abductions.

Over a period of time the foursome and perhaps a fifth person join the investigations into the secured areas and items found on the ground near their work place or the trailer. Rick and his entourage of friends grow close and all his friends become involved in helping to investigate.

Before I knew it, I had the foursome under hypnotherapy because of what was transpiring with them. The last time I saw the foursome *was* the last time. Each of them separated and moved on to another state because of what they knew and what was happening to them.

Rick left too because he could no longer deal with this type of life. He went into hiding. He did touch base with me to tell me he was safe and trying to deal with his life. He didn't contact me to let me know if he had begun to try to rid himself of the torment. He just wanted to live as normal a life as possible if he could. He knew he had to somehow get the implants out of his body. He did not know how he would heal his brain or even if it was possible to do so. Rick has disguised himself for his own protection and where he is today is unknown.

Gabe Valdez had his hands full with investigations into this phenomenon. He was also there for four other people, and not just these four people, there were many more he helped. Was it through Gabe that Rick finally found safety? My own research into and study of the abduction phenomenon was furthered through Gabe's tools of teaching, investigations, and the video films he took on his investigations especially in Dulce, NM. He shared his videos with me as a teaching tool. Gabe introduced me to the pueblo people of Dulce, NM whom I guided in hypnotherapy.

Gabe Valdez passed away on August 7, 2011 with a "sudden heart attack." Gabe helped me over the years from the time we met until his death. Since his death I have encountered some strange cases. I've had to rely on the knowledge he gave me. Yes, at times I don't have the answers to give to my clients and now I don't have him to guide, investigate, or follow up with my clients' trials that are put upon them by these universal entities and the governments collaborating with the aliens.

Thank you Gabe for being on my road of life and teaching me your knowledge so I can continue on.

Over the years many clients have experienced alien and/or military abductions and have come to me for their answers, and help in dealing with the experiences that have changed their lives so drastically. Some of my clients would seek me out because they were having a hard time dealing with anger, stress, obsessions or crying for an unknown reason. One woman did not turn to drugs but instead she turned to gambling at Casinos on her long drive home from work until one night.......

Jessica is an intelligent very educated woman. She chose to teach in an elementary school. This particular school was located on one of New Mexico's Indian Reservations. Jessica and her husband did not move closer to her work location so travel would be easier for Jessica as they were quite happy and settled in their mountain home. Jessica had to travel about forty minutes either way to get to her destination and in between her home and her work was a Casino owned by another Indian Reservation.

Jessica was never inclined to patronize and had no interest in Casinos. When Jessica would leave the elementary school at which she taught for many years she had her travel time down pat.

Then unexplained and unknown occurrences changed in her life. Why would she find herself walking into her home one to three hours late at night to a very worried husband? She could not explain the missing time and in her own mind she was on time traveling home from school. She felt there were no occurrences or problems on the way home, but she could not explain the time difference in arriving home late. She and her husband began timing her travels back home one dark winter evening when they had calculated the approximate time she should arrive home safely.

This one particular fall/winter Jessica's tardiness at arriving home became so consistent that her husband would either go out looking for her although he never found her on the highway or on the winding dirt road. Eventually he just remained home and called the Sheriff's office or State Police. At some point Jessica would reappear at home, sometimes disheveled and not knowing where or what had happened to her.

Jessica's life changed as well as her personality and she did not know why. Yes, now on her way home from work she began to stop at this particular Casino and began to have fun "playing the machines" as she put it. She does not know what turned her on to this but thought that the stress of driving home, the arguments at home, being unhappy might be the cause. Jessica started "finding a release for herself" by "playing the machines." She would only stay twenty minutes, and then be on her way home. Then a realization came into play in Jessica's life.

One cold windy evening she just had about one mile to drive down the deserted small winding dirt road that leads toward their home. A very bright light appeared above her car. The car began to twirl around and she had no control over her car. Her memory is blank until she woke up in an unfamiliar place with "Ungodly Creatures" performing some type of work on her body. She found she could not move. She passed out and woke up in her car. These unusual events occurred quite often. She does not have memories of these events. Therefore once again she could not explain why she arrived home late.

Time passed and these ungodly creatures began to let her have some memory. She worried her husband would not understand or would he? One evening on her drive home she made the turn off the main highway onto the winding dirt road to her home. Before she knew it, "it happened again." Her car was lifted up by a rushing strange light and she realized she was awake through the whole scenario. Looking upward she saw something large and black, a hole, a hole large enough for her car to pass through. She passed out, and woke up in her car in an unfamiliar place which she described as looking at a "metal space." She described seeing "ungodly creatures" somehow floating her out of her car. She was taken to an examining room where a small baby was removed from her. Then just as quickly she was put back into her car, with no memory until she found herself parked on the side of the dirt road to her home.

On another night's drive home after leaving the casino she was just about to turn on the road to her home when she noticed a black truck quite close to the back of her car. The truck also made the same turn she did. This concerned her greatly, so she sped up because she didn't recognize the truck following her. The bright light again appeared and Jessica found herself in an open metal space with the ungodly creatures. This time something was different. The black truck was there as well. She saw a man in the truck.

Jessica was allowed memory each time abductions occured. She began her own research and so did her husband into this phenomenon. Her husband had always been interested in these phenomena.

Once again Jessica was taken on her way home from work and this abduction experience was the icing on the cake for her. She thought she was not going to survive because of what they did to her on that night. She was taken to a large room where there was a pie cut shaped round metal contraption. There were about ten compartments within the pie shaped object. Once again her clothing was removed and she was put into one of the compartments in a laying down position as were the other nine humans she saw. She was told this was a blood and brain test. They hooked her up with intravenous lines and some type of connecting line around her head. Then the metal container began to slowly spin, faster and faster and even faster to the point at which she lost consciousness. When she woke up her body did not feel like her body. Her bones felt as if they had been rearranged. The skin on her face felt as it had been removed from her body. The skin on her body also did not feel normal. Lying there for however long on the metal unit she was finally helped up to a sitting position by some of the strange looking creatures. She saw that the majority of the other humans were not awake, or moving. She was told she was the lucky one. The others had perished and were not strong like she was.

Jessica's husband had heard of me and knew that I was a hypnotherapist working in the field of paranormal abductions. He called me with his story and I invited him to come to my home office. We spoke, he cried, then told me of his wife. Could I help her?

I soon met Jessica and together we ventured into her bizarre life with the Greys, Reptilians and other strange creatures.

During the period of my many sessions with Jessica I was contacted by a young man whom I also brought in for hypnotherapy. During his hypnotherapy sessions I was drawn intently into a segment of one particular session as he was reliving a vital part of his memory. I had an audio tape going and I had confirmation for Jessica as well as for this man. This man is the man who was driving the black truck that dark cold winter night. He said he "lost control" of his truck that night and he did not know how his truck was "somehow steering itself" as his arms were thrown away from the steering wheel. He felt as if he was under the control of something or someone else. He did feel a presence in the truck with him, but never saw anyone there in the truck with him. His truck turned down an unfamiliar dirt road and began to follow the car that he described on tape as belonging to Jessica. He lost consciousness and awoke in an unfamiliar place but still in his truck. He was able to move his head but not his body. He spoke of how cold he was, and when he began to look around to see where he was he saw curved grey metal walls. The area appeared to be large. He could not understand why he could not move his body and how he had gotten to where he was. While looking around during his trance experience, he saw the car that he had been following on that dirt road. At that very moment he witnessed two Grey beings, "creatures," actually "floating" a woman from the car. Suddenly, other types of unusual Beings appeared around him. He blacked out.

Jessica was too afraid to meet this man and never wanted to. The man *did* want to meet Jessica but it never happened.

After working with Jessica for some time she asked me if the Greys abducted children. Yes they do, I told her. She told me the reason why she asked this question, and it had to do with her granddaughter.

Jessica and her husband divorced. Jessica and her daughter along with her granddaughter, disappeared as Jessica planned to do. The reason was to protect her granddaughter from the Greys and the 'others.' I never heard from Jessica again.

Jessica's husband became a well known researcher in this phenomenon until his sudden death.

I cannot name this particular Indian Reservation. The pueblo's Medicine Man believed strongly that "pueblo peoples" must remain within their culture, to live within their pueblos/ reservations and not seek outside help. He was the Medicine Man and they should seek help from him. Before the Medicine Man had his way, clients from that reservation were being brought to me by Gabe Valdez, who worked among them in the state of New Mexico. This well known reservation has gained a lot of notoriety due to the phenomenon.

Gabe Valdez had previously spoken with me about certain Native Americans living on this reservation who were having alien abduction experiences. Yes, these few families did seek help, as did most of the pueblo's people, by contacting their Medicine Man. These families did not accept the information given by their Medicine Man as their truth about what they had experienced. They had heard from others about recent occurrences on their reservation regarding this particular phenomenon. Within the pueblo, information about Mt. Archeluta and the phenomenon is common knowledge. However, the pueblo people are told not to speak of this knowledge. Gabe Valdez asked me if I would be willing to work with these families through hypnotherapy and I said yes. Gabe and I were to travel up north to their homes and word got out that I was to be there working with these families. Gabe also found out that I would not be accepted by the Governor nor the Medicine Man of this pueblo. These families were strongly reprimanded. I do not intend to harm any member of this pueblo. I do respect their laws.

There is intense controversy over what is believed to be transpiring deep within this certain mountain. Many clients have sought me out for help to discover their firsthand knowledge, memories and personal truths through hypnotherapy. With the help of my guidance into their "true memories" we have found much conflict about the truth of this mountain. Perhaps people are misinformed. Perhaps some just refuse to research the accounts of what is located there. It's their secret. My clients know their own truth and what they lived through. Through my witnessing of each client's story as I guided them through hypnotherapy not one client can be wrong with his/her memory of what they lived through, saw, and identified in the mountain. Each one of my clients who made their own discovery of this mountain cannot be wrong. Descriptions are found to be the same. Each one has confirmation of their abductions into this mountain. Gabe did confirm to me that he studied the claims and witnessed things spoken of. He showed me the videos and maps of that particular mountain that he himself had researched. How could Gabe have been wrong about his information and my clients' investigations revealed through hypnotherapy and their own research? Before his death but mostly after his death, Gabe's work was being renounced even by his own son Gregg. Gabe's critics say that there are no universal entities (aliens) or government military visiting and/or abducting humans on earth who are mutilating cows. This is altogether a different phenomena. Gregg and the other misinformants claim that there is nothing "paranormal" with regard to this particular mountain. These people have a large following of non believers who are not alien abductees. They say they have the proof of validity meaning they have the logical and justifiable proof that satisfies them. Yes, they are researchers in their own right, but I feel they are overlooking the valid truth of what many humans are aware of and have witnessed at this "famed" reservation.

On Monday of that week in question, Gabe called me from Chama, NM asking if he could bring a family and two other young women to Albuquerque so we could talk and perhaps I could guide at least one person into hypnosis. This family had become distraught with their "secret" because they were told by the Medicine Man not to ever speak about their secret outside the pueblo. There were no telephone interviews with this family to start with. Thursday morning I greeted the family and two young women along with Gabe as I opened the front door to my home. These people were such a delight and brought forth information of remembered experiences not just for myself, but for many of my clients as well. Over the hour of "interview" we gained each other's trust and respect. I needed them to feel safe, comfortable and to know me as a trustworthy person.

I interviewed the mother separate from her family. She was quite open with all her memories of seeing, and being abducted by the Greys' and other universal entities. She related that these happenings with the "Skywalkers" as she would call them at various times go back into their people's ancestry. She spoke of times when she was a child and into adulthood. She spoke of occurrences now being married with young adult children and how these occurrences were affecting her own children and family. She told me of her knowledge of the special mountain in question. The mother maintained much acquired information so I felt the need at the time to guide one of the young women. "Mother" did not want to go through hypnosis.

Louise readily relaxed in her first session and experience of hypnosis. In trance, she began speaking about things she had experienced during the time that she wanted to discover more about. Through her fears and tears she spoke and opened her consciousness to her truth. The information that came out was not new to me but it gave her confirmation and this was hers to have and to hold within herself.

Mary, the other young lady also wanted to learn her truth that afternoon. So family gathered together and left so that Mary could also relate her truth in private as did Louise. Mary went into relaxation and opened hidden memories quickly. Mary was more able to relate and accept what she relived through hypnotherapy. When the family came back to my home to collect Mary, we gathered around and I gave Louise and Mary the opportunity to share their truths if they wanted to do so at that time. Before leaving my home Mary and Louise asked if they could come back for another session, which was agreed upon. The following week another session was set for the two young women.

I remained in contact with the family from this pueblo through Gabe as Mom and Dad did not want the Medicine Man or the Governor to know about our visit. They also did not want either to know that I was guiding the young women through hypnotherapy.

These two young women and I developed a beautiful relationship as I continued guiding them into the memories of their abductions. These two young women were close in relationship. They were cousins. They asked if either one of them had an abduction during the following days/weeks, could they contact me by phone the next day? I readily said yes.

Gabe followed up with me on their hypnotherapies. He knew that I could not share any accounts of their memories that they relived or spoke about. That information is strictly confidential. If the family wanted him to know any information that information had to come from them and not me. Gabe knew and respected this confidentiality. Yes, the family shared with Gabe continually.

Over the following days and weeks I began to receive phone calls of occurrences of abductions from these two young women. This happened while each was lying in her own bed in her own home located on the pueblo. One night they were both taken from their beds up into the space ship where both were experimented on. Another night one young woman was lying restless in her bed and couldn't sleep. Outside her bedroom window a bright light appeared that lighted the grounds outside. She then saw a small, skinny Grey with a large head walking toward her. She blacked out. Yet on another night once again a bright light appeared, she saw her mother being floated out of the large bedroom.

Early one evening the two women asked two of their friends to go with them on a "discovery" drive up the dirt road that led to the top of this special mountain. These two women wanted to see for themselves in "reality" that this had been the mountain they were taken to. All four ladies thought this would be a fun thing to do. They stopped at the general store located on the pueblo and bought soft drinks and munchies. They began their "secret" trek up to the special mountain. They knew there was some kind of a door, perhaps a sliding door into the mountain that they both experienced being taken through. They needed to know.

It was late Fall. The sun had set and it was very dark and cold outside. The time was around 8:30 p.m. They thought they were all brave driving on the dirt road in pitch darkness. Quiet consumed the car as they travelled. Few words were spoken. The driver of the car felt very confident of the situation and they all knew at this point they were high upon the mountain because of the terrain. Then suddenly a very bright light lit up the area around their vehicle. They could see outside. The light just became brighter on the inside of the vehicle and each young woman saw fear on the other's faces. Some of the women began to scream when they felt the car being pulled upwards. They hollered, "Push harder on the gas, push, push!!!" The car continued upward and then there was no more bright light. As they looked down they saw the small dirt road disappear. Bushes and lights of what they thought was the pueblo disappeared into darkness. Here their memories end.

Much later they woke up in a strange place asking themselves, "What happened? Where are we?" They thought they were still on the dirt road heading up to the top of the mountain. Their memories at that time were quite sketchy and it seemed like each one of the women had different memories of where they were. A full moon outside indicated to each one they were no longer on the dirt road leading up to their planned destination. One lady got out of the car to see where they were. She exclaimed, "We are not on the dirt road, but on some type of mesa! I don't see a road to get onto to get us back home! I don't see any other cars around!" One young lady glanced at her watch and her watch had stopped at 12:00 a.m. Hysteria soon set in with all of them. Then the emotionally stronger woman hollered for everyone to be quiet and get contained. Memory soon came back to each of them about what had transpired. They all remembered seeing the bright light and feeling the car being lifted upward. They each had some memories of seeing the small dirt road and the bushes disappearing. They recalled seeing some lights down below but yet they all said they were still in their car! "Where is the cell phone?" one young lady called out. The cell phone was later found underneath the back seat. "Call your Mom Louise, call your Mom!" The cell phone did not work. They sat for awhile thinking they would wait until day break to find their way home.

They all became nervous and afraid that their mothers would be quite worried now and concerned about their daughters' whereabouts. "Start the car." someone said. The lady who was not the original driver started the car, although it took several tries to get the engine started. "Okay, which way do we drive? Are we in an arroyo or what?" No one knew their whereabouts but came to the conclusion they should follow the path that was lit by the brightness of the moon. There was not full agreement on this. The young lady with the cell phone tried to turn on the phone again. The light on the cell phone came on. "I've got a signal! I've got a phone signal!" One girl urged, "Louise call your Mom!" Louise dialed the phone number twice as the first time she dialed the cell phone died. The phone rang. Her mom picked up the phone. "Mom, mom!"

"WHERE ARE YOU LOUISE?"
"We are some place, and I don't know where we are!"

"IT IS 2:00 A.M. WHERE HAVE YOU BEEN? GET HOME NOW! WHO ARE YOU WITH!?"

"I am with Mary and her other two friends." she told her mother. (I cannot reveal the other two young women's names). Louise explained to her mother that they wanted to take the desolate dirt road up the mountain. She told her mother what had occurred. Louise told her mom they woke up in their car someplace in the desert and didn't know how to get home. Louise's mother asked Louise to get out of the car and survey the area. She suggested that Louise walk a few feet away from the car to get a better look at the surroundings using the bright moon for light. Louise described the area and said that she saw in the distance a small wood "house" up high. After the descriptions, Louise's mother then knew where the young ladies were. Her mother told Louise, "I've been there before myself. I know where you are. Just follow my directions. There is no road near you, but I will guide you to a dirt road that leads to the highway. You are quite a distance from home and the pueblo. I think you are on the mesa or near Redding ranch." Louise's mother guided the four ladies back to the safety of their pueblo and home.

Mary came for another hypnotherapy session with regard to this incident. Somehow soon after this last incident, the Medicine Man found out that the family and their daughters had visited me in Albuquerque. He also found out that I had been working with them through hypnotherapy. This was not good news for the family.

The two young women did not heed the warning from their Medicine Man. They continued to make appointments with me on their way home from college in southern New Mexico. They also made appointments during school holidays, and whenever they visited the pueblo. They soon found the information they were looking for; the confirmation that they are alien abductees and did have shared experiences in Mt. Archuleta. These two young women described the same levels within the mountain that I and other abductees had been taken to. Here we were experimented on by various universal entities and saw human men and women who were dressed in camouflage uniforms or military dress.

I learned that many Native Americans who live within this pueblo are abductees. Since long ago until present time they have knowledge of what has transpired within Dulce, NM and their pueblo. This confirmation came from pueblo people who came to me for hypnosis. Information was confirmed by two other people who knew and worked within the pueblo. Gabe Valdez and a psychologist also worked on the pueblo. Since Gabe is no longer alive, am I the only source of information now about what transpired within that certain mountain? I hope not!

Yes, I too have memories of being taken to Mr. Archuleta, New Mexico. I was wide awake and coherent when I was taken into the mountain with its different levels. There I found Universal Entities working alongside of military people. I saw many tables, with abductees lying on these tables having medical experiments done to them. I saw men and women working with microscopes using slides which contained whatever was removed from humans. Different medical equipment was located on different levels of the mountain.

On one level I saw a "tall fish tank looking apparatus" as I called it. This "fish tank" held some type of fluid. Within these units were human beings, both male and female, somehow wide awake and able to breathe.

For some reason the universal entities and the military were interested in my blood. So I had a lot of blood removed at this facility. I think I was taken to this facility twice. On one of the occasions it was explained to me about some of the functions of the various medical equipment. I have not been put through hypnosis to find out more information with regard to any visits to Mt. Archeuleta. Through the years of guiding many of my hypnotherapy clients, my own experiences have also been confirmed.

When Gabe and I spoke of this particular mountain he brought several videos of the mountain for me to look at. I pointed out for him what I thought was the area of my entrance into this mountain. He had studied the area many times as he hiked with his sons and other people at close proximity to where I pointed in the film. During another meeting he told me he had witnessed some type of small airplane or saucer at night flying directly into the mountain. One day time sighting was witnessed by Gabe when he saw a saucer fly into an opening within the mountain. I must mention here that in one of the night time videos taped by Gabe and his entourage while camping in close proximity to the mountain, the camera focused an area of trees. Within the trees stood a small universal Grey! To present date apparently these videos have not been recovered by Gregg Valdez or anyone. I suspect that for some reason these videos are being held in secrecy or have been destroyed because of the information they contain.

I believe I was taken to four other underground bases including Mt. Archeuleta. The underground base in California near Edwards Air Force Base may be somewhat larger than Mt. Archeuleta. Louise, Grace and I were taken to the California underground base. After exiting the spaceship and the helicopter Grace, Louise and I were driven in a military jeep to the facility. We realized we had not been drugged. Our minds were quite clear of any drugs. We were handed over to a General by the military men who were dressed in camouflage. We were not introduced to this General. Louise, Grace and I were walked into a large concrete underground building on the base in California. At some point in our travel that night our night clothes had been removed and we were dressed in brown pants and shirts. I suspect the reason for this was to avoid calling attention to ourselves.

We walked down a large slanting concrete sidewalk. The building had a large concrete facade. The lighting originated somewhere else other than the lights attached to the building. Light poles lit up the area making it appear to be daytime. I remember a heavy glass door to the entrance of the building. When we entered we stepped aside because another man was exiting. After entering the building I saw no reception area only concrete hallways possibly leading to other rooms. We walked down a dimly lit hallway into a large room.

In a large room within the underground base I remember seeing military personnel sitting at tables and desks. Some of these people, both men and women, appeared to be working on large computer boards. I recognized these boards because of the computer work my husband Fred and our employees worked on. Working alongside with military personnel were Universal Entities. I know I have been taken to this underground facility more than once. To date I have not been hypnotized to help me recall these occurrences.

In "Morning Glory" Diary of an Alien Abductee I described an underground base I had been taken to in Albuquerque. I had been taken to Sandia/Kirtland Base at least twice. A man whom I cannot identify in this book because of his position, had contacted me and told me he worked at Kirtland Base. He confirmed information that there were underground facilities at Kirtland/Sandia Base.

HYBRIDS:

Throughout my years of guiding both male and female abductees I've had many females who were impregnated with hybrid babies. Many of these females experienced being pregnant and having the symptoms of pregnancy. Some of my female clients who were not married and said they were not sexually active, did not know what was occurring medically in their bodies. When their menses stopped they questioned their situation. When the second period was missed they became worried and made doctor appointments. However by the end of the third month normal menses had returned. Some of my single female abductee clients who experienced this knew they had been abducted by Universal Entities. When pregnancy occurred they were quite aware of being abducted again and eventually saw a very small unusual looking baby removed from them vaginally.

Several of the single females who were not aware of being abducted by these Universal Entities knew something was definitely wrong in their lives. They could not understand why they were having pregnancy symptoms. It made no sense to them until they expanded their awareness of what had happened to them through hypnotherapeutic process.

Many married female abductees who have had pregnancies with or without viable human babies born to them do recognize pregnancy symptoms. Many women took a home pregnancy test to see if they were pregnant. The test showed they were pregnant. By the third month of pregnancy many of these mothers suddenly and unknowingly "lost" their fetus.

Many women who were allowed to witness their abductions saw needle like tubes inserted into their vagina by the Greys or another one of the entities. One month later they would find themselves pregnant. Sometimes male hybrids would inseminate the human female abductees.

In helping these women to remember through hypnotherapy, I discovered during the second or third session their subconscious minds would throw each one into a "real life" memory of giving birth to a small unusual looking baby. The baby looked part human and part Universal Entity. This was typically a Grey who was involved in the procedure.

In <u>Morning Glory</u> I explained my reliving being pregnant when I could not possibly have been because of having had a hysterectomy. I personally experienced symptoms of pregnancy and yes, small babies just like these women experienced. There is a way used especially by the Greys to implant fetuses in women who have had hysterectomies. This experience is traumatic for women to live through.

These "new" mothers are asked or forced to hold their new babies right after birth. The babies would be taken away, perhaps forever. Some new mothers would have the chance for further contact with their hybrid babies. They might even be allowed to watch their children grow from childhood into adulthood.

Many of these women would be taken to the various nurseries to view their babies. In my experiences I had been taken to some type of nursery where I saw hybrid babies developing in a large, tall, horizontal tank that held some type of fluid. These hybrid babies remained there for over three months. I saw these developing hybrid babies at different stages of development and yes, they were alive. I saw body movement from these hybrid babies. This last statement has been confirmed by my hypnotherapy clients and by researchers within the field of this phenomenon. I was fortunate to be able to have contact with two of my hybrid children both females, whom I delivered vaginally. I will not repeat my experiences about this since I did write about the topic in <u>Morning Glory</u>.

Many of these mothers were allowed to hold and cuddle their young hybrid children. As these children grew the abductee mothers would teach their hybrid children about human life on earth. In turn, they would learn from their hybrid children about their life.

Some hybrid children had vocal cords allowing them to mimic sounds or perhaps even speak their mother's language, though not fluently at all. These hybrid children were not aware of the meaning of the words they spoke. For example, the word cat would be called "dat" and the word dog would be called "cog." Sometimes their spoken words made no sense. Conversation between mother and hybrid children through telepathy allows the mother to hear correct sentences of questions. These hybrid children enjoyed making noisy sounds with their little voices.

I myself rarely saw male hybrid babies. For some reason the male hybrid babies were never introduced to the new mothers. If this statement is correct these male hybrid babies were taken away from their mothers immediately after birth by a female Grey who was in attendance at the birth. The male hybrid baby was never seen again. This could be an erroneous assumption on my part. Perhaps these male hybrid children were kept in other areas of their home ship, possibly in some type of training as the child grew. If the reader of this book knows otherwise, please contact me with your information.

I do know for a fact that many times female hybrid Greys are in attendance at the birth of hybrid babies. For some reason, the male Grey who delivered the hybrid baby does not hand over the baby to the new mother to cuddle and hold. Instead he gives the baby to a female hybrid Grey who quickly walks away carrying the new born hybrid. The new mother is left with a feeling of loss.

I do know if these hybrid children have their mother's genetic DNA. One of my hybrid daughters had polio as I did as a child. This hybrid child was put to death by the Greys. I believe this was because the Universal Entities just want "perfect" hybrid children.

Male abductees are used predominantly for their sperm to inseminate the adult female hybrid. Male sperm is taken from male abductees while lying on a table and made to ejaculate sperm. Many male abductees are taken to a special room where they will meet a female hybrid and have sexual intercourse with her. Over the course of abductions this male abductee will meet up with this same hybrid female many times. The outcome is that the female hybrid does produce more hybrid children. This procedure has become very detrimental to many male abductees.

I have had many human males cry during their hypnotherapy session when reliving this sperm collecting procedure that has been done to them. They find themselves either lying on a table with the alien entities using their tools to excrete semen or they are taken to another room to be with a female hybrid sexually. It touches my heart and soul when I hear either male or female cry during their hypnotherapy sessions during memories of this reproductive scenario. Some married male abductees feel as if they have to inform their wives. Their wives are a support system for them. These males are extremely dedicated and loving toward their wives. They share an open relationship between themselves. Many females inform their husbands of their situation for the same reasons. Both married male and female abductees stay married to their original spouses who continue to be supportive and understanding of the abductees' situation. In other cases though, some wives or husbands cannot accept this fact. They feel as if their spouses are being unfaithful and the marriage fails. Perhaps they both eventually find other mates to live out their lives.

When this procedure is done to an adolescent male, the young man does not yet perceive what is occurring while lying on the table. He knows what is happening to him and knows it is wrong. Or he may be taken to a special room where he is introduced to the female hybrid. He will see her for a long time and have sexual intercourse with the same female hybrid.

When the male abductee's hybrid child is born the male abductee is also taken to the nursery and shown his hybrid children. On the same basis as the female, the male can see his hybrid children grow up and he is allowed to intermingle with his hybrid children.

Many female and male abductees can accept what has transpired and successfully deal with it in their lives. This is a difficult process to go through as I well know. I found it very hard to explain to my husband that I had hybrid children. He somehow understood. Or did he? At times life was unbearable between us. I know life can be unbearable for my married clients of hypnotherapy. Those who experience this type of "use" in abductions, may have a very strong love for their spouse. This allows acceptance of the situation by both soul mates. I have no words to explain what human life is like when you are so in love with and devoted to your life partner. When an unwanted intervention comes into your life like this, tears of sorrow accompany the explanation you give your spouse. It has to be said not just for my healing but for his as well. If only he were here today! "I was forced….it wasn't of my doing…...I did not accept this happening into my life…please understand me as I told you then and asked you to do for us….and as I ask of you today wherever you are in heaven." I know many a tear and sadness was shared by my husband and myself as well as by my hypnotherapy clients and their soul mates. Eventually healing and acceptance do take place. Happiness once again can be shared between soul mates in spite of their different children.

Now is the time to speak about "self medication" by abductees. Many abductees male or female, regardless of age cannot deal with this sexual situation in their lives. This is when many turn to alcohol or hard drugs to self medicate and to cover up their awareness of these creatures, the Universal Beings. Many abductees self medicate for a very long time until they can find help and wellness. Many abductees become sexually promiscuous beginning with adolescence into old age because of what the Reptilians and other creatures have done to them.

REPTILLIANS

Many abductees have found Reptilians to be benevolent, many have not. My feeling about this species is the latter. Within my soul I'm not supposed to hate any species, but I cannot accept these living beings! My opinion of this species is that they do not regard human life as "life." They are considered by me as not worthy creatures. They are distrustful and very sexual beings. I have described abductions with them in this book as well as Morning Glory. Yes, they are shape shifters. They use shape shifting to prey upon human beings. I described a few experiences involving this species. I was taken on board ship to a room full of different age males being sexually abused by this horrible species. Two large Reptilians led me into a room for an unknown reason. I had much disgust for this species as I witnessed what was transpiring. What lesson was I to learn from this experience? I was forced and controlled into having sexual intercourse with a young man. The Reptilians watched this process as part of their study.

I've had some hypnotherapy clients relive some life awakening experiences with this species. A couple of female clients during the relaxed state of hypnosis described the shape shifting procedure these Reptilians can do at any moment. Both females were single at the time. As an example one older lady was infatuated with a well known handsome actor and singer. She would have in-depth thoughts, dreams of meeting him and being with him especially in a sexual manner. Many times this is the way she would fall asleep. Several times while wide awake before falling asleep she had thoughts about the actor/singer. She looked toward her open bedroom door and was surprised to see her dream man. This dream man walked to her bed and sexual intercourse took place. In the depths of this sexual encounter her dream man showed himself to be a Reptilian using her body! I had another female client who experienced the same procedure. Both clients went through several of these shocking experiences before it completely stopped. Both ladies are alien abductees. This experience was life changing for both of these ladies. I have heard of this process affecting both male and female abductees. They were being used by Reptilians, either by entering the abductees' home or by being taken on board ship.

SOME PERTINENT QUESTIONS:

There are many Universal Entities that other abductees and I have encountered. Many of these have been researched, written about in various books. You can study and learn from the internet as well. I suggest however that you just be cautious of devious people who want notoriety or personal gain and put out wrong information.

I am compelled to write this book to touch on a few client cases which represent the ordeals of many of my clients, to help my readers who may be experiencing similar phenomenon. These truths may help the readers understand the known or unknown symptoms they are experiencing in their own lives. They need help to realize the need to awaken this truth in themselves. They need to come forward and seek help within the UFO community. They need to search for genuine, knowledgeable people and or other groups within the UFO field. These individuals will lead them on a path to finding their own truth in order to begin the healing process through hypnotherapy.

Tragic events that occur in life can cause memories to be buried deep within our conscience mind so that they cannot be released or brought to consciousness. Be watchful though. There are many devious hypnotherapists out there as well as "groups." You have to find one that is true to this phenomenon. Seek out those who work closely with people *in their* own truth. Your own guidance comes through learning and your own healing.

I am now at a point looking backward in my life asking the same questions as everyone else in this field. The question is why are so many humans who are researchers in this phenomena dying of sudden illnesses that take life quickly? Why did two individuals who devoted their life's work to this cause die in car accidents? One very well known educator died when he was hit by a car while crossing a street. Another succumbed to her death after suffering from a car accident which took her husband as well. We have asked ourselves are these deaths caused by our government or people who feel these researchers knew too much about the abduction phenomenon? Perhaps it was just their time to meet their Higher Power. Are their sudden deaths planned and executed? Who will be next? Why are people being told not to speak out? Why are researchers who work to validate strange phenomena being threaten? Why is the truth of these abduction experiences being silenced? The effect of these deaths has caused researchers to be afraid. Many humans who are experiencing these unknown occurrences in their lives are terrified. Many are living with their "secret" afraid to come forth and seek help for themselves and their families. Nonetheless many humans are taking this step and coming forth to seek their truth in their lives. Yes, these people are strong individuals and many are active in their work to help others.

I have received many threats to my life and the lives of those I love. I began to seek help for my family and for myself through the UFO abduction community which I wrote about in my book "MORNING

GLORY" DIARY OF AN ALIEN ABDUCTEE." In spite of this, I am once again speaking out and writing about what I know to be true.

The realization "hit home" when I lost my husband in a "sudden death" occurrence. I feel guilt because they did not take me but punished me by taking my soul mate forever. He paid the price. Yes, I became fearful and did stop speaking out at workshops, conferences and places where I communicated with others. Fortunately I did not stop helping clients who would contact me for help in this chapter of life's strange occurrences. As a result my health has been affected more than once and I continue to fight for my life and for my known work within this phenomenon because I care for life. I also care for what is happening within other human lives that have been affected by this phenomenon. I was taught, and now I pray for good health in order to continue my work not just for abductees but for their human and hybrid children.

At the beginning these Universal Beings did abuse not just me but certain members of my family. These certain family members now will not come forward with their known truths. Perhaps one day they will, and I do hope you will listen to them. Now I carry the so called "sole burden" because my family does not understand and accuses me of having "black outs" and that I am not right in mind. Because of this I know now why I cannot "grow up" with one grandchild. I hope that one day they will also know this truth to be true and they will forgive and understand me and perhaps further my known truth unto other humans and the universal species.

MARCH 22, 2002

Another dream experience that included numbers. On board an alien space craft that evening I was shown a panel. On this panel numbers were written in illuminating green colors: 06.10.2006. I focused on the year instead of the day. Memory also has these numbers as well: 06.30.2006. After viewing these numbers on the panel I heard a lady's voice. I could not understand what she was telling me because she spoke in a very quiet tone and very quickly. Some of the words I recognized as English, so I could understand what she was telling me but I did not fully understand her. I researched these dates but found nothing significant.

DECEMBER 29, 2003
FRIDAY'S NIGHT ABDUCTION

When I woke up I found myself lying on a table and heard myself moaning. The room I was in was very dark except for a dim light coming from somewhere behind me. This tall alien Grey walked to where I was lying. There seemed to be something different about him. I stared at his body, face, and eyes. Looking into his almond shaped eyes, they began to glow yellow! I told myself, "This is not a Grey." Still staring into his eyes, I thought, "This is a Reptilian! I have reasons to hate the Reptilians!" I panicked.

When I awoke the next morning I could not recall the full memory of this abduction. In my thoughts, "Yes, he was a Grey, but no… because of his yellow eyes." There was a question in my mind because I had never seen a Grey with yellow eyes!

I wrote an e-mail to a researcher who is a doctor in this phenomenon and asked him the question, "Do the tall Greys have glowing yellow eyes?"

This is the response I received:
"Normally, Zeta Reticulan Star Visitors' eyes do not emit a glow. But the Star Visitors can project imagery to our mind which makes us "see" things differently than they are for awhile.

Alternatively, your "abduction" may have been a military-intelligence faux-encounter with post-hypnotic memory change to misremember the event.

I suppose it is also possible that you were visited by a hybrid Star Visitor. The Reptoid Star Visitors do not have glowing eyes, but the golden/yellowish color of their irises/slit pupils may reflect light.

I suggest you consult a known colleague and review that experience, possibly including regressive hypnosis.

I never did contact this known colleague and did not go through regressive hypnosis on this abduction.

FEBRUARY 16, 2004
ABDUCTION LATE ON THE 16th OR EARLY A.M. OF THE 17th

Once again I woke up lying on a table which seemed to be attached to a silver wall. The room was small. I immediately knew where I was. Opposite from this table was a lady with blondish hair. She was sitting in a chair. I had seen this lady before and I believed I knew her. This lady also knew the male person who eventually was brought into the same room we occupied. After she curtly said "hello" to me, she began a one sided conversation with me. She knew that I had been told by the male person in question that he was leaving for Berlin and should be in Berlin at this time. She indicated to me that this male person was not in Berlin as he had told me. Secondly she said this male person does not want to correspond with me anymore both by phone or e-mail and he asked me to leave him alone. The lady told me that "I was just in this male's way." Yes, she was also well aware of the last telephone conversation I'd had with this male person several days earlier.

The male, was my long time friend, Jack. Yes, we would call each other at least once a month or so. The e-mails and phone calls were just friendly correspondence. There was nothing more to our relationship than just being friends.

I know that Jack has a way about him. When asked a question he does not want to answer, he will avoid answering that particular e-mail or verbal question. Before he left for Berlin he was in a different mood, and did not want to converse much. Because of our friendship and knowing him as I do, I know when to back off.

Jack was brought into the small room by a Reptilian who held onto his arm. Jack saw the lady and recognized her. He asked, "What are you doing here?" Then he looked at me while I sat on the side of the table. Jack appeared to be very "sleepy" or drugged. He just looked at me in a daze, like I was not supposed to be there.

The Reptilian told the lady to remain sitting in the chair. I don't know how, but I heard the directions the Reptilian gave to the lady. Was I meant to hear this statement from the Reptilian to the lady?

The Reptilian opened a door which was located next to the chair the lady was sitting in, and Jack and I were walked down a familiar hall.

Approximately two or three weeks later, Jack and I had phone contact. He said yes, he had been in Berlin and that he had just arrived home and called me. I had the opportune time to ask if he had been abducted the evening of the 16th or early on the 17th of February, by the Reptilians. Unfortunately, his response was that he did not think so.

I was disappointed at his response and did not further the conversation on that subject. But I know for a fact he was there because when I was taken down from the table, Jack grabbed my hand and held it until we were taken to another familiar room.

DECEMBER 26, 2004
A TRUE OCCURANCE

I don't know how I got onto the beach. But there I was, standing near the water's edge alongside a familiar man of Asian ethnicity. I had to be dressed in my night clothes. Perhaps that was why many of the people, that beautiful sunny warm day, were staring at me. The beach was full of people who were enjoying the sun, sand and water. The people were Asians. In close proximity to the beach were two- and three-story white buildings that apparently were resorts. These resorts were beautiful with native trees and vegetation surrounding them. People were sunbathing, playing with their youngsters in the sand or in the ocean waters.

I did not understand what I was witnessing at the moment, but looking out over the waves and down at the ocean, I realized the tide was quickly receding. As the ocean water washed back violently onto the shore it came further onto land than the normal beach area. Once again, the water receded back into the ocean. The receding ocean water left many sea shells and sea weed on the wet sand. Children ran to the shore and collected the sea shells that were left behind in the wet sand.

The man I was standing next to, realized what was transpiring. Quickly and as loudly as he could, he hollered for everyone to run. "Tsunami! Tsunami!" He knew about Tsunamis. Confusion overwhelmed everyone. People were in a panic as they searched for loved ones who had been surfing or swimming in the ocean waters. They could no longer see their loved ones as the waves became stronger and higher. People quickly began to run. Others stayed and ran into the water looking for their loved ones. By then, it was too late for them to reach safety as the thunder of huge waves roared in toward the beach.

My friend realized what was happening. Hollering another warning, he quickly took my arm and told me to run. He actually pulled me along because I could not run as fast as he could. When I failed to keep up with his pace, he pulled me along and my legs moved even faster. I stumbled a couple of times and he picked me up and held onto me, shouting in a panic for me to hold onto to him. We needed to find safety. People were scattering, running into nearby buildings, and/or higher places from the shoreline. The ocean came inland very fast and strong.

My friend led me up a steep and sandy hill. Running was difficult because of the vegetation and our feet sinking into the soft sand. He pulled and yanked at my arms. I was out of breath and my lungs hurt. I had the feeling I was not going to make it to wherever he was running for safety. The water was getting deeper and stronger. It pulled at us and tried to carry us back into the ocean. People screamed and the ocean thundered. We reached a building far above the beach that had a covered porch with white poles holding up its roof. My friend shouted for me to grab onto a pole as he held me even tighter against the pole. I looked out over what used to be a beautiful beach and ocean that was no longer there. Then it happened! The angry ocean sent huge, strong, mean looking waves to destroy whatever was in its way. Horrible! Extreme fear washed over me as I realized we might not survive this ordeal. I felt the pressure of salty water pushing and pulling at our legs as if it was about to carry us away! I saw the devastation of broken buildings, floating people, and vehicles being pushed by the huge waves that came far into the land. Destruction everywhere! I had never experienced anything like this before.

The next morning, I woke up feeling so very tired. The muscles in my body hurt as if I had run, climbed, perhaps exercised profusely. I stood up from the bed and noticed that Fred was not in bed or in the house. "I must have over slept." I said out loud. I could not comprehend what had transpired in my dream during the night. "Was it a dream? Where was I? What happened? What had I just experienced?" I could not quiet my mind. I had many questions. Then I began to examine my body. There was no dried sand on my legs or feet, no visible sand in my bed. My short night clothes had no sand and did not smell salty. I had no sand on my body!

What type of dream was this? I am considered to be psychic. So was this just a psychic vision of a forewarning of a tsunami to happen? Then reality set in. Before falling asleep I had symptoms (like a forewarning) that something was going to happen. These are the symptoms that most alien abductees experience before their abductions.

Unknowingly, I had been abducted and once again put through a hologram test of a tsunami. I was forewarned of a tsunami that actually did occur later in the year. This tsunami is what I experienced that evening. I still could not decipher if this real life dream was a psychic vision or if in fact, I had been abducted. Had I been abducted that evening by one of the universal aliens and been subjected to a hologram test? These hologram tests are used for studying human reactions; to get the abducted person's response and emotions to such a situation. I had been put through several prior holograms by the Grey's and also by our military.

The tsunami I experienced in the hologram test did occur during the Christmas season - 12/26/04. An earthquake occurred somewhere in the Indian Ocean causing a catastrophic situation from Banda Indonesia to the islands of Thailand.

When I awoke on December 26, 2004, I turned on the T.V. to listen to the news. I could not believe what I heard and saw about this situation that was being broadcast on T.V. My heart just fell. I was shocked to see what was happening and to know that I had experienced what I believed was a hologram test about this occurrence. I just could not believe it. I could not believe I had knowledge of this! It tears up my soul and wounds that which makes me human.

I stood in front of the T.V. and began to utter the words, "They exploded the bomb. The bomb went off." At the time I did not remember previous memories of India and the American Counselor. I just uttered these words quietly for a period of days. I could not figure out why I was saying those words. Something just kept eating me up. I had to keep saying the words. Suddenly, the memory came to me about the experience I had in India. I quickly researched my documents and found what I had written of that experience in India. Was it possible then, that the experience I had in India was a true experience? Is what I was told (by the Counselor and my military guide) true of a nuclear explosion? Why, why, why? What would this have accomplished? What was the purpose and reasoning behind this project? Why me? I have no answer to all these questions. So many people lost their lives just because of some horrible test? Are the Universal Entities involved in this plan as well? Was this experience true??

FEBRUARY 2, 2005

I received this Open Letter in 2005. The author does not want to be identified. The person who wrote this letter was told of my tsunami experience as well as the experience in India with the American Counselor. I am not part of this rogue "Cabal" group nor do I desire to be in their presence.

OPEN LETTER

You are being contacted because I feel that you may be in a position to react appropriately to the enclosed information, and exert your influence in the proper channels of government and international decision-makers to address the international security threat presented by a powerful rogue group.

The threat is the occurrence of further Great Quakes, such as the anomalous pair which occurred Dec. 24 (8.1 at Macquarie ridge south of New Zealand) and Dec. 26 (9.0, the Sumatra Great Quake, which launched a tsunami that killed a quarter-million people.)

These quakes were not accidental. They were caused by the testing of time-distortion technology by a super-powerful international group of geoplutocrats bent on world domination. This group is popularly referred to as The Cabal.

The Cabal hijacked time-distortion physics and technology from an innocent conventional scientist, Dr. Ronald Mallett of the University of Connecticut. His work in controlling time has been published in the May, 2000 paper in Physics Letters, Vol. 269, p. 214, entitled "Weak gravitational field of the electromagnetic radiation in a ring laser."

Dr. Mallett, with his UConn colleague Dr. Chandra Raychoudri, has come upon a physics principle, and concomitant technology, which can create a "time machine," but with enormous distortion of space (matter) in the local area of the (space) time-distortion effect.

The "enormous distortion of space-time" had deadly results when the power-greedy Cabal operatives conducted time-travel experiments on Dec. 24 and Dec. 26 with mega-deaths results.

Dr. Mallett's approach is innocent. But the hijacked version dovetails with reports of highly-classified and "dangerous" research leaked to me by a CIA official, who stated that extremely powerful holographic fields were being created in top governmental classified labs. Los Alamos National Laboratory (and Lawrence-Livermore/Sandia National Laboratories), which would serve as a "time-portal", i.e. an engineering time-distortion field through manipulation of photon particles to increase their energy as their inertia is increased by recently-developed light-slowing technology.

Dr. Mallett has found that when light comes to a stand-still, its energy reaches exponential levels in such a generated super-powerful field, not only is time slowed down, but space is distorted as well. These distortions had profound and ultimately deadly effect along the Macquarie Ridge tectonic plates junction 12/24/04, and then again in the Sumatra-region place on 12/26/04.

The Cabal hijacked Dr. Mallett's physics ideas, and engineered them into an unshielded device without proper protection, and their "successful" exercises in generating a time-distortion field (a time-travel portal) had the side-effect of causing huge tectonic plates to shift suddenly, generating enormous earthquakes.

Unfortunately, the Cabal scientists who had success in achieving time-distortion, are drunk with success at achieving the beginnings of time-travel technology, the ultimate international security threat. These Cabal engineers are bent on conducting further tests, regardless of the fact that they have not stopped to figure out, and include, protective technology against major distortion of space, (i.e., violent wrenching of Earth.) Because these power-greedy types intend to pursue unshielded experiments more Great Quakes will ensue, and most likely cause further significant loss of life and environmental damage.

But you can do something about it. If you do nothing about it, the blood of future victims is surely on your hands.

I have notified you carefully-selected governmental insiders and "good-guy" scientists I know that the Cabal has wrongly appropriated Dr. Mallett's work and mal-engineered it into an extremely dangerous device. And I have cited that the two great Quakes are illustrations of the danger of Cabal misuse of this technology, which could only be used with proper protection in place, which these power-drunk operatives have not slowed down to develop.

It is my intention in so notifying such well-intentioned people I know, that this will cause them to intervene with the right people, and for those officials to move into action to intervene and bring a halt to unsafe experimentation of this kind.

The great poet, Dante wrote that "the lowest rung of Hell was reserved for those who, in times of great moral crisis, stoutly affirm their neutrality." I am confident that you will not want to be counted among such cowards.

Do everything you can to mobilize those you have contacts with to apply pressure on the Cabal to back off these wanton and reckless time-travel experiments with poorly-understood and dangerous technology.

This threat is so serious to human well-being that certain Zeta Reticulan spokespersons have contacted me to inform me, and urge action.

I hope that you will take this situation with commensurate seriousness.

Thank you

This open letter raises many questions for me with regard to what I was shown and told by this American Counselor. Are the American Counselor and the military guides part of this Cabal group working with the universal aliens and receiving alien technologies? For what purpose? Power? Money? Control? I'm unsure if this American Counselor and the military escorts are Cabal. Perhaps they are just merely informed of the Cabal's plans and planting information into my subconscious mind.

I have to stop and think though, was this American Counselor who he said he was? Did he work for the American government? If this "Open Letter" is the truth about the tsunami and earthquakes that occurred and were caused by the rogue Cabal, could they then be the cause of past and future disastrous occurrences? Are they also involved and working alongside our earth governments? This group needs to be disrupted and interrupted quickly! I wish I could pray that all humans who inhabit this earth could get along through peace and love. Perhaps I have let it be known through the universal entities (who have taken me), this is the wish I have. This earth belongs to us, all peoples, all cultures. It has to be made into a peaceful existence with peace, love. But we do not see this happening on our world. We do not need one more "Cabal group" to invade and destroy us! We are only on this earth for a very short life span.

MY ROAD OF LIFE IS ONCE AGAIN TURNED
IN A NEW DIRECTION

Since "Morning Glory" Diary of an Alien Abductee" was published in 2001, the International UFO Museum and Research Center in Roswell, New Mexico invited me to come to the Center with books in hand and to meet me. I stated earlier the great support I received from Julie and Sandy and basically everyone that worked at this Center. The librarians were so helpful and just getting to know each one at the International UFO Museum and Research Center was extraordinary! Over the years I had been invited many times for personal book signings, during the UFO festivals that are held the first of July, and this is where I gave my first workshop. Meeting so many people that came to the Center from all over the world was phenomenal! I met many authors and researchers at these venues. The radio station located in Roswell invited me to speak on the local radio station, and Julie came and supported me. I just cannot say enough about Julie and Sandy who gave me "that push to venture on!" Yes, they all became my new found friends who accepted and believed in me and my "secret life."

I had previously and very briefly met Mr. Don Schmitt and Mr. Tom Cary, two well known researchers and investigators during the early days of the UFO Festivals. On August 26, 2002 I received this e-mail from Don Schmitt:

Hello Gloria,
Sandy at the Roswell Museum described a number of fascinating items from your book which she will forwarding to me for my attention. She may have also mentioned our returning back to NM next month. If your schedule would permit, we would like you to join us for dinner the evening of Sat. Sept. 14 at the home Nate Twining Jr.. Nate is the son of the Five-star General and has had a number of his own UFO experiences. He has also been a tremendous supporter of our work.

I would truly like to talk to you personally about your own events and if we can be of any help to you. I await your response.

Don Schmitt

Don Schmitt and Tom Cary are the current investigators (experts) concerning the Roswell incident and they are recognized as such by the International UFO Museum and Research Center.

On September 13, 2002 I did received another e-mail from Don with the time of 7:30 p.m. at Nate Twining Jr.'s home for dinner. I was given the directions and phone number just in case I could not locate Mr. Twining's home.

I arrived back in Albuquerque on September 13th around 5:00 p.m. from a trip to Seattle, WA. I had been so unsure of attending this dinner that I became very nervous because I did not really known Mr. Nate Twining Jr. or really know Don and Tom that well. I had asked a couple of friends who are researchers their opinion of this dinner. Their response was "negative." This did not help matters for me. On that Saturday evening, my husband Fred, said I should attend this dinner and to take his cell phone and call him if I needed to.

"THE SHAKING IN MY BOOTS SYNDROME"

While driving myself to the unknown, I said to myself, "Gloria, you have experienced far worse than being invited out to a dinner." Cell phone in hand, I was feeling rushed. By the time I got home from the airport, washed myself up, and went to choose a nice cocktail dress, I discovered that the only choice in my closet was limited to one "old" cocktail dress!

Hmm, okay just follow Don's directions….. The autumn sky was dark now, driving over the bridge, I could not find the turn off…..I drove a little further, still could not find the turn off…. I turned my car around and drove over the bridge again….Darn, I am late now…..I called the phone number Don gave me. Oh, I passed up the road again! I was told to look for the first road located on the west side of the main street from the bridge and make that turn. *Again* I missed the turn off, traffic was getting heavy, so I turned the car around and drove *very* slowly…..There was the turn off! If only there were street lights!

I turned and passed by a huge iron gate. "This is not the house." I told myself so I just kept driving. Something told me to turn around.

No one told me this gate was electric and had a camera. Okay, there was a pole, that looked like a speaker. I pushed the button, and a man answered! "I said I'm looking for Mr. Twining's home." "Your name please?" I said "Gloria Hawker."

The gate began to open, and I was given directions to park in the curved driveway in front of this humongous mansion! I was told to walk up the stairs to the very impressive door of this beautiful "glorious" home! "Oh Dear God" I thought to myself "What have I done! Too late to turn back!" The door opened quickly and the "BUTLER" who was dressed in a tux, welcomes me into a most beautiful home decorated completely in marble floors, walls and ceilings. And all's I could think of was I need to pee!

The rooms! My house would have fit into *one* of Mr. Twining's rooms. I was led to a large living area that had the most elegant, expensive furniture and a large beautiful grand piano. Gosh, was Liberace going to show up to play this piano? (Now I *really* needed to pee.) "Okay, Gloria," I said get a hold of yourself! I wondered where are Mr. Schmitt and Mr. Cary? Why was I seated here alone, one stage away from critical "flood"? I was so very nervous and shaky! Thank God the butler walked back into the room. I asked him if he could please show me the guest bathroom. He led me down the hallway. When I entered the bathroom, I feared I might pee on the floor until I noticed the marble and gold. It would *not* be polite to make a mess in such a beautifully appointed place.

I found my way back to the living room and sat down to wait. Before I knew it, a man entered from some other room. Reaching for my hand he introduced himself as Nate Twining Jr.. He was a very pleasant soft spoken man who made me feel "right at home." He said he read my book and had wanted to meet me! He sat down in another one of his chairs and we spoke for about ten to fifteen minutes. If memory serves me right a dinner bell was rung, and a servant instructed us to come to the dinner table.

The first thing I saw was an enormous crystal chandelier above the dining table. I've never seen a dining table as long as this one was. There were many place settings. I felt so intimidated but yet so very special. I said to myself, "Where are Don and Tom?" Mr. Twining sat at the head of this exclusive dining table and I was seated at his right side.

Then from another room, I believe, four to six men entered. They were all dressed in black suits! Oh my Gosh "Men in Black." I remember thinking "I will just get up and leave now!" But then, Don and Tom, came into the dining room thank God, but who are the other men I wondered? Following these men were the wives of some of the men. Whew. They introduced themselves. Mr. Twining made me feel so very comfortable as did Mr. Schmitt and Mr. Cary. The other men and their wives treated me like "old friends." I noticed two empty chairs at the end of the large table that had place settings. I did not catch the names of the missing people, when they were asked about. Mr. Twining said they were en route. Mr. Twining instructed his servants to begin serving dinner.

The large entry door soon opened. A man and lady entered and were greeted by everyone. As of today, I still do not know who this man and woman were, but they looked so familiar. Were they someone in the political field or perhaps maybe an actor and actress? I still don't know who they were.

I had never experienced the honor of *being* the "honored guest." Most of the conversation that evening focused on "me" and my life experiences and the "The Big Dig" to happen at Corona, NM where in 1947 a space ship crashed and Grey beings were found dead with one alive. The evening ended late around 1:00 a.m. I excused myself and shook everyone's hand. Mr. Twining (Nate, I was to call him by his first name now) extended another dinner invitation to me. He said, perhaps it would be even before the Big Dig.

Much sooner than I imagined, I received another dinner invitation to the home of Mr. Nate Twining Jr.. I felt more comfortable about accepting his dinner invitation which was to be held on a weekday just before the "crew" left for the dig in Corona. I was to park in the same place as before. Feeling more comfortable after exiting my car I looked around at the surroundings. I saw two other large guest houses opposite Nate's home.

Once again the "Butler" as I called him, opened the door and standing next to him was one of the other men that I had met at the last dinner. Both men welcomed me in. Mr. Twining was right there to welcome me as well. The same people were there with the exception of the man and woman whom I cannot identify. We all sat in the living area, and someone asked Nate to play a piece on his piano. He played beautifully. During the evening I felt as if I were the special guest once again.

Nate told me more about himself and his father during dinner. His father, the "Five Star Air Force General" Nate F. Twining Sr., was the commander of the Air Material Command at Wright Field in 1947. This is where the debris from the Roswell incident was sent. Wright Field was spoken about in general during the evening. After dinner we were all invited into Nate's den where different conversations were taking place. The dig took precedence as Don and Tom explained procedures and new techniques that were going to be used. This was another new experience for me. Once again, another dinner invitation was extended, perhaps after the dig.

At the time, I had these wonderful friends, Bruce and Barbara. Barbara was an abductee. I introduced them in "Morning Glory" Diary of an Alien Abductee. Barbara is now deceased. Bruce, Barbara's husband, worked with and became good friends with Mr. Gabe Valdez, whom I previously spoke about. Bruce had some knowledge of the Roswell Crash site in 1947, plus he and his wife knew one of the lost nurses whom Mr. Schmitt and Mr. Cary were looking for. I had given this information to both Don and Tom. Don wanted to speak with both Barbara and Bruce. I received an e-mail the end of January, 2003 from Don asking to set up a time to speak with Bruce and Barbara as he was going to make a quick trip to Albuquerque on his way to Roswell. We met and information was exchanged. Don was to continue speaking with Bruce and Barbara at a later date.

Approximately two to three months after the last dinner at Mr. Twining's home, I received yet another invite to dinner from Mr. Twining. I told Mr. Schmitt that I was going to have company during this planned dinner and did not think it was going to be appropriate for me to attend and leave my guest at home. My guest was promptly invited to dinner. My guest was Jack, the film producer who made a documentary regarding Al Bielek and myself. I gave this information to Don. The group at Mr. Twinning's home was most anxious to meet and speak with Jack.

After entering Mr. Twining's home Jack saw the grand piano and he immediately sat down and played songs he knew. Jack is a terrific piano player. This caused Nate to walk into his living room and take a seat to listen to his piano being played. The other well known people soon appeared and sat and listened, and then introductions were made. Jack is a very easy and comfortable person and he greeted these new friends. We enjoyed the evening and Jack answered many questions about filming and the documentary he'd made.

Another time when Jack was visiting, we were invited by Nate to visit his oil fields between Belen and Los Lunas, New Mexico. Jack and I accepted his invite. When we were out at the site one morning, we were told that when Nate and the crew where out working the oil fields many days and nights, a space ship would appear above them. The ship would be so close up in the day or night sky that they could see, it was a round space ship. They don't know why this occurred so often over Nate's oil drilling fields.

SUMMER, 2003
A MAN NAMED ELIAS: (A PROUD INDIVIDUAL)
PAULA B.

I was unaware of a special "following" I had by two ladies here in Albuquerque who were interested in this phenomena. Over time, as we became friends, I soon learned that these two women were my "followers." When I had a large crowd of people at book signings here in Albuquerque, I would try to talk to each person after speaking about my life that was written about in "Morning Glory" Diary of an Alien Abductee. People then would line up to buy my book. I did not realize that several times I encountered the same two women at different book stores for book signings. They always wanted to speak with me even if it was just "hello."

A few notes were taken on these first occurrences. I failed to document the full phone call that morning in 2003 when I received a special phone call from a lady who gave her name as Paula B. I cannot identify her last name because she has disappeared out of my "present" life now and I don't know how to contact her. Where she may be now is unknown. I must include Paula's dear and close friend whom I also became friends with. Paula and I lost this beautiful lady several years ago in death.

This particular morning was the beginning of an era of new direction in my life. This was to be something I never dreamed could happen in my life, as my life at the time was still very "hectic" with abductions and guiding other abductees, helping them to recognize and live with what was occurring in their lives. I thought my life was quite full, but as time went on, I realized I could do more!

"Hello," I said to the female voice on the other end of the phone. She introduced herself, "This is Paula B. I work for Baldridge Lumber Co., here in Albuquerque. I used to work for K Mart on Montgomery Street. We have been to your book signings. I know you will recognize me and my girlfriend." I believe Paula got my phone number from the hypnotherapy cards I hand out at book signings. Paula was quite nervous on the phone. "I've some information to give to you, Gloria, but I don't know how true the information is. I have gotten to know this particular couple who frequent the lumber company and I do know their names." Paula continued on with the description of this couple. I listened intently while Paula told me about a particular conversation the three of them had several times and this conversation had to do with Roswell, NM 1947 crash. Paula said the man did not speak a lot about this, but the woman did. In fact Paula received all the information from this woman.

The couple told Paula they lived in Roswell, NM while the lady's husband was in military service at the Roswell Army Air Field. The lady described what her husband saw in 1947. Paula said to me, "I feel these two people are quite honest with regard to what the lady has told me." She also added that most of the information came from the lady but that at times, the husband would insert just a small bit of information.

"Paula, do you think they would talk to me about this?" I asked. She said she would ask them when they came in again, and she would ask for their phone number so I could call them. A week or two went by and I did not hear back from Paula. Then I got another morning telephone call from her. I was quite surprised.

Paula told this couple about me being an alien/military abductee. She said she had spoken with me and that I would like to speak with them. She did get their phone number.

Meanwhile, since I had done some hypnotherapy work for the UFO Research Center in Roswell, I decided to give them a follow up call to see if they wanted more information to give people on the subject. I called the UFO Research Center and spoke with Sandy and also spoke with Julie Shuster (the director) with regard to this information. I felt I had done my work and they would know better who might need follow up information.

MR. DON SCHMITT AND MR. TOM CARY

At this point, I will go back and tell you about my face to face meeting for the first time, Mr. Don Schmitt and Mr. Tom Cary (2001) at the yearly UFO Festival, held the end of June and the first few days of July. I did not know who Mr. Schmitt and Mr. Cary were at this first meeting. This meeting was quite brief. Sandy and Julie had wanted me to meet these two gentlemen and this meeting was about two years before receiving the phone call from Paula. I already told you about the contacts made by Mr. Schmitt's e-mail and the events I attended at Mr. Twining's home and getting acquainted with Mr. Schmitt and Mr. Cary.

After I received Paula's phone call in the summer of 2003, I attended another UFO Festival that summer. I was sitting at the author's book selling and signing table in the UFO Museum when Sandy came and invited me into Julia's father's office. When I entered the office Mr. Schmitt and Mr. Cary were standing alongside Julie and her father. I was asked about Mr. Benjamin and the story Paula gave to me on her telephone call. Mr. Schmitt and Mr. Cary asked if I would take it upon myself to call and try to meet with Mr. Benjamin and his wife.

Mr. Schmitt and Mr. Cary gave me their personal phone numbers to follow up with them with regard to Mr. and Mrs. Benjamin. Before this UFO Festival Paula had given me the Benjamin's phone number which I called several times, but to no avail. The phone just rang. I later found out that the Benjamin's had been in California and Mr. Benjamin had been in the hospital. When I was able to reach them Mrs. Benjamin answered the phone and I introduced myself and told her that Paula had called me with regard to the information they had given to Paula. I also said that Mrs. Benjamin had given Paula their phone number so that I could call them.

"Oh, yes, Oh yes." she said. Mrs. Benjamin spoke with warmth and appeared to be a very gentle woman. She informed me that she and her mother were nurses. She spoke somewhat of her husband, Eli.

"May I speak with Mr. Benjamin?" I asked. "Well, let me see if he will speak with you, Gloria." I heard her say, "Honey, telephone." He asked who was calling for him. Mrs. Benjamin told him who was on the phone. I heard some hemming and hawing sounds from Mr. Benjamin then, "Hello." I introduced myself to him, and again told him how I'd heard about his involvement with the 1947 crash in Roswell, NM. "Oh yes, oh yes. My wife talks too much." he stated. "My wife and I just got back from Roswell this last weekend! You know we have family there, and we normally go for a visit during the festival. We did walk through the museum. Were you there?" My answer was yes. Was I at the Center? Again I answered yes. "I wonder if we saw each other? But we did not stay long at the UFO Museum. We have seen it so many times. Where were you?" he asked.

I told him I was sitting at the Authors' table. "Oh yes, oh yes." he responded. "Well what can I do for you?" he asked. I then informed him of the phone call I received from Paula and the information she had given to me with regard to his military duties at Roswell Air Force Base and the unusual events which he was involved in one particular day in July 1947. "Listen, I'll just say a little over the phone. I don't feel comfortable talking about this, he said." He told me that he did not have much to say with regard to the Roswell incident. I thought perhaps if I told him a little bit about

209

my knowledge and experiences with these entities, he might feel more comfortable. Maybe just getting to know me better would help. So I interrupted him and told him about myself and my own abduction experiences.

Quietly he listened to what I had to say. I went into the history of also being a hypnotherapist guiding alien abductees. He listened intently. I told him I would like to share more of this ongoing life with him in person, if he would be interested, and I would also like to hear his story. "Well I just don't know!" he exclaimed. "Can you call me back?" he asked. "When would be a good time to call you back?" I asked. "Oh, maybe in two weeks." Mr. Benjamin presented himself over the telephone as a pleasant and friendly individual.

Two weeks passed and I did return the phone call. No answer. I waited for about one week then called again. His wife answered the phone again. Complementary expressions were exchanged. "I wish my husband would consider talking to you about this. He needs someone to talk to." she said. She began to tell me a little more history about herself and her mother, and what her mother witnessed as she worked in the base hospital that night, but her mother would never speak of this situation again. The doctor her mother worked for was on duty at the hospital the day when the Beings were brought in, and this doctor called her mother to come to work that day at the base hospital. Mrs. Benjamin's mother is deceased. Mrs. Benjamin accidentally told me at this time she was one of the nurses also working there and what she saw. She realized what she had said and quickly changed her thought on that statement.

"Honey, telephone it's Gloria." "Hello" in his Spanish accent. "I just don't know, Gloria." I reaffirmed to him that anything he told me was to be held in strictest confidence. He would also be helping me in confirming what I know if he would just sit and talk to me. He had many excuses and became quite stern over the phone with regard to my phone call. We said our goodbyes. I waited for perhaps another two weeks and I called again. (In the meantime Mr. Cary called and spoke with Mr. Benjamin. The phone call was not productive).

Mr. Benjamin was in a better frame of mind. He told me that when we spoke last he was not feeling well and he was very busy at that time. He apologized. He was quite talkative on this day. He told me that he and his wife would be leaving for California again and would be back in two weeks. I was to contact him then and yes, he now wanted to meet with me and talk. I kept in contact with Tom and Don during this time. Tom gave me a list of questions to ask Mr. Benjamin at our prospective meeting. After two weeks I called and we set up a meeting to meet at the Senior Center. He gave me the directions to the Senior Center and asked could I meet him the following morning at 10:00 a.m.? I said, yes, but how will we know what each other looks like? I described myself and what I would be wearing, and he did the same.

I expected both Mr. and Mrs. Benjamin to be at the Senior Center, but only Mr. Benjamin showed for this meeting because Mrs. Benjamin was at home getting ready for the dance later in the afternoon.

Entering this Senior Center, I noticed a man sitting in a chair. He stood up and walked toward me. "Are you Gloria?" he asked. I replied "yes" and he proceeded to shake my hand, then gently said let's go to the back room. I have a lot of friends here and I don't want anyone to hear what I may say. We walked to a back hallway and into a room, and yes, as we walked down this hallway he introduced me to many men that are his friends. I brought a paper tablet along with me as well as my book within a folder so as not to give away to anyone what the topic of conversation would be.

As we sat in the room, questions were asked of me. Where was I born? What high school did I graduate from? Did I go to college? Was I married? How many children? Etc. etc. He told me that he and his wife go to the Senior Center on certain afternoons to dance. They liked to dance and I should come to dance. He also told me that he volunteers at the VA Hospital. The conversation was "just getting to know each other."

At that point I pulled out my book "Morning Glory" Diary of an Alien Abductee and he carefully looked through it. I asked him if he would like to take the book home to read and he responded with

"Yes." I noticed a slight relief in his posture and in his voice. I reinserted the confidentiality factor that he could feel comfortable telling some of his story to me. He began to speak casually about "his life," and then he asked for a piece of paper and pencil and proceeded to draw the face of a "Grey."

"This is what I saw." I questioned him on how large these Beings were, how tall, their skin color. What exactly was his job there? I received no answers. He became quiet. I had not yet told him that I had been in contact with Mr. Schmitt and Mr. Cary.

During this meeting Mr. Benjamin became uneasy with the conversation. He just stared at the drawing he'd made of the face of this entity and asked me questions about what did I know of them. Again I went into my abduction experiences with him. I found it hard to speak of this at that moment, perhaps because of talking just to one person who holds memories of events of not just that day.

As relief for Mr. Benjamin, he began speaking of his friends there at the center and how much he and his wife enjoy coming there. They had many friends there. He shared more about his family and his and his wife's involvement in their church. I asked him if we could meet there next week. He readily said yes, same day and same time.

In a phone conversation with Don I told him of our meeting and the drawing Mr. Benjamin made for me. Not much information was given during this meeting. Knowing I had to hold onto my promise of confidentiality to Mr. Benjamin, I could not give any more information to Don. I somehow had to work this out with Mr. Benjamin and myself.

Mr. Benjamin and I met for a second time without his wife. He was waiting for me and gave me a tight hug as I entered the Senior Center. We walked back to the same room as before and sat down. He was quite relaxed and more comfortable. He was able to read part of my book. He stated he just could not put my book down. The pictures I drew of the "Greys" in my book affected him the most.

I don't know how this man had lived with his secret and torment since that day in July 1947. Mrs. Benjamin apparently was the only one he had told his secret to. He said he trusted me and felt he could talk to me. In sketchy detail he told some of his story and spoke about threats he received from the United States military if he ever spoke of the events of that day. The threats that did occur while he was still in service were short lived and he survived but even now his fear was still real and ongoing. Many years have gone by and perhaps now, he finally felt, was the time to talk.

Private first class Elias Benjamin, 390th ASS at the Roswell Air Force Base, 1947 was processed to Top Secret clearance. He was authorized to provide security support for the most highly classified operations of the 509th Bomb Group. His primary position was guarding the Silverplates, his secondary duty was that of a recovery specialist. This secondary duty involved grim activities which were associated with the aftermath of plane crashes.

I saw tears in his eyes and his voice showed some shakiness as he began telling the beginning of his story to me. His story in full covered at least two more meetings at the Senior Center. This I realized was so hard for him to talk about, but I saw within him a release of his soul as he finished the whole story. He'd kept this secret (other than telling his wife) for some 60 years. He had withheld his unusual life experiences for so many years in order to protect his family and himself from any terrible threats that might have been carried out to them.

I put together my notes after each meeting I had with Elias. I used his words as I wrote my notes. I immediately believed his story and I knew he was telling the truth. The period of the early meetings with him as he discussed his life and his life story of so many years ago, seemed like just yesterday to him as he spoke. He had tears in his eyes, and his shaky voice would choke up when he talked. He would speak looking directly into my eyes, and then at times, so I would not see him cry, he would look down. He was very afraid of telling his story as he still thought I was from the government! I know he thought in speaking even now, something terrible was going to happen to him and his family because "he talked." I constantly reassured him that I was not any part of our government, military or otherwise and I was in the same position as he, because of my status.

Yes, I too was afraid of our government because of the two different experiences he and I shared within the truth of this phenomenon. Elias is a very strong, intelligent, very gentle and kind human being.

The following is compiled from my written notes of the meetings with Elias, his wife and myself. Elias' full story is confirmed in "Witness to Roswell" which is written by Thomas J. Carey and Donald R. Schmitt.

"Monday July 7, 1947. I just got off duty and I was walking back to the barracks after a night of guard duty on the flight line. I just had breakfast at the chow hall. I was very tired from duty that night and just wanted to sleep."

His location at that time was near the base headquarters. As he walked back to his barracks he remembers hearing the National Anthem being played and the raising of the American flag. He stopped, saluted and was at attention, but he felt something was not right. After this procedure of the anthem being played and the flag being raised that morning, while standing there, he realized there were too many staff cars and vehicles located at the base headquarters. Staff meetings were only held on Tuesday mornings by the base commander, Col. William Blanchard. When he arrived back at his barracks he remembers his squadron received word that they were on alert for special duty. He knew then sleep was secondary now. He soon was given orders to get his gun and report to Hanger P-3 for guard duty.

"I saw them there!" "Saw who?" I asked. "These strange Beings."

He did not remember if it was late in the afternoon or early evening when he reported to the large hanger as ordered carrying his gun. He searched for his officer in charge to get his instructions for the duties he was to perform at the hanger. At the entrance of the main hanger there was quite a commotion. He saw some MP's who were trying to subdue an out-of-control officer who appeared to be drunk. Later he found out the alleged officer in question was from his squadron and was the officer to whom he was to report to for a special detail. This officer was to oversee the transfer of "Top Secret items" from this main hanger to the base hospital.

"There was much confusion and I was told that my officer in charge had been to the crash site then when he was at the hanger he saw small bodies. I guess it was too much for him to see and handle so he just 'lost it.' I had just arrived at the hanger myself and I was told I was going to help with the transfer to the base hospital. At that moment a Major or a Lt. Colonel came out of this hanger and looked toward me and pointed directly at me. 'Come over here, you are now in charge of this detail.' he hollered at me! 'Get these to the base hospital!' He then pointed to the three or four gurneys that held something covered up by sheets. These gurneys were in the hanger. I saluted my acceptance and understanding of the orders given to me by this Major or Colonel. I walked to the gurneys looking at them then I saw something on one of the gurneys that was covered up by a sheet. This 'something' was moving!"

Eli continued, "I then instructed the other men who were to help me with this detail to load this 'payload' into the back of the truck that had just arrived. I did not know what we were to transport to the base hospital but when we were loading the gurneys onto the truck one of the gurneys slipped and the sheet covering fell off. I saw a gray face, swollen head that had no hair on it! This thing did not look human! We took the gurneys to the base hospital's operating room ramp." Eli told me he was to remain in the operating room with the gurneys until he was relieved.

When they arrived at the emergency room ramp, they proceeded to unload the gurneys. Eli walked into the emergency room with the first gurney where the medical and non medical people took over. Eli stood near a doorway and when the medical and non medical people removed the sheet covering. Eli saw a small, thin child-like Grey Being. The Being had a large egg-shaped head, slanted eyes, two holes where a nose should be, and a slit for a mouth. Originally Eli told me that he had to escort the covered species into the "operating room" area where the medical and non medical officers were standing and waiting for the arrival of these gurneys. His new orders were to remain there in the operating room while the procedures on these beings were going on. All of the other gurneys were not yet in the operating room.

This is when Eli said he saw the species being uncovered. One dead grayish colored species and two live, grayish species, of which one died on the operating table. He described how swollen these "Beings" faces were and how he was able to see and was even able to touch one of the species' bodies at the hospital. Eli described this non-human being that he saw: "A small like person, thin..., with a large head....shaped...shaped like an egg. 'His' head was too large for his body. This being had large slanted eyes, and two holes where a nose should be, a slit where its mouth should be."

"He's alive....he's alive!" Eli said out loud as he told me this account. Eli has never forgotten these beings' facial features to this day. Seeing their eyes and swollen faces is what has remained with Eli and has bothered him since.

He does not know what happened to the live being that night, but apparently the live being he was told later "...was taken to Alamogordo, NM, then shipped to a base in either Texas or Ohio." Eli was dismissed and he was told to return to his squadron which eventually he did. Eli said, first though, he was taken to another hanger where he saw the wreckage in question. When he finally arrived at his squadron Eli said he was debriefed and he was made to sign a nondisclosure statement regarding what had just taken place. He was told and instructed more than once if he ever spoke about this situation he and his family would be killed.

Elias often wonders if this being is still alive and if so where is he?

On our next visit I was invited to their home to meet Mrs. B. Benjamin. When I arrived I found a very warm lovely home where I was immediately welcomed. Mrs. B. Benjamin presented as a lovely warm lady. It felt as if we knew each other already. I was taken to the den in their home and made to feel quite comfortable. Mrs. B. Benjamin and I spoke mostly while Elias sat there listening to us, interjecting into the conversation briefly. Mrs. B. Benjamin spoke of their life in Roswell and of their marriage in 1949. She is now a retired nurse who worked for a doctor in Roswell and then here in Albuquerque. Her mother was also a nurse working at a hospital in Roswell. Mrs. Benjamin and Eli agreed they were not closed minded with regard to other species in or outside of our universe, because they were very religious. They both said in part of the Bible you find verses talking about this phenomenon. She stated to me that when Eli saw and witnessed these events he was not shocked and he was open to the fact of this phenomenon. She was not shocked when he came to her with this information but believed what he told her. I feel this statement is incorrect because of Eli's expressions of grief and the movements of his hands and body when he told me of his involvement.

Mrs. B. Benjamin then began speaking of what she knew with regard to this strange event when Elias had finally opened up to her privately and secretly soon after their marriage. Mrs. B. Benjamin confirmed the events that Elias spoke of during our (Elias' and my) two to three meetings at the senior center.

Mrs. Benjamin could never speak about this secret until just the past few years because of fear for the lives of family members and her husband and herself. She stated this information is not spoken out to just anybody at that time.

Mrs. B. Benjamin's wish was that Elias would have spoken to someone earlier. Mrs. B. Benjamin said, she tried to get Elias to speak with someone at the International UFO Museum and Research Center located in Roswell, NM. One time while they were visiting the center, Mrs. Benjamin took it upon herself to speak to the director at the center about Elias, but when she turned around Elias was not there and not to be found inside the Museum. Elias was not ready to tell his story to anyone, so he took off and went outside.

I found Mrs. B. Benjamin to be as understanding and trustworthy as her husband, Elias. She has a beautiful personality. Over these past years I've been welcomed into their home many times, getting to know each one of the Benjamins quite well, and hearing the repeated account of Mr. Benjamin's involvement with new information coming forth each time we spoke. At one point Mrs. Benjamin repeatedly said that her mother was one of the nurses on duty when these alien bodies were delivered to the operating room, but quickly would retract her story and say that her mother worked for the *doctor* who was there in the operating room of the base hospital that day. This same statement occurred several times.

On 11/28/07 Mrs. Benjamin once again changed her story regarding her mother who was a nurse. She said her mother worked for a man who had worked many years at Ballard Funeral Home. Her mother told Mr. and Mrs. Benjamin what this man did. His involvement was to get small children's caskets and measure the caskets, then go and pick up these small bodies from the hospital. There is much confusion with Mrs. Benjamin's stories or involvement and of her mother's involvement. So was this man the infamous doctor who worked that day in the operating room on these species? We will never know now. Perhaps this is the confusion Mrs. Benjamin wanted understood so the real truth would not be known because she still feared threats.

When I first met Elias, speaking with him, gaining his trust, informing him that his story would be held in confidence by me, then eventually speaking to his wife, I found myself in such a dilemma. Having been told of such accounts from Mr. Benjamin created deep conflict within me as his valid important information had to be given to Mr. Schmitt and Mr. Cary. But how do I do this without betraying confidentiality?

Once again sitting in the Benjamin's den I spoke of two investigators within this phenomenon whom I trusted, explaining that these gentlemen "worked" alongside with the International UFO Museum and Research Center. These two men would like to help out the Benjamin's with this account of involvement that transpired in July, 1947. I asked if one of the men, either Mr. Schmitt or Mr. Cary, could call them. They were uncertain, unsure if this should happen, then Mr. and Mrs. Benjamin finally agreed.

From the beginning of this journey for me, Tom and Don stayed in constant contact with me with their advice, prompting, giving me advice as to how not to lose the Benjamins. I had never done anything like this before, but I soon learned. Tom called Mr. Benjamin before I made the first contact with Mr. Benjamin. Below is that e-mail.

I previously e-mailed both Mr. Schmitt and Mr. Cary.
On 10/22/2003 I received an e-mail from Mr. Cary.

Gloria,

*Yes, Mr. Benjamin finally answered his phone, and it was the guy
we were looking for. He wanted to know "who talked" so that we
could find him. Well, it was obviously his wife who told the two
ladies who in turn told you. Anyway, we had a nice conversation
during which he would only give me hints at what he knows (a lot).
He said that he would talk more but only face to face. He could
prove to be a very important Roswell witness indeed. Don and I
are planning to visit him ASAP (before he has a chance to get "cold
feet"). In preparation, I would like to talk to the lady you were
going to contact about this if there was no answer on the phone.
Can you get her phone number for me? If she doesn't want to talk to
me, can you either record her information or take notes so we have
some idea as to what Mr. Benjamin story is?*

Thank you,

Tom

NOVEMBER 14th THRU THE 16th of 2003

A date had been set up for Mr. Schmitt and Mr. Cary to come to
Albuquerque to talk with the Benjamins. This meeting did not take
place as scheduled.

Mr. Cary spoke with Mr. Benjamin a second time before 11/18/2003.
At this time Mr. Benjamin expressed his desire not to meet with Mr.
Cary or Mr. Schmitt so he expressed his concerns to Mr. Cary with
a number of excuses. Mr. Benjamin was to call Mr. Cary back but
never did. Mr. Cary and Mr. Schmitt felt that Mr. Benjamin was the
most important witness ever in this case.

It was suggested that I call Mr. Benjamin and assure him that Mr.
Cary and Mr. Schmitt were not government agents. Once again Mr.
Benjamin said to me that he thought that Mr. Cary and Mr. Schmitt

were government agents. I had my work cut out for me. I did understand the Benjamin's position of being fearful.

We had planned another meeting between Elias and his wife. A date for this meeting was set up but when I called to say I was on the way there was no answer to the phone. I called for several days. At a later date Mrs. Benjamin answered the phone. Mr. Benjamin was in the hospital. I told this information immediately to Mr. Schmitt and Mr. Cary.

Mr. Cary thought I should take advantage of asking Mrs. Benjamin some questions that Mr. Cary wrote up for me. I was able to speak with her again soon after and did ask her the stated questions. She answered the questions promptly. I asked the questions in my own thoughts and words and used the questions in conversation form. I related the answers back to Tom.

In another conversation with Mr. Cary, he gave me the name of another person who was also involved in this event of the Roswell Crash. I was to ask Elias if he knew him.

Elias had been home from the hospital for several days. I called to see how he was doing. He was feeling great! During our conversation I asked if he knew this person. "Oh yes, I do. Over the years we have spoken. Yes, he was there at the hanger working along with me and he knows."

Mr. Schmitt and Mr. Cary would plan now to visit the Benjamins early next year. I wrote back telling them not to wait that long, they should come ASAP if I could get the Benjamins to concede to a meeting. Both the Benjamins and Mr. Schmitt wanted me at this meeting in case I could help to change the Benjamins minds about being interviewed by Mr. Cary and Mr. Schmitt. Both Mr. Schmitt and Mr. Cary felt they were going to lose this potential witness.

Elias did agree to meet with Tom and Don, not just once but many times. The first meeting took place in my home and many times after that we met either at my home or where Don and Tom would be staying. As always both Mr. and Mrs. Benjamin were there together. When Don and Tom came to Albuquerque, specifically to speak with the Benjamins, I was always included in these meetings as well. Mr. and Mrs. Benjamin were also invited to a dinner at Nate Twining's home along with Don and Tom and myself. They were very nervous as I was at my first dinner at Nate Twining's home. I drove them to Nate's home and they experienced the warmth and welcome as I always did. The Benjamins felt quite comfortable with Mr. Twining and getting to know each other. The questions asked of the Benjamins that night were answered with their honesty and truthfulness. Over the years, the Benjamins and I have grown close to each other.

Mr. Benjamin has come a long way with Don and Tom over the years. The three of them have such respect for one another, as well as for Mrs. Benjamin. There have been documentaries, and filming projects, which I have been invited to attend as well. Eli's involvement has been written in Don and Tom's book "Witness to Roswell." This is a book everyone who is interested in this involvement of July, 1947 should read. In this book there is a lot of history about the many people found who were connected to this Roswell incident. As investigators Tom and Don did their constant hard work over the years on this subject as described in their book. I highly recommend reading "Witness to Roswell".

Don and Tom taught me a lot working with them. They are courageous men who are searching for the truth. I highly respect these two men whom I have gotten to know over these years. Information on specific names and other information that I felt I could not write about is shared in Tom and Don's book.

Sadly to say though, Mrs. Benjamin has fallen victim to a disease of dementia. She and I do not communicate now, and that I do miss.

SEPTEMBER 23, 2004
JULIUS A.

Mr. Cary asked if I could try to contact Julius A. who lived in California. This name was given to me either by Tom or Mr. Benjamin. I had Mr. Benjamin call Julius because both Julius and Mr. Benjamin were in contact with one another over the years. I asked Mr. Benjamin to place a phone call to Julius A. and ask him if I could call him with regard to the same involvement that Mr. Benjamin had lived though. I asked Mr. Benjamin to bring Julius up to date about my having spoken in detail with Mr. Benjamin and his wife regarding Eli's involvement on the day of July 7, 1947. Mr. Benjamin complied with my wishes to contact Julius A.

Julius A. answered the phone that day. I introduced myself and asked if Mr. Benjamin had called him as well. The answer was yes. He wanted to know why I was calling him. I asked him if Elias informed him of the reason for this call. He was just double checking he said. Julius stated that he had just recently returned home. He had been living with his son because of illness. He was quite proud that on the following Saturday he would be 77 years old. Julius confirmed he was in the Army for three years. He was stationed at the base in Roswell, NM for one and one-half years.

"My wife died in 2001." he said. We kept the conversation light, just getting to know each other. During our conversation, Julius mentioned that a man from back East called him. (He did not remember what state the man had called from.) I asked him if Mr. Don Schmitt or Mr. Tom Cary called him because they also had Julius' phone number. Julius said no, he did not remember the name of the person who called. He asked who the people were that I had just mentioned. I explained that Mr. Don Schmitt and Mr. Tom Cary are Investigators, Researchers who are involved with the International UFO Museum and Research Center in Roswell, NM. I immediately took the opportunity to stress the fact that Mr. Schmitt and Mr. Cary are not with any governments. They are just who I said they are.

Julius explained that he did not have much to say about this matter. During our phone call he informed me that yes; he was there at the base working on that date. I detected shakiness in his voice. He then told me he could not talk about this because of his life being threatened. He needed to think this through and would talk to his son about speaking with me. He asked if I would call him back in a couple of days. At this time I informed him that a proclamation in 1994 absolved anyone with knowledge about the Roswell incident who believed that they were still subject to security or secrecy oaths regarding this matter. I placed a second phone call after speaking with Don and Tom and they reminded me of this proclamation and to reaffirm it with Julius again.

Julius presented as a coherent, mentally stable person with memories of that day in 1947. He became excitable when asked to share his memories of that particular day. He said he would have to talk this over with his son and ask him if it would be okay to share his memories. I asked if his son would like to speak with me as well. I told Julius his son could call me if he would like to and I would answer any of his questions. I never heard back from Julius or his son. Two weeks went by and I called Julius. No contact was made until......

January 2005, I made contact with Julius. He was quite talkative. He'd had an accident and had three broken ribs. Suddenly, as if he'd become frightened, he said because of the medication he was on, he would like for me to call him back in February.

In an e-mail from Don, he thought it might help break the ice with Julius if he knew that Don had spoken with Cpl. Downs. During the next phone call to Julius I mentioned the information Don had given me about Cpl. Downs. Julius was just leaving for a doctor's appointment. He said he would return my phone call and that he did want to talk to me. This was a "put off."

Several phone calls and approximately one month later Julius did not answer his phone. Don and Tom felt that Julius was very frightened about the threats made by the military. Tom reaffirmed that those people who have "talked" to them have received no threats, nor has anything ever "happened" to them.

On a later phone call to Julius, I reaffirmed this information. This phone call was short. I feel as if he just wasn't confident about speaking with me. Don and Tom agreed perhaps I should go to California and speak to Julius in person - face to face.

On the morning of May 17, 2005 I was once again able to speak with Julius. What came out of this conversation was affirmation.

He was in the Army assigned to the Roswell Base during that period of time, either in 1946 or 1947. He said memory failed him now about exactly when he had been stationed in Roswell. He had been a policeman turned paramedic. He remembered 390th Air Service Squadron. Don and Tom have a resource that confirms that Julius was assigned to this base in 1947. In our conversation Julius said he remembers Mr. Downs. Julius once again stated he is still very frightened to say any more even if Mr. Benjamin has "talked."

THE DISAPPEARANCE OF JULIUS

I would place monthly calls to the phone number I always used to make contact with Julius but no one answered the phone until October 2005. He answered the telephone and had many excuses for me. We shared a pleasant conversation, and I asked him if I were to fly out to where he lives, would I be welcomed and would he talk to me about his involvement with the 1947 incident. He said he would feel comfortable with this, but he does not remember much anymore. He asked if I could come toward the end of November. Julius wanted me to call him the middle of November to schedule my visit.

Don and Tom were to fly out to California the first of the new year and they were looking into funding so that Eli and I could go and interview Julius. This never occurred.

The last and final phone call I placed to Julius in late November to let him know of future plans for Eli and myself to visit him. He said he was getting ready to move in with his son and that he would call me when he got settled. I never heard back from Julius and his phone had been disconnected.

THE INFORMANT

In the last couple of years a well known doctor from Albuquerque was in Roswell I believe, during the UFO Festival. He had given Julie Shuster some important information. Don called me on this and asked if I would follow up. I did. I found the phone number of his medical office but was only able to speak with his nurse the two times I called. After introducing myself, I asked if I could speak with this well known doctor. (Once again I cannot reveal his name). She asked what I needed, because he was not able to come to the phone. I told her that I had a message from Julie Shuster the director of the Museum in Roswell. He had given vital information to Julie and I was to follow up on the information. The nurse said she would give him the information and if I did not hear back from him by the next day, for me to call back. I called back and the phone was given to the same nurse. He has changed his mind about "talking" was the message. Interesting, I thought. I wondered if someone had gotten to him or if he had just changed his mind. Perhaps the information he'd given was false?

JUNE BLAIR

Once again Mr. Don Schmitt and Mr. Tom Cary asked if I could contact Mrs. June Blair as she now resides in Albuquerque. I did not know much history about Mrs. Blair, only that she had been Col. William Blanchard's Executive Secretary. I was given an address and Tom and Don filled in the missing information on Mrs. Blair. I was ready to follow up and hoping to meet this lady.

One afternoon driving in the area of her home I did stop at the address I'd been given. I pulled into a parking spot and noticed that each home had an "A", "B", or "C" number. I then proceeded to walk toward my destination. Mr. and Mrs. Blair's home had a tall iron fence around their front entry. There was a door bell on the tall iron doorway, so I rang the bell hoping someone would answer. I waited, and no answer then rang the bell once again. This had given me time to look over their front yard walls and green plantings. I thought they had a beautiful front yard. No one responded again to my ringing the doorbell. I walked back to my car and left the area. Arriving home, I called Tom and Don. They had many questions for me about what I had observed in the Blair's yard, walls etc.

One week later, I received another phone call from Don and Tom asking me to try going to the Blair's again and perhaps taking Eli Benjamin with me. I called Eli and explained to him the plan. Eli was quite willing to do this with me so we set up a day and a time to meet.

DECEMBER 2009
A COLD WINTER DAY

I met Eli and Mrs. Benjamin in a furniture company parking lot. Eli rode in my car to the Blair's home. We both were somewhat nervous and just hoping that someone would answer the front door. I parked my car and we got out and walked to the Blair's home. I rang the door bell twice. To our amazement an elderly lady opened the front door and came out to where we were standing. She was small in stature, had short gray hair and a soft spoken voice. I asked her if she was Mrs. June Blair. She asked who needed to know and why? I introduced myself and then introduced Eli Benjamin. I explained to her what we were doing there at her gate, hoping she might invite us into her home. The wind began to blow making the temperature even colder. The woman had on a sweater with her pant outfit. Of course she did not invite us in; I could just imagine her thoughts about us. I don't believe I would have invited two strangers into my home either.

Eli once again introduced himself and stated he had been a private first class with the 390th ASS at the RAAF. He possessed Top Secret clearance. He had provided security for the 509th Bomb Group and the Strategic Air Command. Eli openly began to tell a brief story of that early Monday morning of July 7, 1947 as he walked back to the barracks. When he arrived at his barracks his squadron was given orders to be on alert for special duty. He was told to grab his gun and report to Hanger P-3. Arriving at Hanger P-3, he encountered MP's holding the drunken officer to whom he was to report. Instead, a Major or Lt. Colonel (at this point Eli cannot remember the name of the Major or Lt. Colonel) gave Eli orders that he was to be in charge of this detail and to get into the hanger and begin transporting "gurneys" to the base hospital. Eli followed those orders and twice he saw small grey bodies that were not human! Having finished his story, he said to Mrs. Blair, "I need to talk to you about this." After hearing the important highlights of his involvement, Mrs. Blair said she had an appointment she needed to attend to. She said her goodbyes to us and quickly went into her house and shut the door. Eli and I just stood there. We looked at each other then walked to my car and left the area. We both felt good about making the first contact with Mrs. Blair. Perhaps we could try again on a warmer day.

I had her address and took advantage of the information to write her the following letter.

December 29, 2009

Mrs. June Blair
Albuquerque, New Mexico 87106

Dear Mrs. Blair,

I want to apologize for the inconvenience on a cold wintery day that you graciously opened your front door to a couple of strangers and to speak with us. Mr. Tom Carey and Mr. Don Schmitt who are authors had previously tried to contact you in their research with their forth coming book on the Roswell incident of 1947 in regards to the UFO Crash with alien bodies. They had asked me if I could go and visit with you with the accompanied of Mr. Elias Benjamin. Since I had no phone number to contact you and introduce myself I took the chance of just appearing at your front door.

Mr. Elias Benjamin witnessed (saw) an alien body (ies) in hangar P-3 at Roswell while being loaded into the back of a truck and his orders were to deliver these bodies to the hospital emergency room (Bldg. 317). His story is written in Don Schmitt's and Tom Carey's book "<u>Witness to Roswell</u>". When I first met Mr. Benjamin he was unsure and frightened to talk to me and he did not feel safe, because he too, thought that I was government trying to harm or threaten him and his family. (A proclamation in 1994 that absolved anyone with knowledge about the Roswell incident who believed that they were still subject to security or secrecy oaths regarding this matter). Mr. Benjamin asked for another visit and as time went by he gained his trust in me and the reason for seeking out his information of what had transpired on that night/day of the incident of the UFO crash with alien bodies. Mr. Benjamin was in the Air Force at the time and stationed at the base there in Roswell. Mr. Benjamin would now like to help the many people who were involved in this incident. Many important people have already spoken out and spoken to Mr. Schmitt and Mr. Carey and to myself and have not had any problems *of harassments, threats, intimidation etc. coming from any source of government or government agencies.*

I too, have a selfish reason for finding the truth which one day I would gladly sit down and tell you my story. But for now, knowing that time is running short as many people yet who have vital information are growing older and dying. Mr. Schmitt and Mr. Carey know that you were a private secretary to the infamous Colonel who I believe gave a death bed confession. Knowing Mrs. Blair, you would not only be helping Mr. Carey, Mr. Schmitt with their research or myself with your vital information on this incident, but realizing the large populace who needs the truth to be told and the truth to be written in regards to this incident. If you would not want your name published in this new book, providing you would give information your name would be published as an anonymous name. I would like to someday soon be able to meet you and talk to you, and hopefully gain your trust in me too. Until that day will/would come as you gain your confidence to come forth. Until then, I pray, and thank you again for your time spent on this letter and please consider in getting to know me and speaking with you. Yes, Mr. Tom Carey and Mr. Don Schmitt would one day like to meet you as well.

Thank you,

Gloria Hawker
Phone #

For some time I waited for a phone call from her, wishing she would call. I often wondered if she had read my letter. Did she even receive my letter? I happened to be driving in her area one day and thought I would give this a "shot." I drove into the parking lot where her home was located. I got out of the car, went to the large iron gate and rang the bell twice. I could see through the window but saw no movement. After ringing the bell twice I left.

Sometime later I wrote her another letter.

September 2, 2011

Mrs. June Blair
Albuquerque, New Mexico 87106

Dear Mrs. Blair,

It has been one year and a half that I made contact with you through an outdoor visit and a letter. Over this time I had hoped for an opportune time that you would have contacted me through either the mail or telephone. I'm getting older and time is passing quickly as I am sure you realize how the time is passing quickly too. My wish still is to be able to sit down personally and just talk to you in regards to this known phenomenon of what transpired in July of 1947 in Roswell, New Mexico.

I would like to be up front with you at this point of my interest in gaining your knowledge and confirmation that you withhold. It does not matter if you think I am "insane" because of what I am going to inform you of. This is my life and my truth. I know you are aware of humans who have been abducted by extraterrestrials from within our universe. Some members of my family and mostly myself have been taken many times over the years by several different extraterrestrials. Yes, my life story is long and at first frightening until understanding and acceptance was made by me. I too, then shortly after the first year of encountering these different cultures, began the most frightening part of my life and that was because of humans abducting me too. I am also known as a MILAB. Military abductee. You behold your knowledge and known truth of what occurred and with your knowledge it would be such great confirmation for me. I took the chance and put myself out there to the public with my personal experiences because I wanted to share and help other humans who were/are experiencing the same. Yes, thinking that they are alone and insane in this matter. I wrote a book on my personal experiences with these different cultures from other planets and I became a hypnotherapist guiding many humans throughout the United States and Europe to regain their health, knowing their truth. Many people in New Mexico have experience in their lives what I have experienced and the rewarding part is the gratitude and love given back to me by these many peoples. This is such a rewarding gift of life. May I one day very soon come by your home for a visit with you, or perhaps you could please call on the phone? My number is---------. You are a very gracious lady; I once again thank you for your time and waiting for contact with you.

Thank you,

Gloria Hawker

I never heard from Mrs. June Blair with regard to my letters. On March 10, 2013 her obituary was published. She took the knowledge of her involvement in the Roswell crash incident with her to her grave. Perhaps she told a family member or a close friend of her involvement and perhaps one day that person will come forth. In 1946 she and her husband returned to Roswell, NM and transferred to the U.S. Army Air Corps. She became Executive Secretary to Col. William Blanchard commanding officer of the 509th Atomic Bomb B-29 Wing. This is the reason for contact being made.

BLAIR, JUNE S. BLAIR Mrs. E. Frank Blair Jr. died Friday, March 8, 2013 in Albuquerque, NM. A native of Roswell, NM June Blair was born April 25, 1926, the daughter of Henry C. and Versa Stephens Sorrells. She graduated from Roswell High School in 1943, where she ranked third in her class. June married E. Frank Blair Jr., of Roswell, August 18, 1944 in Chicago where he was serving in the US Navy aviation cadet program. Later he was transferred to Norfolk, Virginia where they remained until the end of WWII. While the Blairs were stationed in Norfolk, June commenced a 41 year Federal career working for the US army at Hampton Roads Port of Embarkation. When they returned to Roswell in 1946, June transferred to the US Army Air Corps and became Executive Secretary to Col. William Blanchard commanding officer of the 509th Atomic Bomb B-29 Wing. June took a leave of absence following the birth of her son Stephen. When he started school she returned to the Federal service at WAF Base as a court reporter. Active in community affairs, June was a charter member of the Assistance League of Roswell and of her church, St. Andrews Episcopal Church. Upon the closure of Walker Air Force Base, the Blairs moved to Merced, California where June continued her career as a Federal Court Reporter with the Air Force. During her career she traveled throughout the Southwest, sought after for highly classified cases, as she was one of the few court reporters with top secret clearance. When the opportunity arose in the late 70's the Blairs returned to Albuquerque, where June continued her court reporting duties at Kirkland AFB. She retired there after 41 years of federal service. Shortly before her retirement she was honored to have a new court room at Kirkland Air Force Base named in her honor.

In Albuquerque, June was a member of the Lew Wallace Chapter of the Daughters of the American Revolution and of Saint Marks on the Mesa Episcopal Church. She is predeceased by her husband Frank, son Stephen, her parents, and her sister Ada Robinson. Survivors include her nieces Whitney Blair, Kelly Robbins, Lane Leadingham and nephew Dr. Chris Robinson. The family request contributions are made to a charity of choice.

ABOUT GLORIA, *the author….*

The realization of a second book that has come forth is unbelievable to me but here it is. My further experiences within this phenomena had to be told because of the many requests since "Morning Glory" Diary of an Alien Abductee was published. It took many years for me to even begin writing, and once again, as I wrote my experiences, healing was realized.

When "Morning Glory" Diary of an Alien Abductee was published I found it difficult to be able to just get my story into the book stores here in New Mexico. I had many appointments with book managers in top line bookstores as well as the smaller bookstores in Albuquerque and around the state of New Mexico. Many times I would find their attitude to be a "snickering" response. I felt that these people considered my story unacceptable to grace their bookshelves. After sending out press releases and other forms of marketing tools I knew that I could not just give up. My story needed to reach out to others. I was soon contacted by the International UFO Museum & Research Center in Roswell, New Mexico and a well-known bookstore located within this center.

I had my first productive book signing at the International UFO Museum and Research Center with many people in attendance. I was invited back to the International UFO Museum & Research Center many times. I was surrounded by all of the wonderful people who were employed there. They offered support and love which made me stronger to be able to venture out on my own. I was asked by Julie Shuster to speak at the center and this was my first opportunity to speak to a large crowd relating my experiences. This was the great beginning of my realization to reach other alien abductees and to listen and guide other humans with their own "secret life" experiences.

Since then, Morning Glory has been readily accepted into the major bookstores here in Albuquerque and around the state of New

Mexico. Some years ago Morning Glory traveled to other countries and is still doing well in the United States.

How fast word traveled! People ordered <u>Morning Glory</u> resulting in enough of a demand that many stores now carry my book on their shelves!

I never dreamed that <u>Morning Glory</u> would touch other countries in Europe, Japan and China, Sweden just to name a few. I've been quite fortunate to receive letters from many people throughout the world that I have touched and who have requested my help. I am so astonished by the outreach and my determination to continue with a goal I had in mind; to not let defeat win over when I felt <u>Morning Glory</u> was being segregated by bookstores here in Albuquerque or even in the State of New Mexico.

<u>Morning Glory</u> began selling by word of mouth and through Amazon. com and Barnes and Noble.com. I cannot say enough thanks for the outcome and outreach that the International UFO Museum and Research Center has provided to promote my life story. This is where I did step into a new life in my outreach. The sincerity, love, and belief I was shown from an outstanding organization truly encouraged me to move forward with my goal to help others.

This outreach I refer to has led me to speaking at many conferences, workshops throughout the United States. I have reached out further, having been invited to be a guest on many radio programs that broadcast further than the United States. I was filmed by the Discovery Channel for a segment. This segment was called "Aliens Cloned my Husband." I lived my goal while maintaining friendships and guidance for others who are involved within this unusual phenomenon, guiding them through hypnotherapy. Over the past years I have guided many alien abductees, contactees. I have seen much growth and knowledge gained by my abductee clients through my hypnotherapy support. I am touched by the sincerity and love, concern throughout these past years I continually received from you all. I propose now that my second book "<u>MORNING GLORY</u>" Ever-After (<u>The Story Continues</u>) will touch even more who may need to read and be helped by my life experiences. They may contact me through my e-mail Damom15165@Aol.com or Facebook: GLORIA HAWKER

I believe Mr. Budd Hopkins may have been correct when he explained to me that this special journey I have accepted into my life for many years, would come to an end at a certain age. Thus, I think he may be right. But as I look out my second story window toward the Sandia Mountains, I still witness (as most recently with a blink of an eye) small round alien flying crafts, disappearing into a side of the mountain. I can be traveling in my car with a Southwest Airlines jet flying above and witnessing still another silver alien flying craft. So is this unusual life really over for me?

My wish with this last book is "Those who have been touched either by this book or my first book, may you reach out and touch another who may need your guiding hand."

Gloria

GLORIA'S NOTES

1. Mr. Donald R. Schmitt and Mr. Thomas J. Cary I extend a special thank you for asking me to be involved in your investigations for your cause. Your research and investigations bring forth the known truth and validation to humans who are involved in a phenomenon as I am. From all of us "thank you" for the work you both have done in giving us the absolute truth in your research.

   To my readers you will find truth in "Witness to Roswell." Authors: Mr. Donald R. Schmitt and Mr. Thomas Cary.

2. Eve Lorgen, Author of *"The Love Bite: Alien Interference of Human Love Relationships*,(Elogos and HHC, 2000) and *"The Dark Side of Cupid: Love Affairs, the Supernatural and Energy Vampirism* (Keyhole Publishing, 2012) is a 20 plus year researcher and hypnotherapist in anomalous trauma. This spectrum includes alien/ET encounters, paranormal experiences, MILABS, and other dimensional visitations. The focus of her two books reveal taboo aspects of how love relationships have been orchestrated, interfered with or disrupted by paranormal sources.

   Eve also holds a B.S. in Biochemistry as well as a Masters Degree in Counseling Psychology. Her scientific and intuitive skills have contributed to her success in understanding these otherworldly experiences. While research is important, her priority is in support, healing and empowered sovereignty for her clients.

   Her inspiration into the anomalous started early in life with her own paranormal experiences. Her inspiration came through the work of the late Dr. Karla Turner and the UFO and alien abduction researcher, Barbara Bartholic.

   Eve, in appreciation for your contribution in your research *"The Love Bite: Alien Interference of Human Love Relationships."*

3. To the special people who sought me out for their guidance. The very few examples of clients which are given in this book I did not identify you, but did use your experiences to help others come to terms and deal with their truth if they identified with your experiences. You are quite special and dear in my heart. I know for a fact that some of you are already reaching out and helping others, for that I graciously thank you for giving of yourselves.

4. Ms. Julie Shuster and Sandy thank you for your belief in me and your guidance.

5. Over the years the support, understanding and love I received from new friends both non-believers and believers within this phenomenon. Within this realm new and old friends have carried me through this unusual life experience. There are too many to name here, the list would be quite long. You know who you are and each of you reside in my heart and soul. Thank you for being and walking with me on "My Road of Life." I love each of you individually.
Gloria

FURTHER COMMENTS

Gloria Hawker has bought great insight to the NM UFO/Paranormal forum Group. Gloria has been on the executive committee since the group's beginning in 2006 to date. Her sincerity and desire to seek out the truth make her a creditable figure in the UFO field. The fact Gloria has always been there for abductees and contactees shows her desire to help those whose lives are greatly affected by this phenomena. She is a guiding light for those who have nowhere else to go.

Michael Wisotzke –Chief Editor TruthSeekerForum.com